SS Intelligence

SS Intelligence

The Nazi Secret Service

Edmund L. Blandford

CASTLE BOOKS

This edition published in 2001 by

CASTLE BOOKS
A division of Book Sales, Inc.
114 Northfield Avenue
Edison, New Jersey 08837

Published by arrangement with

Airlife Publishing Ltd.
101 Longden Road, Shrewsbury, SY3 9EB England
E-mail: airlife@airlifebooks.com
Website: www.airlifebooks.com

Copyright © 2000 Edmund L. Blandford
First published in the UK in 2000 by Airlife Publishing Ltd.

ISBN 0-7858-1398-5

Printed in the United States of America.

CONTENTS

INTRODUCTION

The products of human culture, the achievements in art, science and technology with which we are confronted today, are almost exclusively the creative product of the Aryan. That very fact enables us to draw the not unfounded conclusion that he alone was the founder of higher humanity and was thus the very essence of what we mean by the term man.

Adolf Hitler, *Mein Kampf*

Adolf Hitler, architect of Europe's 'New Order'

Reichsführer *Heinrich Himmler*

It was from the above premise that Hitler planned to depose the 'sub-human' nations to the east, via a huge programme of resettlement which would result in a Greater German *Reich* populated exclusively by Nordics numbering 180 million. This figure had been arrived at by a German doctor in a prize-winning essay devoted to the rebuilding of a greater, purified Germany following the blood-letting of World War One. It would be some years before the world woke up to the fact that Hitler and his band were perfectly serious in their pursuit of this dream.

'Three hundred colonies would produce a yearly influx of one hundred thousand unbroken human beings and cause a turn of the tide throughout the life of the nation', the good doctor had written, continuing the theme of German emigration first espoused long before. This need to expand was not of course exclusively German; others had explored, settled and populated new lands around the world for centuries. It was part of man's destiny. But for Germans some other, almost mystical, urge drove them to dream of moving on to the vast, open territories beyond Eastern Europe, lands

Reinhard Heydrich – the most dangerous man

that were fertile and sparse in population, even to the Urals. Millions of Germans had long spilled over into several neighbouring states: Bohemia, Romania, Hungary – and Russia. All these countries, long before Hitler came to power, had by and large absorbed these immigrants peacefully. However, once the Nazis began their programme of hate, such people became 'harassed' minorities and more.

None of Hitler's aims could be achieved without war. He knew this and relished it, feeling thwarted when peaceful settlements were thrust upon him. A start could not be made until absolute control had been established in his adopted land – Germany. He entrusted this task to Heinrich Himmler, one of his closest adherents, whose own instincts leaned towards such control by repression and the furthering of the Nordic race. Himmler was a great admirer of the Soviet manner of secret policing, though he felt he could improve on them. However, Himmler's SS was not that kind of force, so even before Hitler controlled Germany as Chancellor he had set his mind on taking over the small, rather inefficient political branch of the Prussian police in Berlin. It was a goal not to be achieved without problems. Beyond that, Himmler decided he needed a small intelligence unit within his SS, which would monitor both Nazi Party members – no small job in itself – and anti-Nazi factions. He had not progressed further than drawing up a short-list of possible chiefs for such a unit when he was confronted by Reinhard Heydrich.

Though Heydrich was to create the SS Security Service, the *Sicherheitsdienst*, or SD, and through it a spy system which extended its activities outside Germany, he began as an amateur. He was long preceded by the man and service already well versed in such matters, Canaris. For the chronicler of such history, it is fascinating that the veteran took the fledgling under his wing, only to find he had harboured a monster.

It is inadvisable to ignore the achievements of Wilhelm Franz Canaris and his *Abwehr*, or military intelligence service, in the years before Reinhard Heydrich achieved prominence.

In describing these events it is worth noting that Canaris blossomed under Hitler, as did many others, notably in the military. He may not have been a 'National Socialist', but the Nazi regime afforded him the opportunities to prosper. In this sense, as with Rommel, his falling foul of the *Führer* is irrelevant.

1

THE *ABWEHR*

While Admiral Canaris could never be regarded as a career spymaster, at the time of his appointment as head of Military Intelligence (the *Abwehr*) he could look back on unusual adventures overseas and experience which well suited him for the task in hand. He had also gained command of a U-boat in World War One, firmly believing in the submarine as a war-winning weapon; this sided him with Doenitz, rather than the Chief of the German Navy, Grand Admiral Raeder.

Canaris's portrait photograph discloses a face of guile and wariness, a man capable of intrigue. To those who knew him, either personally or by reputation, he was the fox, 'Old Whitehead'. It seems strange, but just before his appointment to the *Abwehr*, Canaris seems to have been shunted into a dead-end position, to command the land forts at Swinemünde. That was in autumn 1934. His previous command was aboard the old training battleship *Schlesien*. At Swinemünde, the garrison consisted of marines manning a few coastal batteries covering the mouth of the River Oder beside the Baltic Sea. The nearby town of Swinemünde was a popular seaside resort; any officer of his rank sent to such a spot could only look forward to retirement on reduced pay. There were several able officers already in the *Abwehr* who might have been appointed chief.

Earlier in World War One, Lieutenant Wilhelm Canaris had served aboard the cruiser *Dresden* as part of the Imperial Navy's force which won a victory against the British at Coronel in the South Atlantic. The Royal Navy caught up with the German force, and only *Dresden* escaped – to be bottled up in Chilean territorial waters. Lieutenant Canaris was sent to the British commander of the cruiser *Glasgow* to try and negotiate; by coincidence, this had been the only British warship to escape the Battle of Coronel. The negotiations failed, and *Dresden* left its haven to be scuttled by its crew.

Canaris then entered the spy game. He was fluent in several languages, including English, and was sent to Spain in 1916, where he was soon brought to the attention of the Allied Intelligence services. Canaris fled, using the odd alias 'Reed Rosa', but was caught aboard an Italian freighter and jailed. Intervention by influential Spanish friends earned his release and deportation to Spain via Marseilles. The Italians never

Wilhelm Canaris – doomed chief of the Abwehr

discovered his real identity. Canaris, certain the French would seize him once the ship called at Marseilles, was determined to avoid them. He actually persuaded the Spanish captain on the ship not to call at the French port at all, but to sail straight to Cartagena.

Lieutenant Canaris longed for a sea command, preferably a U-boat. Succeeding, to his chagrin he found himself sent to serve as an instructor. Not until spring 1918 did he succeed in escaping to command a submarine sent through the dangerous Straits of Gibraltar, into the Mediterranean. Yet he was frustrated, as the only safe ports to call at for supplies were taken by the Allies; Canaris managed to escape back to Kiel.

It was a disastrous time for Germany, the end of an era. A mutiny instigated by Bolsheviks dressed in sailors' rig started the fleet uprising in 1917, and after the Great War ended German troops and marines were combating the various armed factions that threatened to plunge Germany into bloody revolution. In Berlin the police chief was deposed and revolutionaries set up the first 'Soviet'. Plundering and murder and street fighting became daily events as those loyal to the old order attempted to wipe out the Spartacists and other revolutionary forces. In these confusing, dangerous times, officers like Canaris naturally sided with law and order and did whatever possible to combat the Reds. In doing so he was accused of irregularity during a trial of revolutionaries and sentenced to house arrest – pending further investigation. This entailed his sojourning for a short time in the Royal Palace.

The Bolsheviks set up another 'Soviet' in Munich, being eventually put down by regular forces, but not before they had shot hostages. Most of the Reds were put up against a wall and themselves executed. Ex-Corporal Hitler was in Munich and witness to much of this chaos.

It can be seen, therefore, that Canaris, by 1934 of higher rank, was eminently suited to take over as chief of the *Abwehr*, a fledgling spy service compared to that of Great Britain, which dated from Elizabethan times. Its terms of reference under the new Hitler regime included a bar on any activity directed against the State and *Wehrmacht*. It was forbidden to spy on any Party organisation, and the *Gestapo* and SD were not supposed to spy on the *Wehrmacht*. The three secret services would ignore these rules; the *Abwehr* proved to have leaks later. It was always Himmler's and Heydrich's intention to absorb the *Abwehr* eventually, but success was long coming. To succeed sooner by infiltration proved impossible.

Aged forty-seven, Canaris gave the impression of a wise old man, white-haired, rose-cheeked, and an Anglophile. For him it was impossible to reject the chance of becoming Nazi Germany's spy chief, though according to one source as early as 1934 he thought his country was on the road to ruin. Available evidence indicates that Canaris did everything he could to help Hitler's aggressive schemes, and little if anything to thwart him. Certainly, once ensconced in his headquarters he began to learn a good deal more about Nazi methods, and especially about the gentlemen across the street – Himmler, Heydrich and Müller.

The German Navy had taken command of Military Intelligence; the Admiral and his naval aides worked well enough with the Army officers in the department. Army Intelligence operated only within the military sphere on the continent, not outside the *Reich*. A crisis between *Abwehr* and the Nazi secret services would soon develop, since the former were of the regular, old school, who regarded the Nazis as gangster upstarts, amateurs and far removed from the old concepts of gentlemen spies. Nevertheless, being patriotic professionals they stuck to their guns. There was never any question of resigning *en masse*, which would have suited Himmler and Heydrich admirably. From the start their dislike and jealousy of the military extended to the *Abwehr*. Heydrich was hardly forgiving after his dismissal from the Navy.

But the problem which propelled Canaris into the top spot first emanated through Hitler's chief of the defence staff, General von Blomberg, who had easily accommodated himself to the new regime. Though of the more traditional Army hierarchy, he complained to Grand Admiral Raeder that the *Abwehr* chief Captain Konrad Patzig must go. Patzig could not get along with his opposites in the Nazi security services and was therefore unacceptable to 'the Party'. The *Abwehr* contained Army personnel, but perhaps on account of their experience of the wider world, the sailors were looked upon as more suited to take senior positions. Men like Canaris had always had the greater opportunities to gather information during their voyages. In the event, Raeder, after consulting his staff and files, decided the new *Abwehr* chief had to be the then Captain Canaris. He was believed to be of brilliant mind, experienced and resourceful, with a talent for man management. However, Raeder is said to have been hesitant, not quite able to fathom the true character of this candidate, who always displayed a kind of reserve and secretiveness. But Raeder knew it was better to maintain the Navy's dominance and get one of their men into the seat before Hitler appointed one of his own Nazi nominees.

In a sense, being of the old school himself, Canaris was now out of his depth, entering a world where ruthlessness and murder were already becoming the order of the day. He was obliged to meet Heydrich, the young man he had known in 1925 as a cadet on his own ship, the quite talented violin player who had fitted so well into the Canaris family soirées. When they met again the far older man's reaction was one of fear, a feeling that never left him. Yet Heydrich, now head of the Nazi secret service, would again hear *Frau* Erika Canaris play her cello and, on the surface, the two families would re-assert their ties. To his wife Lina, Heydrich remarked how pleased he was that Canaris had been appointed chief of the *Abwehr*. He had not been able to get along with Captain Patzig. On the other hand Canaris confided that the younger man was 'a born criminal'; yet their odd relationship continued despite such assessments. For Heydrich's part, whatever charm he genuinely displayed, whatever pleasure he derived from the family get-togethers, he remained determined to get the better of the older man and especially the service he had taken over. The SD file on Canaris grew steadily, from the naval man's early history, including the violent verbal attacks made on him by left-wingers, the Reds and socialists of the immediate post-World War One era.

Canaris never met Himmler; what he knew of him gave rise to the opinion that the *Reichsführer* SS was a jumped-up nonentity. But with Heydrich it was different. The old *Abwehr* chiefs had established a good relationship with both the German Foreign Office mandarins and the *Reichswehr*, with the exception of a few generals who had become 'browned' (i.e. they had willingly fallen in with the Nazi regime). The *Abwehr* professionals belonged to the same military caste as the *Reichswehr*. This alone distanced them from the new Nazi hierarchy, including the bombastic von Ribbentrop, the former wine salesman who had bought his title ('von'), and bamboozled Hitler into believing he was an expert on other countries and their peoples – especially Britain. Incidentally, all *Abwehr* staff were exempt from the Nazis' 'Aryan' screening process; some at least of its own 'V' men would never have passed it.

Canaris commented after his reunion meeting with Heydrich that his old acquaintance was 'an inherent criminal, but one with a high intelligence'; he was 'a clever beast'. An entry in his diary read, 'a brute fanatic with whom it will be most difficult to collaborate frankly and with confidence'. His fear of Heydrich stemmed not only from his noted cleverness and cunning, but from his sheer physique; despite rather broad hips and a high pitched voice, Heydrich was a big man and in excellent physical shape. Adding to prowess in horsemanship, fencing and other sports, he also learned to fly after joining the SS, and would go on to master the Me 109 fighter plane. This made him a most unusual figure among the Nazis and a formidable character to deal with.

Once appointed chief of Military Intelligence, Canaris was obliged to move his family from Swinemünde to Berlin, where, early in February 1935, he found a house in Doellerstrasse. He then discovered that Heydrich lived in the same street, and, allegedly for professional reasons, by that summer he got into the habit of strolling with his family to the Heydrich residence, to play croquet in the garden. Thus the extraordinary relationship between the two intelligence rivals continued. Each played the family man, while behind the façade actively scheming to circumvent the other, Heydrich forever the predator. His true feelings towards his old CO were expressed more than once to close aides: 'That old fox you can't be too careful about.' Indeed, one glance at the older man's portrait photograph confirms Heydrich's view of Canaris as just that. A year later, in August 1936, the Canaris family moved into a small house bought in Dianastrasse, located at Schlachtensee in the capital's south-western suburbs. Six months later, Heydrich moved his family to an unfinished house in Augustastrasse, just two minutes' walk from the Canaris home.

Even in Nuremberg jail after the war, Walter Schellenberg continued to spin tales, telling fellow inmates that Canaris had obtained proof of Heydrich's 'non-Aryan ancestry'. (The facts on this aspect are given in Chapter 3.) In their meeting in 1935 Canaris opted for the friendly approach, and since the meeting was designed to iron out any problems between the two services apparently created by the new chief's *Abwehr* predecessor, Heydrich was permitted a few apparent concessions. In fact, Canaris gave way on no important points as they tried to hammer out lines of demarcation between SD and *Abwehr*. The resulting agreement came to be called 'The Ten Commandments', and allowed the *Abwehr* to control all military espionage abroad; it also permitted Canaris to carry out all counter-espionage at home, though the *Gestapo* would make arrests. But secret political intelligence from foreign *sources* was declared the SD's prerogative, this being one area of action that had already created friction between Captain Patzig and the Nazi service.

In reality, the supposed agreement stood little chance of being adhered to, as in practice it proved impossible for either side to stay entirely clear of each other's area of responsibility. Further, there were complications which should have been eliminated, such as Goering's own private spy service, the so-called *Forschungsamt*, or 'Research Institute', apart from von Ribbentrop's own Intelligence Department at the Foreign Office. Then there was the Party's own Foreign Political Office, and of course Goebbels's spies. This was the reality of the gigantic bureaucracy that Hitler allowed to develop, a hugely wasteful multiplicity of effort, which when war came proved to be to the Allies' advantage.

As most are now aware, spying never stops: all the major (and some lesser) nations maintain spy services whose agents, whether accredited as such, or 'diplomats', convey intelligence of one kind or another to their governments. Whatever the state of the ex-Kaiser's Germany in the lean years following the country's defeat and collapse in 1918, it is certain that some leading figures in the German intelligence service maintained links and work in some way. This is tantamount to saying that whatever disaster befell the nation, the men who had managed the spy nets were unable by reason of their nature to cut themselves off from 'the game' entirely. Indeed, as is well known, from the time of the signing of the Treaty of Versailles, military and political elements in Germany began working to circumvent its clauses. This involved intrigue, secrecy and an atmosphere of plotting, into which the agents of both sides (German and Allied) could fit very nicely.

The *Abwehr*, as it became known, survived in some form in the uncertain years before Hitler and his Nazis gained power and began building their 'Third *Reich*'. Once the new regime got its hands on the nation's Treasury, the *Abwehr* was assured of adequate funding to build up a far greater organisation.

The building occupied by the German Secret Service became well known to foreign agents even before Reinhard Heydrich gained his foothold in Berlin. The stone quay known as the Tirpitzufer beside the Landwehrkanal contained Nos. 72–76. It was near the great Defence Ministry complex in Bendlerstrasse which stretched almost to the very

Canaris wined and dined his deadly rival –

16

who planned to supplant him

pleasant Tiergarten park. Following his promotion to chief of the *Abwehr*, Admiral Canaris could sometimes be spotted hurrying into his headquarters via a side entrance, usually clad in a shabby raincoat and trilby, resembling more a seedy private eye than boss of a large national spy service. Canaris was not the only important figure noted by foreign agents, who apparently were numerous and entirely brazen in watching out for military notables in that area. Indeed, they could often be seen trailing higher officers along the street, keeping close behind in blatant efforts to overhear snatches of worthwhile conversation. These spies even followed groups of German staff officers to the bus stop in the hope of picking up confidential gossip.

All the potential enemy states maintained spy outposts nearby: the Poles, Czechs, French, British, and US Naval Intelligence, since America had no overseas intelligence gathering agency as such, apart from diplomats, that is.

Canaris was so anxious to start work as *Abwehr* chief he arrived at the Tirpitzufer at 8 a.m. on New Year's Day 1935. He was obliged to have an aide summon his predecessor Captain Patzig from bed. This officer arrived

17

two hours later to deliver (apart from congratulations) commiserations and warnings about the 'other people' who had set up shop across the street – the Himmler-Heydrich SD HQ. Though named in the German press in 1928 as the schemer behind anti-government plots, Canaris thereafter managed to stay out of the limelight, as befitted a spy chief in the pre-'open' era (which exists today). He would, however, be cited by a British periodical in 1939 as head of Nazi Germany's spy service. Though sometimes referred to as First Officer of the training cruiser *Berlin* during his naval service, Canaris was in fact ADC (aide-de-camp) to Baron von Gagern, commander of the Baltic naval station which even as early as 1920 was part of the German military conspiracy to re-arm. Part of this effort involved liaising with friendly foreign shipyards, which were willing to supply Germany with warships, etc., Canaris acting as liaison. During the twenties he adopted two roles, that mentioned, travelling in disguises, and also conspiring with others against the democratic government. Canaris was bent on subverting any government he felt leaned to the left, which implies he was supportive of right-wing factions of all shades.

As an aide, and not without irony, the Hungarian-born writer Ladislas Farago was actually interviewed by Canaris only a few weeks after taking office in 1935. His first notion that Farago might prove a potential agent was soon dispelled, the German quickly sizing him up over lunch and soon losing interest. This was a small disappointment, as such travelling journalists were sometimes useful. For his part, Farago admits he made the mistake of dismissing Canaris as an 'honest dullard'.

Canaris went out of his way to fulfil the hopes of the Nazified Army staff, to work more harmoniously with them and the new security services than his predecessor. He appointed a Nazi sympathiser to liaise with the *Gestapo*, and soon began wining and dining Heydrich in the *Haus der Flieger* (House of Flyers), adjacent to the *Gestapo* building in Prinz-Albrecht-Strasse. When he was first appointed chief, the *Abwehr* was simply a department or division of the *Reichswehrministerium*, or Defence Ministry. Only after the fall of Field Marshal von Blomberg and reorganisation in 1938 did the *Abwehr* attain a greater size as a more independent group of departments, its three Divisions most directly concerned with gathering foreign military intelligence, sabotage and subversion, and counter-intelligence. Canaris found his own sanctum in the Tirpitzufer, a 'little office'; his own room continued to be that, frugally fitted, with a worn carpet and filing cabinets, the empty ones sometimes used by his long-haired pet dachshund Peppi. The man who was entrusted with many millions of marks had no love of ostentation, and important guests had to make do 'as found'.

Canaris must have dedicated all his waking hours to his job, and certainly kept up with the times; he commissioned the Telefunken company to design and produce a special, easily concealable 'spy' radio transceiver. Over the first eight months of 1935, he despatched agents to various parts of the world to commence operations. In London, sums of money were drawn through Barclays Bank for agents' use. It seems odd, however, that despite his undoubted cunning, shrewdness and experience, Canaris allowed his spies to be rushed out before they were properly trained, a trend that would in time cost him dearly in operations against England. As an example of *Abwehr* rashness and incompetence, the French caught no fewer than twenty-one agents during their first ten months of operations.

When in that first year Canaris met Hitler he contrived to spark the dictator's interest by lacing reports of spying successes with a few juicy tales. Hitler appreciated this, as he had already become bored with the dull dossiers delivered by his diplomats. One particular triumph Canaris reported to Hitler was the penetration of the Austrian Secret Service; Major Erwin von Lahousen was a man in that service who was perfectly prepared to sell out his country for the Nazi cause. Surprisingly perhaps, at first Canaris was only mildly interested in England and USA as targets for operations, preferring to concentrate on France, Poland and Czechoslovakia. This was perfectly agreeable to Hitler, who had been working for an understanding with the British and in 1935 had achieved (through von Ribbentrop) the Anglo-German Naval Agreement. The *Führer* felt this was a triumph, though he would declare it null and void once it suited him. In the case of America, Hitler had remarked that two-thirds of that country's engineers were of German origin; these and millions of other expatriates were seen by the Nazis as highly susceptible to propaganda from their homeland. Canaris was surprised to discover on taking office that his 'firm' already owned a flourishing operation across the Atlantic.

The German spy net in America had originated from former World War One aviation leaders' desires to rebuild their broken air arm. German Intelligence despatched an ex-air-force mechanic and unemployed designer under the alias of 'Wilhelm Schneider'. His job was to send back reports and blueprints on worthwhile aviation developments. For some undisclosed reason, this probe was called Operation 'Sex'. Schneider proved to be one of Germany's greatest spies, and lax security in the States enabled him to despatch a mass of material to Berlin.

Canaris made his first big mistake in 1936. The *Führer* was enraged to learn that despite his warnings not to cause waves in England, a certain 'Dr Goertz' had been arrested for spying and would stand trial in London. The British had intended to treat the matter lightly, perhaps cautioning the spy and deporting him. Two facts emerged to change this. Dr Goertz had travelled around England with his 'secretary'; while he sketched and photographed airfields and other installations, the woman flirted with an RAF man who eventually reported the matter to his CO. Dr Goertz's landlady at Broadstairs called the police on discovering suspicious papers with his briefcase which the incompetent spy had left around while away. These proved to be *Abwehr* orders and cyphers; this, plus Hitler's deployment of troops into the demilitarised Rhineland ensured a spy trial in England. Goertz was jailed for four years and Canaris had to answer to his *Führer*. Hitler placed a complete ban on *Abwehr* operations in England, which would last until 1937. It is interesting to note that Canaris had the *Abwehr* foot the bill for the defence of Goertz in England, and arranged a monthly sum for his wife and a payment to the secretary. Then, refusing to believe the British had caught Goertz 'red-handed', Canaris set his old naval sleuth Richard Protze to work to uncover the mole in the *Abwehr* whom he believed had betrayed them. It was Protze who would figure later in uncovering a highly successful Polish spy.

After Goertz had served his jail term he returned to Germany, to be signed up again by Canaris for an even more luckless venture, this time in Eire. Parachuted in, he was betrayed by the very people he hoped would help him – the IRA also stole his bankroll. Goertz committed suicide in jail.

Hitler's determination to woo the British into an understanding and so free his hand for eastern designs included strenuous attempts by various Nazi organisations, who utilised friendly persuasion, propaganda and subversion. None of this was equated with actual spying. Organisations and highly placed individuals from Berlin did their work in London, fostering Anglo-German friendship, anti-Semitism and fear of communism. In London, organisations such as The Link and Anglo-German Fellowship were part of this effort, which achieved a certain degree of success, mostly among the upper crust of society and some right-wing politicians. Curiously, Hitler did little or nothing to establish ties with Mosley's Fascist movement. The connections and influence made among British converts, mostly via social gatherings and printed works, was solid and undoubtedly might have been of greater importance had Hitler used more guile.

It was not the *Abwehr* or Heydrich's SD, however, which prised open some of the most promising contacts. As shown, Canaris had got his fingers burnt and been warned off again by Hitler. The Goertz operation had only come about at the request of *Luftwaffe* chiefs – he had naïvely believed that if things went wrong they would take the blame.

The Nazi Party 'philosopher', Alfred Rosenberg, discovered a certain Baron 'Bill' de Ropp, a Balt from Lithuania, who had been educated in Germany and had lived in England since 1910. He had served in the Wiltshire Regiment and in the mid-thirties had been introduced with his English wife to Hitler. The Baron was recruited as an agent and 'met' Squadron Leader Fred Winterbotham, who seemed delighted to know him, evincing great sympathy for Hitler and his 'Third *Reich*'. Winterbotham was a prime target, as he worked at the Air Ministry. The Baron's excited reports to Berlin soon resulted in a *Luftwaffe* officer being sent to pump the RAF officer for all he was worth concerning strategy in the air and armaments, etc. Squadron Leader Winterbotham was indeed friendly and chatty, but in truth he was employed by Air Intelligence *and*

MI6. He was playing a double game with the Germans, finding out all he could about the *Luftwaffe*, whose agent Obermüller became so intrigued by progress following a high-level meeting at the Air Ministry that he recommended Winterbotham as new Air Attaché in Berlin.

Alfred Rosenberg was completely duped into believing he had penetrated into the highest circles of the RAF leadership, which had not only agreed (behind the backs of the Foreign Office) to enter into technical co-operation with the *Luftwaffe*, but proposed a two-way exchange of officers, delegations who would be shown the latest developments. Rosenberg believed he had triumphed where the *Abwehr* and others had failed.

The outcome proved a great joke on the Germans, who showed visiting RAF military a great deal of their *Luftwaffe* and associated installations. When the truth dawned, accusations flew among the Germans of treachery, Hitler lamenting his officers had disclosed the secrets of German radar development. Squadron Leader Winterbotham never went to Berlin as Air Attaché, being sidetracked by his chiefs. As for the Baron, he had known Winterbotham as a friend since the earlier war.

Canaris had kicked the *Abwehr* into life on taking office, and though Hitler placed a ban on actual spying in Britain, the admiral went ahead by installing *Forschers* on the island. These scouts would worm their way into British society under innocent-sounding cover and await the signal to start their real work. They were 'sleepers' in the Soviet manner. Strangely, a kind of free-for-all developed as the various *Abwehr* stations across Germany began to send such would-be spies to England, all quite uncoordinated by the Canaris HQ. The result was inevitable. Foul-ups led the chief to call a halt and insist that all operations be cleared through his HQ.

Other foreigners were willing to assist efforts to undermine the British, notable among them Irishmen and Welsh Nationalists. One Joseph Kelly persisted in badgering the German consul in Liverpool, Reinhardt, an old school diplomat who, like his British counterparts, wanted nothing to do with undercover work. Finally, the exasperated diplomat passed the Irishman's name to the proper quarter, the *Abwehr*, who sent Kelly a return ticket to Osnabrück. He sold the *Abwehr* plans of an important munitions factory in Chorley, Lancashire, for which he received the derisory sum of £30. Kelly aroused British suspicions after his return, with the result that he was arrested, tried and received seven years in jail. Consul-General Reinhardt was expelled. This displeased the Germans, who responded by expelling the British Passport Control Officer in Vienna, by then occupied under the *Anschluss*. This was unfortunate and hardly a fair exchange for Britain, as Captain Tom Kendrick had organised a widespread spy network covering Austria, Poland, Czechoslovakia and Hungary.

Also in this period, following the lifting of the ban on *Abwehr* spying in Britain in 1937, a 'seedy racing journalist' named Donald Adams sold the Germans various military information, including details of the new 4.5 in-AA gun. Adams, however, was netted by MI5, who also caught four

Russians working for the Germans in Woolwich Arsenal. Canaris lamented these setbacks, but the British were wrong to believe they had the situation well under control, for the *Abwehr* alone was operating no fewer than 253 spies in Britain by August 1938. Indeed, the amount and quality of intelligence was so high that Canaris could claim his agents had mapped every RAF airfield, and photographed and sketched every major harbour installation, docks, oil tanks, warehouses and other military and economic targets from London to Hull. In accordance with custom, all such data was passed to the relevant *Wehrmacht* department, much of it providing very full and accurate target maps for the *Luftwaffe* when war came.

Much credit for this work went to Captain Joachim Burghardt, chief of Department AST X in Hamburg, who, with the aid of capable executives, organised agents and operations. These were arranged as an 'R' and 'S' chain: *Reisen* were travellers (vacationers), the *Schweigen* were 'sleepers'. Some of the spies employed by the *Abwehr* are of special interest. One called Charlie Diggins tried to subvert British seamen calling at German ports, especially Hamburg. Another, an alleged 'eccentric Londoner' calling himself Captain Fox Newman-Hall, sent several reports to the *Abwehr* before he was put on ice, presumably during Hitler's 'no-go' era. However, when the Germans tried to reactivate him he failed to respond. An Irishman called Brandy had worked for the Germans in World War One. By the late thirties he was in his sixties and still eager to serve them, being an ardent admirer of Hitler. However, after receiving his orders in the *Reich* he returned to Dublin and dropped dead.

The skipper of the Neptune Line ship *Finkenau* acted as a courier, receiving spy reports when he called at British ports. Then there was an engineer called Fritz Block who gave up his usual employment to start up a ladies' garment business in Holland, with most of his customers in England. Block was married to an American woman whose parents lived in London. Recruited by the *Abwehr*, he found it expedient to visit England often, and by the end of 1938 he had delivered 130 reports to his masters, plus 400 photographs covering all manner of military and economic targets, including airfields, aircraft factories, electrical and water pumping stations, even fire-fighting methods. Fritz Block was one of the most successful spies ever used by Canaris in what must be regarded as the 'golden age' for German espionage in Britain.

Block even persuaded an English journalist friend to let him have copies of the government 'D notice' topics which were forbidden to the press. They were obviously sensitive subjects and of interest to an enemy. Described as a 'Walter Mitty' character, Block was never highly paid. The *Abwehr* only gave him about £7 a week, not much more than most professional people earned in Britain at the time.

Friedrich 'Freddy' Kaulen, a slim, bespectacled young man, was another very successful *Abwehr* spy in Britain. He had come to the *Gestapo's* notice earlier as an amateur radio ham. Cautioned but left alone, he ended up on the *Abwehr* books by chance, after showing holiday snaps taken in England to a friend. Kaulen made three very successful trips to Britain, working mostly in the north-west, and even hanging about in pubs to listen in on what the *Englanders* thought about various topics – particularly politics, etc. Kaulen escaped on the last steamer to Ireland before war was declared. He was so highly valued by his *Abwehr* controller that a recommendation was given that he should be awarded the Iron Cross, but it was not deemed appropriate for a civilian.

In the last years before the war there was much talk of German spies among the media and public. This was at a time when very many genuine job seekers were coming to Britain from Germany, mostly domestics hoping to land decent employment among British society. Naturally, some of these people were on the *Abwehr* payroll. One who took a job as cook for a family in Manchester spent her off-duty hours trying to recruit sub-agents; one of these was the aforementioned Irishman Joseph Kelly. Two middle-aged German females found posts as housekeepers with naval officers in London, and another actually worked in the house of the First Lord of the Admiralty.

Once the Hitler ban was lifted in 1937, Canaris pulled out all the stops, recruiting every ship's officer (including captains), he could find, especially among the well-known Hamburg–Amerika Line, North German Lloyd and others. These men were given cameras and instructed to photograph British and American harbour installations. Other 'DK' (*Dämpfer Kapitänen* – steamer captains) were detailed to take pictures along the Thames into London. When these ships' officers returned to continental ports (even in Belgium and Holland), they found special *Abwehr* debriefing officers waiting for them, and in Rotterdam for example they could well be Dutch Nazis. The work carried out in this manner included anti-submarine defences at the Firth of Forth and photographing the British seaplane base at Harwich.

Despite all the successes, once war came *Abwehr* efforts foundered, and after the summer of 1940 proved a disaster. Nineteen would-be spies were taken over by the British security services and run by the Double-X Committee to feed largely false information back to the *Abwehr*, which continued to be duped until the end, even after the execution of its chief in 1945.

Yet, what can be regarded perhaps as the greatest German spy coup of World War Two was not initiated by the regular spy services at all.

One cutting among many clipped from newspapers in New York by a German agent and sent to Berlin in October 1939 began it all. The news item referred to 'scrambled' telephone calls made by President Roosevelt to his envoys abroad. The communications division of the *Abwehr* was intrigued enough to put brains to work on the possibility of eavesdropping on such talk, to tap into the cable which ran across the Atlantic seabed. Goering's *Forschungsamt* also became interested, but neither agency found the problem solvable. The idea lapsed until summer 1941, when the head of the German Post Office (*Deutsche Reichspost*) set his chief engineer, *Herr* Vetterlein, to look into the induction system called ciphony. The engineer quickly constructed two pilot models, one of them a scrambler, and during the evening of 7 September 1941, succeeded in his first experiment. But it took several more months' effort until Vetterlein reckoned he had cracked the problem, and by March 1942 he had set up an interceptor station near Eindhoven in Holland.

The system worked, and from that date onwards the top Nazi leadership, including Himmler, became privy to all transatlantic telephone conversations conducted not only between President Roosevelt and Prime Minister Churchill, but many others made by their advisers and other aides. Though none of the Allied leaders knew the Germans had made such a breakthrough, they were always conscious of the possibility and tried to speak guardedly. Transcripts of their conversations were sent by classified teletype (B-Schreiber) machine to Berlin. The whole process took some two hours, far swifter than the early decoding attempts in the British Ultra system, though later of course the latter often resulted in German Enigma signals being routinely read within minutes.

None of the Atlantic messages reached the *Abwehr*, however; Himmler sent copies to Walter Schellenberg after Heydrich was assassinated. Great though this success was from a technical point of view, overall, in terms of strategic gain, the enemy achieved little. Recipients such as von Ribbentrop were often quite unable to gain anything from the information, solely because of the Allied callers' habit of camouflaging their conversations. The most important fact learned by Hitler which was of real value was the coming Italian perfidy and defection, which enabled him to take countermeasures. A lesser example was a transcript of Roosevelt and Churchill discussing the build-up of US combat forces in Britain in May 1944.

The Atlantic 'phone cable was of course not actually 'tapped' into, the means of access used was electronic. Some Germans had favoured a more direct method, actually using engineers delivered by U-boats to 'clip' into the cable itself.

As indicated, whatever successes the *Abwehr* gained on the continent of Europe, its gains from the UK were stifled once war came. Ambitions to set up a widespread spy network in Britain were not fostered by the SD under Heydrich – his small but successful efforts will be mentioned later. Perhaps it is for this reason that one massive tome (over 650 pages) on this spy era makes no mention of Heydrich's work in this direction through his SD. In fact, the very name 'Heydrich' is omitted from the index, an error in itself since his name does crop up just once. Most written works on the man concentrate on the legacy of horror, not spying, the terrible atrocity of Lidice committed after his death, and the implementing of the 'Final Solution' against the Jews. It is hardly accurate to link the first deed directly with Heydrich, and, terrible crime though it was, many more innocents were put to death through the hostage system of reprisal before and after Lidice.

Both Canaris and Heydrich provide very interesting character analysis – friends then deadly rivals, the old fox against the ruthless upstart perhaps. How far one should take the stance of 'Nazi vs non-Nazi' is debatable. In the sense that both willingly jumped on the Hitler bandwagon they were both 'Nazis', happy to further their careers via that regime. Heydrich has been vilified as, to quote one eminent journalist, '. . . a young man of diabolical, arrogant and ruthless character'. The writer was William Shirer, recording his years as an American correspondent in Germany. Others have called him 'Hitler's most evil henchman', asserting that every cunning, evil ploy that emanated through Himmler actually originated with Heydrich. This may be true, though just how far Heydrich's ambitions reached and how much power he actually had is debatable.

In terms of guilt, there can of course be no comparison. Heydrich was unquestionably responsible for very many deaths. But loose, unsubstantiated ideas put into print concerning Canaris's pro-Allied sympathies, and even suggestions he was working for the British, seem absurd. Most spies caught by the admiral's *Abwehr* counter-espionage operations were put to death, unless they agreed to turn their coats. When Hitler put his war plans into action it was the Admiral's *Abwehr, not* the SD and *Gestapo*, which, one can allege without fear of contradiction, despicably engineered the first 'incident' against the Poles. This was one of a series of 'incidents' involving *Abwehr* and special forces (i.e. Brandenburg troops) apart from the Nazi groups designed to throw responsibility for war on the other side. In other words, it was the *Abwehr* of Admiral Canaris which seems to have been perfectly agreeable to providing part of the means to launch dirty tricks. When Hitler was forced to postpone his scheme in late August 1939 it proved too late to cancel one *Abwehr* team who had already gone into action.

It may seem fruitless to conject what course Reinhard Heydrich might have taken had he not become over-involved with one blonde too many and been dismissed from the German Navy (see Chapter 3). He seemed dedicated to his service career, though doubtless his restless dynamism would have urged him on to something beyond the post of mere radio and communications officer. His many talents were such that, had he stayed clear of the hatred generated by Nazism, he could well have gone far.

2
THE *GESTAPO*

In 1946 Colonel Story of the American prosecution team in the Nuremberg trials began his case against the *Gestapo* and SD in this manner:

> The Gestapo and the SD played an important part in almost every criminal act of the conspiracy . . . the category of these crimes . . . reads like a page from the devil's notebook.

The conspiracy referred to was that of the leading Nazis to plan and wage aggressive war, plus of course war crimes. To the accused, even if they considered themselves guilty, the whole process was a farce, in so far as some of the judges in court were themselves representatives of a regime which had carried out far worse excesses. The latest tally of Stalin's murders is some fifty million.

Whatever the arguments (and there were some) against the legality of the Allies' own case at Nuremberg, they were determined to establish a precedent, that the international community could no longer allow such gross acts of 'terrorism', the deliberate making of war to achieve conquest and territorial gain. Until that time, no international laws existed to outlaw such acts, and even if there had been, men like Hitler would have ignored them. There was nothing new in making war for gain, absolutely nothing, any more than it was new to terrorise and put to death opponents. The only

Ultimate badge of authority – Gestapo i/d

'laws' in print were those intended to govern conduct in the making of war, the Hague and Geneva conventions.

No matter what acts those in the dock at the various war crime trials after 1945 were accused of, they pleaded 'Not guilty' on account of their belief of having acted under orders passed by the legal authority of the Nazi German State. In other words, their deeds may have seemed repulsive to outsiders, but in their eyes they could not be guilty of any criminal act, even when written authority for some actions seemed lacking. As servants of the State, they were merely the executors of the legally appointed government. They may too have recalled the words of the Nazi lawyer and one-time chief in Denmark, Werner Best, who proclaimed in the thirties that so long as employees carried out the will of the leadership they were not acting illegally.

There are those today who can argue persuasively that the Allies had no legal or perhaps even moral right to sit in judgement at Nuremberg. It is an argument that can last for ever and need not concern us here. The various security police forces of Nazi Germany were used, unlike those in Britain, USA and other democracies, as instruments of repression and death.

Prior to 30 January 1933, when Hitler gained power, the *Gestapo* had not existed as such. It was merely a small and, according to some accounts, in-effective Branch 1a of the Prussian Police department in Berlin. Though staffed by professional detectives, they were not over-zealous in the Nazi manner in pursuing plotters or saboteurs and were in any case confined to their own 'manor', Berlin and the state of Prussia, having no jurisdiction outside.

When Hitler took office he began handing out rewards to his closest supporters, and although Wilhelm Frick was made Minister of the Interior, it was Goering who achieved command of the police. For a man like Hitler, so filled with hatred for various sections of society, it seemed natural that the ex-air ace who had developed into an overblown example of brutality should wield the big stick in the new Nazi state. Frick had been one of Hitler's early supporters, acting as a spy in the police in Munich during the attempted *Putsch* of 1923. Later, having advanced under Hitler's wing Frick had become a National Socialist member in the *Reichstag*, yet he lacked the brutal zeal and capacity for action common to Hermann Goering, who, until becoming worn out during the war, had always proved to be the one man Hitler could rely on for radical measures – especially against the Jews.

Goering loved repression, the taking of drastic action against opponents or those suspected of anti-Nazi tendencies. He was a military man used to the notion of putting people to death, inured to harshness and capable of what most decent people would see as criminal acts – or at least, the inciting of them. For example, in his usual impetuous fashion, having taken charge of law and order, Goering declared 50,000 SS and SA men 'auxiliary policemen'. They wore white armbands to show their authority for seizing,

27

questioning, beating up, torturing and killing anyone they pleased. There was apparently nothing the existing police forces could do about this, and if such regular, professional policemen abhorred using force or hesitated then Goering had this to say to them:

> Even if we make mistakes, at least we are acting. I may shoot a little wildly, one way or the other. But at least I shoot!

He also said:

> Every bullet that leaves the barrel of a police pistol is my bullet. If one calls this murder, then I have murdered. I ordered all this, I back it up. I assume responsibility, and I am not afraid to do so.

The sanctioning of police terror across Germany was the Nazis' way of rooting out not only the Reds and Jews, but all who doubted the new regime, or at least, carting off the most feared – the 'Bolsheviks'. Others were dealt with at leisure, while the rest of the mostly decent German population was cowed into submission. Hermann Goering, once developed as Hitler's Chief Executive and ornately rigged out in an ever-expanding range of outfits, became one leading Nazi some British and American periodicals liked to portray as the pet-lover, the grand family man who owned a super model train layout. This was the other side of Goering, the oft-noted overgrown, fat, fun-loving schoolboy who, when drug-taking, took to hiding his facial defects with make-up. Whatever the brutal side of the man, he gained popularity, and, unlike one or two at Nuremberg, showed no contriteness for his crimes. As for Hitler's Minister of the

Himmler confers with Rudolf Diels

Interior, Wilhelm Frick, despite his mildness compared to Goering, he was judged just as guilty in 1946 and did not cheat the hangman.

As an independent body, the new *Gestapo* under Goering did not last long, little more than a year. From a few dozen personnel, it expanded to employ some 40,000 men and women, including clerks, but not including of course the huge number of unpaid informers across the Reich. In 1933 it faced a mammoth task in trying to infiltrate the lives of some seventy-five million Germans, soon to become the *Grossdeutschesreich* through annexation and conquest, thus stretching the *Gestapo* and other security forces to far greater limits.

As a rule, the *Gestapo* made the arrests: in the dock at Nuremberg, Otto Ohlendorf of the SD testified that his men only acted as the 'long-range intelligence service' for the *Gestapo*. In fact, both forces overlapped in action, whatever agreements and rules were made, resulting in wastefulness.

As noted, it was the usage and of course scope of the Nazi political police branch which distinguished it from similar departments in the democracies. It is impossible to note when such organisations were first used, since individuals of course had acted as internal spies for centuries, probably longer. One can cite with certainty Sir Francis Walsingham as one of the first to organise political spying, both at home and overseas; his Queen Elizabeth I was kept informed of plots and political undercurrents in her court and among foreign establishments, as far as the insufficient funds allowed. The Soviets naturally exercised huge repression, probably the greatest known, through their own secret police, organised on a vast scale to oversee everything in Stalin's empire. Heinrich Himmler hoped not merely to emulate him, but to surpass the Soviet model with his *Gestapo* – once he laid hands on it.

One early chronicler of the *Gestapo* has pointed out the 'extreme youth' of the men who first frightened the German people into submission before 'trampling on the flower of European culture'. The men who gained almost total power in Germany, Himmler and Heydrich, were still only thirty-three and twenty-nine years old respectively in 1933–4. When Heydrich's successor Walter Schellenberg took over the SD and later the *Abwehr* he was around thirty-five. It was young men like these who cowed older and elderly men of the military into compliance – or withdrawal from Germany's affairs. They proved capable of trapping almost anyone into situations that resulted in death, imprisonment or banishment. They knew no limits in their pursuit and use of power.

For the historian, witnesses who were on the spot and involved in *Gestapo* (and for that matter, SD) methods and actions are virtually impossible to find – and for obvious reasons. The army of agents, clerks and administrators vanished into obscurity once the war ended, seeking anonymity in most cases. If the *Gestapo*, like the SS, was blanketed with the charge of being a criminal organisation, then it hardly paid for the thousands of humbler employees to stay in view to be arrested or interrogated by the Allies. Very few were captured and charged, mainly executives carrying out the death programmes, who were often not actually members of the *Gestapo* itself. But some of that band were often incorporated into the *Einsatzgruppen*, the travelling murder gangs who actually did most of the mass killing in the East. It proved impossible and fruitless to try and pursue clerks and typists who were always given employment in *Gestapo* offices, and even more pointless to even consider rounding up the huge number of informers across the former Greater German *Reich* whose whispers had resulted in arrest and possibly death for many.

A notable exception was Hans Bernd Gisevius, who knew the truth from inside experience and wasted little time telling his tale after the war. As an official in the Prussian Ministry of the Interior, Gisevius got to know much. He testified at Nuremberg that the idea of setting fire to the German State Parliament building (the *Reichstag*), emanated with Goebbels and Goering, and that they arranged it through the *Gestapo*, with probably some help from SA brownshirts. The whole sordid business was cooked up as an excuse to clamp down on the Reds and anyone else thought to be anti-Nazi. Goering used the fire to declare the event as the start of a communist revolution. He took the measures he loved best to implement, using SS and SA policemen, and made the utterances quoted. Goering not only had the fire started, he had in advance prepared a list of people to be arrested by the *Gestapo* for committing or being implicated in the crime. As scapegoat Goering used the Dutch halfwit Van der Lubbe, who later faced trial in Leipzig.

The above testimony from Gisevius is perfectly believable as it ties in with other evidence. Problems arise with his testimony since he was one of those who pleaded 'idealism' as the basis of all his participation in events under Hitler's rule, when he was an alleged 'career policeman' at the heart of things. The problem with Gisevius was not atypical, for having kept his life he found himself hauled up in the Nuremberg courtroom as the 'darling' witness for the American prosecution. Like others, he did everything he could to whitewash his own past, while helping to damn those Nazis in the dock. He may not have been a member of the *Gestapo*, but he was without doubt privy to much of both its methods and masters.

One commentator's view was that Gisevius joined the Nazi Party (hardly a crime) through 'idealism'. He felt happy to continue to work as a policeman under Goering and then Himmler under the same feeling, then turned against the Nazis in similar vein, presumably on discovering their real nature. It is not unbelievable. However, his reasoning begins to seem suspect when we learn how he allied himself with Artur Nebe in plotting against the Diels-run *Gestapo*. (Nebe, the old Nazi CID chief, latterly a police commissioner, went on to command one of most 'successful' murder groups in the East – an *Einsatzgruppe*.) Gisevius stated in his memoirs that while working in the Berlin police building, 'We were living in a den of murderers'. He hardly dared leave the room to wash his hands without tele-phoning a colleague beforehand to inform him 'of our intention to embark on so perilous an expedition'! This was his way of describing the working atmosphere which he claims developed in the *Gestapo* and police complex in the thirties. One can be excused for taking such evidence with more than a pinch of salt. Gisevius tried hard to establish himself as an innocent living in perpetual fear, entering and leaving the building by the rear door, always clutching a pistol in his pocket, sidling along the wall when moving up or down the stairs, fearful of showing himself near the banisters. 'It was so usual for members of the *Gestapo* to arrest one another that we scarcely took notice of such incidents.'

Perhaps Gisevius felt safer befriending Nebe in such an atmosphere of terror, an experienced detective who would be removed to a far dirtier and infamous job.

As noted, the bulk of the *Gestapo* came to comprise administrative personnel, clerks, typists and index keepers. Of the agents in the field, it would be misleading to assume they were all trained detectives, ex-CID men. Among the *Gestapo* were to be found ex-brownshirt SA men, such as Heinrich Baab, an apartment block supervisor (*Blockwart*), in other words a neighbourhood *Gestapo* spy. As a volunteer informer he received fifty marks a month, a worthwhile sum, and having proved worthy he received promotion into the security services – first the *Gestapo* in Frankfurt, then the SD. He has been described as 'plebeian', loutish, and excelling in his new-found authority. It would not be long before this hooligan graduated to the most loathsome of duties as a rounder-up of Jewish families. This involved him in the worst incidents, when children were torn from their parents during the days of the Holocaust murder programme.

Men like Baab often had chips on their shoulders, especially if they were

The half-wit van der Lubbe

31

among the 'have-nots', that class of society lacking the better luxuries of life. As a *Gestapo* agent all things became possible. Agents of the *Gestapo* not only arrested and tortured victims in various diabolical ways, they killed – and at times profited materially. Like a handful of other small and larger fry, Baab ended up on trial in Nuremberg, which ended his career with a new kind of notoriety.

Above such types who did the dirty work were the officials, often quite well-educated men, the *Kriminal Inspektors, Kriminal Assistants, Kriminalrat* officers and above them the chiefs – the *Regierungsrat*. How the *Gestapo* executive-in-chief arrived at his job is explained later. Heinrich Müller, like Himmler, was an advocate of the Soviet system of repression. The *Gestapo* under their guidance (and that of Heydrich) built up the cell system whereby thousands of dutiful citizens who loved scandal, whispers of it and anything faintly untoward could report their suspicions to the *Blockwart*, or nearest *Gestapo* supervising agent. The system spread even into the ARP and labour groups – everywhere in fact.

By this means the *Gestapo* induced a feeling of extreme caution among ordinary citizens, of unease. People feared being found out in a slip of the tongue among their fellows or even friends that might betray them as suspect in any way.

Himmler is said to have expressed surprise over the growing bad reputation of the *Gestapo*, allegedly more than once asking foreign visitors why this should be so. Presumably he was referring to unkind foreign press reports.

Both *Gestapo* and SD hounded dissidents among Germany's factory workers, especially the hard core of communists and socialists of the non-Nazi kind. This was done by infiltration, SD spies posing as workers, joining such groups in order to ascertain the truth. They would pinpoint the ring-leaders and then the *Gestapo* would swoop. There were many such incidents after Hitler came to power and the German trade unions were swept away by the Nazi German Labour Front with its compulsory dues and corps of blue-uniformed supervisors.

In 1936 a much larger workers' group of dissidents was broken up, with no fewer than 280 factory workers being arrested by the *Gestapo* and police. They were locked away in prison for eleven months 'on remand'. When they were finally brought to court the charges were:

> Reading prohibited newspapers (sentence: one to two years)
> Using private dwellings as meeting places (sentence: three years)
> Enrolling new members (sentence: three to four years)
> Working on an illegal newspaper (sentence: four to six years)

The case, which was publicised in Germany as a warning to others, was also picked up by the press outside Germany, so the democracies had no excuse for pleading ignorance about conditions in the new Nazi workers' paradise. In an article published in Goebbels's own newspaper and likely to have been written by him, it was admitted that 'the number of criminal proceedings continually pending in the People's Court for treasonable acts against Land or Reich is the result of this work' (i.e. work done by the *Gestapo* and SD). The article, simply a glowing exposé of the guardians' work in protecting the Nazi State, went on to emphasise that 'all open struggle and all open opposition to the State and leadership is forbidden', and that opponents of National Socialism had not been eliminated by a simple Act of prohibition, therefore the secret police were necessary to ferret them out. The writer could hardly have been more frank, going on to explain the 'ideal' behind the term 'protective custody', which usually meant an indefinite spell in a concentration camp. It was not possible to appeal against a decision of the *Gestapo*, whose 'law' overrode all other authorities – a Decree of 10 February 1936 saw to that.

Neither was the Church immune from *Gestapo* visitations and arrests. Monasteries and other religious institutions were raided and, it is said, the agents rarely left empty-handed.

Gestapo techniques during interrogations ranged from verbal bullying of the worst screaming, 'sergeant-major' type, to actual physical torture which included beatings with rubber cudgels, the use of electrodes to the most sensitive parts, immersion in scalding-hot and then ice-cold baths, removal of finger and toenails and experiments with drugs. One man who, surprisingly, survived to describe his capture was Captain Payne Best, kidnapped by the SD inside the Dutch border in November 1939. Though considered a 'privileged' prisoner, he was greeted in the typical secret police style, not by one of the men detailed to beat him up, but 'Stapo

Heinrich Müller, executive head of the Gestapo

33

Müller' (then chief of the *Gestapo*) himself. This was before he was turned over to Heydrich.

Best, somewhat kindly, described Müller as an exceptionally good-looking man, dressed 'like Hitler', in a grey jacket, black riding breeches and top boots. He began his *Anschnauzen* (a kind of bullying, snorting shout), as soon as he entered the room, 'increasing the pitch and volume of his voice with great virtuosity', and by the time they were almost nose-to-nose, the *Gestapo* boss was tearing his vocal chords to shreds.

> You are in the hands of the *Gestapo*. Don't imagine that we shall show you the slightest consideration. The *Führer* has already shown the world he is invincible and soon he will come to liberate England from the Jews and Plutocrats such as you!

Müller then tried to intimidate Best by drawing up a chair and sitting close in front of him, fixing him with his 'rather funny eyes which he could flicker from side to side with the greatest rapidity and I suppose that was supposed to strike terror into the heart of the beholder'.

It was then the turn of Heydrich, who also began with verbal bullying, working up to a great pitch when the captured British spy calmly enquired of Müller, 'Who is this excitable young officer?'

Yet Best was very fairly treated, as explained elsewhere (see Chapter 12).

Legal rights for *Gestapo* action were established as early as 28 February 1933, barely one month after the Nazis gained power. Article 2 of a Decree issued by the *Reich* President gave the *Gestapo* the exclusive right to send people into protective custody. Furthermore, and even though the *Gestapo* had no hand in running the concentration camps, it was given the job of categorising such camps, from the mildest (*Dachau*), to Mauthausen, which became an extermination camp. The *Gestapo* also provided 'political advisers' for such camps, which as is well known were extended after 1940 to handle the increasing number of victims.

The actions of the *Gestapo* against the Jews was, however, somewhat unorganised and spasmodic until the passing of the various Decrees incorporated as the 'Nuremberg laws' and published yearly in the Nazi Party's handbook. Even then there were discussions and arguments about what should be done with the Jews, with no authoritative views put forward by people like Müller, who was a mere executive. It was left to others of higher calibre and weight to forcefully present ideas that seemed feasible. While thousands of Jews were forced out of the *Reich* by intimidation, threats and physical means, being taken into other countries, men like Heydrich advocated taking ransom money. Finance Minister Schacht was all for milking the Jews via their capital and other assets. Thousands of Polish Jews were removed to the fields of the German-Polish border area by Heydrich, remaining there because the Poles refused them sanctuary.

The senseless assassination of a German diplomat in Paris by a Jewish youth in 1938 gave the Nazis an excuse to unleash more terror against the

Jews in Germany. Müller instructed his *Gestapo* to arrest 20–30,000 Jews, preferably those who were well-off. When Heydrich submitted his report to Goering, some 20,000 Jews had been taken into custody, 191 synagogues and 171 apartment houses burnt down, and 7,500 shops looted or destroyed. Thirty-six Jews were killed. Goering, Goebbels and other Nazis were shocked, not by the damage to Jewish property, but the accidental ruin of neighbouring non-Jewish premises, etc. Of course, as Propaganda Minister it was a disaster for Goebbels, who weighed the damage in terms of hostile foreign opinion.

Once Himmler had taken over the police, their files would become open to the *Gestapo*, who would extract the names of known informers for their own use. Heydrich's SD found its own spies. When Himmler and Heydrich began overhauling and expanding the *Gestapo* after January 1933, the SD chief made sure to install his own spies in the secret police departments. They had access to Müller's card indexes, as Heydrich wanted to keep abreast of events in the *Gestapo*. But the reverse did not happen.

Heydrich sought spies beyond the calibre of the usual police 'narks' and stool pigeons, men of greater intelligence who had 'front' and could move in the right military and political circles – including those of the Nazi Party. Watching over the Nazis had been Himmler's idea, but Heydrich had far bigger vistas in mind.

It would be wrong to assume that Heinrich Müller, once pulled in to act as *Gestapo* executive, employed only semi-idiots or back-street layabouts as spies. The *Gestapo* developed very good ears in all walks of German life, from the top to the bottom of society. Nevertheless, Müller spies were generally of a lesser calibre than those well paid by Heydrich.

Dr Werner Best, Gestapo overseer

Months passed before Himmler was satisfied his new-style *Gestapo* was functioning well enough in Berlin. He then set about, with Heydrich, duplicating it throughout Germany, despatching representatives to every town and city to explain to police chiefs the need to set up local *Gestapo* offices to replace the existing restricted political police departments. It was not difficult, as everyone was aware of the 'Bolshevik' menace, which was played up by the Nazis at every opportunity. Though by 1933 the power of the communists had been largely broken, both Hitler and Himmler feared a 'second revolution' by some Judean-Marxist-Freemason plot, a backlash that would dislodge the foundation stones being laid for the 'Thousand-Year *Reich*'.

The civil police were largely sympathetic, but not entirely, as some officers were already committed socialists and even tuned in to communist propaganda. How far such policemen were prepared to go is hard to say, but once discovered they had to be removed. This was done by presenting them with facts; if they agreed to switch loyalty to Hitler they were placed on probation and watched until their superiors were satisfied they posed no threat. However, in a few cases more severe measures had to be taken. In one instance, a known Red informed on 'his man' in the regular police, disclosing how the man (a captain) had been keeping the local Communist Party office informed of plans to get rid of them. Everything the police did or planned was known in advance by the Reds. The police captain was arrested, charged, tried, and sent to a concentraton camp.

Generally, the fullest co-operation was provided by the civil police throughout Germany, so that as early as mid-1934 a very effective *Gestapo* organisation had been established throughout Germany which swiftly informed its Berlin headquarters of any matter of importance. If the matter became priority, Müller sent a report to Himmler, who in turn ordered a representative to investigate further. This would usually be a plain clothes *Oberkommissar* who had Himmler's authority to act in any way he saw fit, and that entailed overriding any high police authority or Party boss in that area.

All of the usual *Gestapo* agents wore civilian clothes, and the majority were ex-police detectives or men offered the chance to escape from the run-of-the-mill CID work. The rest of the personnel were 'apprentices', trained in Berlin classes under professional detectives. These tutors were carefully vetted by Himmler and obliged like everyone else to swear an oath of secrecy and allegiance to Himmler and the *Führer*. In these highly secret matters Himmler made it clear that as far as the *Gestapo* was concerned, no one below the *Führer* was sacrosanct. The secret police and SD had authority to delve into anything, no matter who was involved. Naturally, those in higher positions had to be treated with respect, and investigations among top Nazis had to be conducted with the utmost discretion, with any findings presented to Himmler and the *Führer* for their decision.

Lower down the scale it was different. Anyone suspected of illegal activities, which after 1933 covered a very wide range, could be arrested for questioning, or taken into *Schutzhaft* – protective custody. The bedrock of the *Gestapo* system became the 'V-man' – the *Vertrauungsmann*, or trusted one. V-men were informer-agents paid weekly to report to the local *Gestapo* officer, who was often located in the police station, a mere room provided with desk and telephone. This *Gestapo* representative would call weekly, from town to town, collecting reports for evaluation and taking action whenever needed. The V-men (and sometimes women) ranged far around their own territory, though never allowed for the sake of tidy organisation to work outside their zone. These employees were encouraged to use sub-agents, who in turn reported to them regularly. The informers included the street and flat *Blockwarts*, caretakers, or simple neighbours with long noses and large ears who relished gossip and could be relied on to pass it on to the right quarter. In this manner, over the course of the years every citizen in Germany found it wiser to remain mute on certain matters. Despite this, as the SD opinion monitors found, people did talk, and quite freely at times, especially when the war took a downturn in Germany's disfavour.

The bottom-of-the-tier spies were of course not on any official payroll, but once enrolled expected to work as patriotic, loyal Germans. Even the V-men often remained unpaid, though at times expenses if incurred could be helped with. Himmler kept a very tight rein on expenditure, despite the rapid growth of his empire. He insisted on overseeing details, and that included the accounts of every department under his command.

In all *Gestapo* investigations, the help of the civil police could be called upon, both in personnel and vehicles. The local 'general' SS could also be called upon if more men were needed, for large-scale searches for example – but never the SD. The *Gestapo* agents became very professional. Every single male or female *Gestapo* agent was of pure German nationality, though those they used were at times otherwise. In fact, in one exceptional case an English subject turned willing informer in France and worked for both *Gestapo* and SD.

Himmler made regular reports to Hitler on his progress in building up the German police forces, including both SD and *Gestapo*, the latter being his prime mover in the war against subversives. Being the kind of man he was, Himmler saw Reds and other undesirables under every bed. He had an inborn fear and suspicion of almost everyone, even those of his own flock, no matter how well he knew or treated them. His use of the term 'comrade' meant little, no one ever became a very close friend of Himmler. If he thought a comrade suspect in even the slightest degree he would turn on him at once.

Despite Himmler's zeal, the kind of blanket surveillance coverage that he had envisaged across the *Reich* proved impossible, or only achievable by using many thousands of trained agents. The training class in Berlin was small: what was needed was a national academy for secret policemen. It was not feasible to train them on the job, as there were not enough officers to act as tutors. At one early conference the idea of an academy was mooted, but owing to the cost the scheme faded to nothing, and the many *Gestapo* officers across Germany were forced to make do, directions coming from Berlin.

The regular *Gestapo* agent's pay was based on that of the civil police detective force, subject to the usual norms of experience and length of service. Only the officers carried rank titles, *Inspektor* and *Kommissar*. Every *Gestapo* agent carried an oval-shaped disc made of brass or zinc which bore on one side his number, and on the reverse the eagle-swastika and *Geheime Staatspolizei* – Secret State Police. The only other item issued was a pistol, usually the Lüger, Walther or the much smaller Walther PPK, which fitted much more neatly into jacket or coat pockets. Anything else needed was his (or her) own affair, handcuffs and notebook for example. In terms of character, the successful secret policeman needed unending curiosity, the ability to keep ears and eyes open – and his mouth shut – plus of course an absolute dedication to the Nazi cause.

Much of the above applied to Heydrich's SD sleuths, as in the field the work was more or less the same, though they were not given the power of

The former Communist Party HQ taken over by the Gestapo

arrest, which remained – initially at least – the prerogative of *Gestapo* and police.

As the number of agents grew in Germany, so did the amount of paperwork. An ever-increasing flow of reports reached Berlin, which in turn meant SD and *Gestapo* were obliged to take on more staff. Himmler allowed ordinary civilians to be enrolled through the usual employment channels, but vetted them all and had them sign the usual oath of secrecy. Heydrich did his own recruiting, and made even stricter checks on his staff's background. No difficulties were experienced in using such staff, whose work was usually routine office work of the kind found everywhere, and most were female. Both *Gestapo* and SD expanded their offices once the large building in Prinz-Albrecht-Strasse was occupied, fitting them out with all the usual paraphernalia of office equipment. The scale of this national effort meant an increasing budget, but there was never any problem, Hitler saw to that. However, the sheer bureaucracy of it all became staggering, and when much later the Allied air raids caused much damage to the *Gestapo* building in Berlin, great confusion resulted as thousands of files went up in smoke.

Each department of *Gestapo* and SD needed a head man, or woman. These posts were mostly administrative and easily filled by people used to office organisation. But the directing brains above them were of course Himmler's picked men, each allowed certain executive powers within his own sphere. Those of the *Gestapo* worked under the ex-policeman Heinrich Müller, who in effect became executive head of a large corporation. However, without the cash profit motive to drive this concern the most obvious comparison is that of a government agency of today. These agencies, like the *Gestapo* and to a lesser extent the SD, employ large staffs and spend freely, and being by nature expansive, end up as gigantic, wasteful bureaucracies.

Müller never went into the field, of course; as 'corporation' boss he sat behind a desk, and since his mental capacities were seen by some as limited, he was provided with a guiding hand above, another Himmler man, Dr Werner Best. Another Nazi 'thinker', Best was an alleged admirer of the philosopher Ernst Junger – and of Hitler. A senior civil servant and jurist, he provided the wider view, the strategic direction for Müller. Surprisingly, he is said to have disapproved of certain tendencies in National Socialism, and of the war. However, he accepted the post of Hitler's Plenipotentiary to the 'Model Protectorate' of Denmark in 1942, when he saw fit to don the Diplomatic Corps uniform.

A much more favourable view of the sometimes alleged clod Müller was given by Rudolf Hoess, ex-chief of Auschwitz concentration camp, who managed to pass himself off as an ex-sailor until tracked down and arrested by British military police soon after the war ended. After a few beatings mixed in with his interrogations, he was turned over to the Poles for his part in the extermination process and permitted to write his memoirs before being hanged. According to Hoess, Müller played a 'decisive part' in the *Gestapo*'s development, and though he did not care to be associated with actual operations or actions, he was responsible for organising all the larger and most important of them and planned their execution. He became well informed about all major political events in the *Reich* and had many trusted friends in all kinds of official positions. Hoess also alleged that though Müller always referred only to the *Reichsführer*'s wishes in every-thing, in fact Himmler and later Kaltenbrunner depended on him in many matters, including that of appointments, and the details and fate of pris-oners. According to Hoess he was a tenacious worker, versatile, ever available, obliging and friendly, never standing on rank – yet impossible to get close to. He was in fact, as one senior British commentator added, an ice-cold executive of all the measures Himmler saw necessary for the security of the *Reich*.

Did the *Gestapo* ever operate in Britain before the war? Proof is lacking, but one ex-MI5 agent, Joan Miller, remarked in her memoirs (*One Girl's War* (Brandon Books 1986)) that the Elizabeth Arden cosmetics building in London (where she worked), was used by the *Gestapo* as a rendezvous point. While her tale dwells too much on irrelevancies and too little on spies, it is illuminating on some points and comparable to the main theme of this work.

Miss Miller was prodded by her mother, long before war came, to find something useful to do for her country in an emergency. She therefore succumbed to a female chum's suggestion to try for a job at the War Office. Her interview took place months before September 1939, and on the very day war was declared a telegram arrived inviting her to be at a request bus stop opposite the Natural History Museum, where she would find an unnumbered bus which would transport her to 'Room 005'. On the bus she found other girls and a few aloof men in bowler hats, all recruits bussed to the War Office, in Miss Miller's case MI5. Surprisingly, the counter-espionage department was moved to Wormwood Scrubs prison, the staff taking over converted cells as offices. When the air raids came the following year one wing was struck by bombs and files were lost – much as the *Gestapo*'s files were lost in Berlin later on during Allied air attacks.

Her attractive looks ensured Miss Miller progressed immediately. She was soon the pet of 'Captain King', the chief of MI5 Section B5(b), alias Maxwell Knight, who was known as 'M'. He began using his new recruit most successfully to penetrate and uncover pro-German plotters in London. Maxwell Knight also wasted little time romancing Miss Miller, and setting her up in a flat as his lover, all strictly against the rules. But, no doubt much to her dismay and lasting bitterness, 'M' saw fit by 1945 to end their relationship by 'brutally' informing her that if an enquiry was held into an important file *he* had lost, then because of his more important repu-tation she would have to shoulder the blame. She ended her six years of war effort under this cloud and retired to Malta, where she died in 1984.

Hermann Goering, first chief of police and Gestapo

Hermann Goering, first chief of police and Gestapo

How the *Gestapo* netted one of its own female operatives is described in *Under Hitler's Banner* (this author, Airlife 1996).

The story is most interesting from several aspects, illustrating as it does not only *Gestapo* methods, but also the fact that the agency also duplicated *Abwehr* and SD efforts in espionage – this time against Germany's supposed ally, the Italians.

The young female had worked as a cook in a private boys' college in Hanover; when it was taken over as a leadership school by the Hitler Youth she continued in the same job. Catering for some two hundred youths was hard work, and though provided with a boy helper, she was overworked, became bored and quit. She had also been astonished and embarrassed to receive a proposal from one of the older students.

The girl next obtained a post as cook-housekeeper through a newspaper advertisement, her employers being one of the city's Nazi Party bosses and his wife. One day, not long after settling into the job, she happened to be alone in the sumptuous villa when two men and a woman called, one of them introducing himself as of the *Gestapo*, his colleagues waiting outside in a car. Following questioning as to her trustworthiness and, having warned her to secrecy, they left. They called again while her employers were

41

absent, telling her she should now accept a more important job – working for the government. Not long afterwards the woman was told to pack up and go home, without saying anything to her employers; and within days she received a further call instructing her to meet the agents who were waiting for her in their car around the corner. Telling her parents she had been 'called up' to work in a government establishment elsewhere, she left home with a suitcase to meet the *Gestapo* trio.

Several hours later she was delivered to a *Gestapo* post in Berlin, completely mystified and apprehensive. She was then told she would take up a post in the Italian Embassy as a kitchen helper and maid. (The same kind of ploy was used by MI5 in Britain.) Her *Gestapo* mentor, called Frank, would meet her on Friday evenings to receive reports on everything she heard among the Italian staff – and pay her a salary. She would also receive the fare to go home once a month, but was sworn to secrecy.

A rather innocent, unsophisticated girl, with no experience whatever with the opposite sex, she now found herself being propositioned by one of the more amorous minor Italian diplomats. Alarmed, she reported this to her mentor, who was delighted, ordering her to agree to the Italian's invitation to spend a weekend with him in a borrowed country cottage outside Berlin. This she most reluctantly agreed to, her worst fears proving well founded when the Italian tried to seduce her in his bedroom. Indeed, success was almost his when three *Gestapo* agents burst into the room to grab the astonished, extremely embarrassed and angry Italian, who was suitably clad for the occasion in a frilly nightshirt. While the female *Gestapo* agent comforted the terrified girl, her two male colleagues set about convincing the hapless, would-be seducer he had better play ball with them. Otherwise, he would face a terrible public scandal when accused of trying to rape an innocent German girl.

The objective of course had been to blackmail the Italian into working for the *Gestapo* in his own embassy, to spy on his colleagues and report regularly to his new employers. One must assume this is what happened. The girl was taken back into the city and put on a train for home, her mission accomplished. She was never again employed by the *Gestapo*, but warned to complete secrecy.

3

AN 'INFORMATION SERVICE'

B orn in Halle on 7 March 1904, the man whose name would inspire fear in Europe was christened Reinhard Tristan Eugen by a Catholic priest. He was the second son of Elizabeth and Bruno Heydrich, a singer and devotee of Wagner's music. Bruno Heydrich was also a composer of operatic works, who by hard effort had elevated himself into the middle classes, which was how he came to meet Elizabeth, herself from a middle-class, prosperous family in Dresden.

In 1899 the Heydrichs opened a conservatory in Halle to teach music to children of the better classes, and it was in such an atmosphere that young Reinhard developed real talent as a violinist. However, his father Bruno's aspirations to advance further were thwarted, possibly because of the anti-semitism rife in the town. Reinhard's paternal grandfather had died young, and his wife remarried in Meissen. She married a man called Robert Suess, which was regarded as a Jewish name. This was the basis of later rumours and indeed belief that the head of the Nazi security services and leading anti-semitic was himself of Jewish extraction. Was Heydrich responsible for having a fresh gravestone made which expunged any mention of a Jewish name? It has been disclosed that a receipt for such a job was found in Heydrich's private papers after his death. Long before, in the early thirties, a *Gauleiter* got hold of some evidence which he passed to Gregor Strasser, one of Hitler's close allies before rivalry led to his downfall. Eventually, the file on Heydrich's origins went into the Nazi Party's *Panzerschrank* (armoured safe), kept by Martin Bormann, with Himmler well apprised of its contents.

All this has been well dug over, with varying degrees of detail, by historians, though none seems to have seized on it as an explanation of Heydrich's own anti-Semitic beliefs. Even if it was true that Heydrich desired to expunge any record of such ancestry, which was crucial to a member of the SS, his 'upbringing' in an atmosphere of virulent anti-Jewish propaganda ensured his 'conditioning' in that direction. There was also alleged suffering at school through the anti-Jewish taunts of other boys. Being Catholic in a Protestant area did not help, either.

The suggestion is, therefore, that the Heydrich family suffered in one way or another on racial grounds, and that Bruno's application to the local authority for permission and funds to enlarge his music conservatory was

The SD (Sicherheitsdienst) sleeve emblem

turned down through such prejudice. *Frau* Heydrich wished them to move to Dresden, believing her better-off parents would help them financially, but this is said to have been frustrated by her two brothers.

Yet, whatever difficulties were encountered by Reinhard at school, he progressed with excellence. Not even the war of 1914–18 nor its worse aftermath in Germany stunted his efforts in education. With Bolshevik revolution in the air, Bruno Heydrich joined the local nationalist *Freikorps Maercker*, whose members were mostly ex-soldiers dedicated to combating the rising tide of unrest and attempts to 'sovietise' Germany spreading from Moscow. It is also recorded that Bruno transferred to an anti-semitic group called the *Deutschen Schutz and Trotzbund*, whose emblem was a corn-flower and swastika, permitting his son Reinhard to join them as a runner. The sixteen-year-old Reinhard was embroiled in what amounted to civil war, as were many enthusiastic youths of the day. But his great vitality enabled him to continue his studies and pass his examinations before reaching eighteen. He had already surprised and disappointed his parents by announcing his intention to volunteer for the navy – the *Reichsmarine* – a collection of small coastal craft permitted by the Allies' Treaty of Versailles.

When Reinhard Heydrich arrived at Kiel to join the old training cruiser *Berlin* as a cadet in late spring 1922, he carried a brand-new, fine-quality violin, a parting gift from his father. Whatever derision came from his fellows, it did not stop Reinhard from practising or indeed making great efforts in his training. Unlike many 'landlubbers', he seems to have taken to the navy life like the proverbial duck to water, surpassing most of the cadets and becoming especially adept in small boat handling. Further, unusually for an intellectual, he showed great enthusiasm and ability in sports, winning prizes in military pentathlons, and even breaking his nose twice while horseriding. He also relentlessly pursued his ambition to become the best in fencing. However, after losing one contest he threw down his épée in a fit of petulance, thereby earning the umpire's rebuke.

For relaxation Heydrich loved to read detective and spy thrillers, and being an impressionable youth, he easily convinced himself that Germany was riddled with foreign spies. By a quirk of fate the man who now took him under his wing later became Germany's spy chief. Captain Canaris was the First and Executive Officer on the *Berlin*, which may have been a cover, for his 'real' job was aide-de-camp to Rear Admiral Baron von Gagern of the Baltic naval station, actually a front for political conspiracies and subversion against both the Allies and the then German democratic government. The plotters harboured impossible dreams of restoring the Kaiser, and above all of rearmament.

An early group photo c 1931–3: 1 – Himmler   2 – Sepp Dietrich   3 – Kurt Daluege
4 – Reinhard Heydrich

Captain Canaris soon discovered he had a most unusual and talented cadet aboard his ship and invited Heydrich home to meet *Frau* Canaris, herself a violinist who held regular musical soirées. There were Sunday evening get-togethers of a quartet to play Mozart and Haydn. Heydrich had been looked on as something of a prodigy at school, and *Frau* Canaris was impressed and invited the cadet to join in her musical evenings. The Canaris family learned of the young visitor's family background, doubtless impressed that his mother was the daughter of a former high official in the court of the Royal House of Saxony.

In 1924, Captain Canaris left the training ship to take up a post connected with foreign intelligence matters in Berlin. He had by then enthused his cadet friend with amazing tales of adventures at sea and thwarting foreign enemies. The captain had a never-ending stock of tales to hand, and escapades and intrigue seemed to be his tools in trade. Reinhard passed out as *Fahnrich*, or midshipman, around that time, gaining the rank of *Oberfahnrich* early in 1926 after studying English, French and Russian. In July of that year he gained his Navigation Certificate and was promoted to sub-lieutenant; he passed intelligence tests in languages and was now permitted to take command of small craft. His career as a naval officer seemed set.

Not unusually for a handsome young naval officer, Heydrich enjoyed several short-lived affairs with young women, though it is alleged his good looks also brought him unwelcome male attention at times, including advances from an officer of superior rank. By autumn 1926 he had been promoted to full lieutenant and was stationed in the *Schnellboot* (Torpedo Boat) Division at Wilhelmshaven base, becoming an assistant on tactics. Two years of this service passed before he achieved his ambition to take a shipboard job as Radio and Signals Officer. He was then put ashore again, joining the admiral's staff at Kiel in a job concerned with naval intelligence.

It was now that his very promising naval career took a downward turn, one that would propel him into unemployment – and then the job. Fate seemed intent on casting him for.

Two romances blossomed, one of the blondes spending a night in his quarters. Before long she informed him she was pregnant, obviously expecting Heydrich to marry her. He did not love the girl and refused. In any case, he had just met a far better prospect, a striking blonde of good family who, though nineteen, was still attending high school at Kiel. Lina Mathilde von Osten was the daughter of a schoolmaster living on the Baltic island of Fehmarn. By Christmas 1930 their relationship had blossomed and they were betrothed. However, his other lady friend's father was determined to pursue the issue, and during a stormy interview demanded Heydrich marry his pregnant daughter. Heydrich explained that this was impossible – he was already engaged to another. Unfortunately, the irate and thwarted father was a wealthy industrialist with important connections, whose friends in high places included Grand Admiral Raeder, of the *Reichsmarine*. Lieutenant Heydrich was summoned to Berlin to face the admiral's inquisition and was sent packing to face a naval court of honour. The stiff-necked officers were less than impressed by the young man's explanation. He was dismissed from the navy.

For Heydrich this came as a totally unexpected and shattering blow to his pride and career. He gave his version of events to his fiancée Lina, and when inevitably her parents learned of the situation they protested she must break off the engagement.

Supposedly of Scandinavian stock, Lina proved tough and determined. She would stand by her man, and the couple were married on Boxing Day 1931. Lina, a member of the National Socialist Party, now urged her un-employed husband to join and find a job through them. But Heydrich had not been impressed by the brownshirt rowdies and other Nazis he had seen. His new wife persisted, telling him of interesting developments in Munich, where she had a good friend called von Oberstein who had joined the SS; being of good background, he was already acquainted with the leading Nazis in Bavaria – including Heinrich Himmler. Curiously, the man had some link, as his mother had been godmother to Reinhard's own mother. Heydrich, after some reluctance, wrote to von Oberstein, outlining his six-year career in the navy. Von Oberstein replied, saying his chief Himmler would be glad to meet him, but he must first join the Party. This Heydrich did, becoming member No. 544, 916.

In mid-June 1931 Heydrich pressed von Oberstein to fix a meeting with Himmler, having in the meantime become involved in street brawls as a serving member of the SS, something Himmler and his aides discouraged. The concept of élitism, an 'apartness', was already being practised in the black order. Himmler, who would not allow his élite to become too em-broiled with Ernst Roehm's SA brownshirt rabble, was already toying with the idea of forming a 'super-élite' within his SS, an intelligence service to spy on both the SA and opponents. He had drawn up a short list of possible candidates to head such a group and agreed to interview the ex-naval officer. However, at the last moment von Oberstein told Heydrich not to travel to Munich, as his boss was unwell. Not to be put off, Heydrich brazenly sent a wire advising that he intended to keep the appointment, so that von Oberstein was forced to meet him off the express train at Munich, his irritation obvious. Still forceful, Heydrich persuaded the officer to call Himmler, and the SS chief made a show of reluctantly agreeing to see him.

Heydrich bussed to the Himmler poultry farm at Waldrudering. Himmler invited him into his house and looked the visitor over as he outlined his history. Heydrich was frank in telling Himmler why he had lost his job in the Navy, his host apparently amused by this revelation. They talked generally about the situation in Germany, which was still unsettled, with constant struggle between the opposing political parties and the armed factions of some. As for the SS, it was but one of the various Nazi uniformed organisations, paramilitaries, and at the time numbered about 14,000 men. Himmler explained his desire to form an intelligence unit, not mentioning that he had another leading contender for chief, an ex-major of the Bavarian political police called Hornigner. But Himmler had savvy enough to see he needed someone better than a mere provincial policeman, someone of perhaps a better background, of superior intellect as well as organising ability. The daring applicant from the north seemed to have the qualities he was looking for. He also fitted in very nicely with Himmler's notions of the blond, Nordic superman.

Himmler gave the visitor just twenty minutes to explain on paper his embryo ideas on the kind of intelligence unit he had in mind. When that time was up he read through Heydrich's proposals and, impressed, gave him the job at once.

Heydrich went home to Hamburg to tell Lina the good news, then packed a bag and departed again for Munich, where he ensconced himself in rooms on the fourth floor of a house at Turkenstrasse 23, owned by *Frau* Viktoria Edrich. The four rooms would serve as both living quarters and offices of the new Department 1c of the SS, its 'Information Service'.

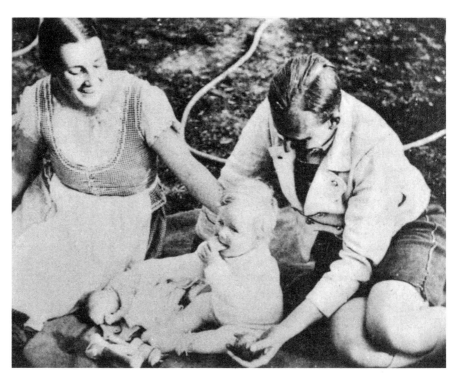

The family Heydrich

Himmler turned over the files he had already collected on various Party members and SA leaders. Heydrich began reading them and then set about starting a card index system. Meanwhile, the SS HQ enlarged its own file on Lieutenant Heydrich (he had transferred from the SA into the SS immediately on accepting the job). He was given three assistants, friends of the SS, enthusiastic volunteers intrigued at being involved in something that smacked of spying, all sworn to secrecy. The 'Information Service' grew rapidly, a fourth helper being acquired; one of Heydrich's early staff brought her own typewriter to the office, and was alleged to be a frustrated novelist. All were as wholehearted as Heydrich in detestation of the Bolshevik menace, this constantly reiterated by their boss who watched over and directed the work. He became something of a friend and mentor to them, so they trusted him. Only later did it become apparent to them that the term 'enemies of the state' covered far wider parameters than a few thousand Red activists. But, initially at any rate, Heydrich's staff believed it was the communists and their supporters who most needed ferreting out.

Naturally, Heydrich's boss had not appointed him to run a mere card index system. Himmler wanted a force of agents, and had all sorts of grand ideas along those lines. He envisaged a nationwide service of spies and informers. This ambition was, initially, to be channelled at the right time into the 'Gestapo', which did not then exist. The problem facing Himmler, and therefore his new spy chief Heydrich, was how to build up such a force, with funds so short it was well nigh impossible to recruit the right kind of men and women as agents. The paltry state of finances became apparent to Lina when she joined her husband in Munich in mid-1932. Heydrich was paid a mere £15 per month, and she had to cater not only for herself and her husband in the small accommodation, but the staff also. Indeed, things got much worse, for the weakening government now tried to ban all uniformed political organisations, and since it had the power of the police to call on, the Nazis were forced to comply. The Heydrich office became the 'Press Bureau', salaries fell or were not paid at all and they existed on bread and potatoes.

By July 1932 the government ban was lifted, and Heydrich was promoted to *Standartenführer*, or colonel. He saw Himmler often, now gaining something of his chief's notions on racial theory, of Nordic heroes in history and the *Reichsführer*'s own researches and beliefs about supposed antecedents such as Henry the Fowler (876–936), the one-time king whose tomb at Quedlingburg became a Nazi shrine – or at least, a place of pilgrimage for Himmler. Anything concerned with the Nordic race, including of course Viking history, was fascinating to Himmler, though anyone less Nordic than himself would be hard to find. Himmler would become renowned for his racial theorising among his fellow Nazis and others, most of them finding him a bore. If Heydrich was among these he never rejected the pet theories of the great menace of Jewish-Bolshevik penetration and desire for world mastery.

Maintaining comradely relations with leading Nazis came easily enough to Heydrich, even with the scarred, tough, ex-soldier and lately trainer to the Bolivian Army whose SA brownshirt corps had been of crucial help to Hitler. Ernst Roehm was a born roughneck and revolutionary socialist, like many of his followers little different to the communists in method. Though he had risen to the rank of captain in the German Army, he was in essence a sergeant-major type, but with brainpower enough to be very articulate, able to set out his tenets in book form. However, he lacked the subtler intellect and cunning of his SS rivals, who would seize the opportunity to get rid of him for ever. Privately, Heydrich detested him, but in the power politics of the time it was most expedient to remain aligned with the brownshirt commander.

Roehm was one of the two godfathers following the birth of Heydrich's first child Klaus. It was July 1933, Hitler had come to power six months before, having been appointed Chancellor of Germany by a reluctant, ailing President Hindenburg. It was a time of deliverance for Heydrich and his small *Sicherheitsdienst* (the SD), for once the Nazis grasped the State Treasury there were funds available for everybody with positions to fill and empires to build. The SD expanded rapidly, not that it would ever match the *Gestapo* in size, for its creators never intended it to. Heydrich insisted his service be run by specialists, carefully chosen men who applied or were plucked from obscurity by himself, certainly not clodding ex-policemen, though such types had their uses. Heydrich needed men with real brains, not Nazi fanatics, men like Otto Ohlendorf and Walter Schellenberg who had backgrounds in law and would almost certainly have remained unknowns had Heydrich not lifted them out of nowhere. These were the clever types with no history of Nazi politics or street brawling; they were not 'old fighters' (*alte Kämpfer*), and were only typical of a number who saw a grand chance to carve careers 'in government', or at least, in one of its agencies. At the start they were little more than administrators, though later on, of course, much changed, especially for Ohlendorf, who would be arraigned in the dock at Nuremberg after the war as a criminal.

Elaborate uniforms, regalia, marches and carefully crafted rituals became part of the Nazi show, though men like Heydrich's department heads shunned these. Indeed, there was one individual in the SD staff who openly gave his view that the Nazi regime would prove to be far from permanent: it was merely one more government – other types of administration would follow. This of course was worse than sacrilege to National Socialists, who really began to believe in a 'Thousand-Year *Reich*' – it was treason. But dogma was not part of these men's make-up; they entered the SD for its job prospects and made the most of it. To Allied interrogators in 1945, men like Ohlendorf presented a peculiar new breed of intellectual killer, cold, calculating sadists who administered murder processes, but normally never touched a pistol themselves.

Whatever their capabilities, in 1933 such men were mere beginners in an organisation Himmler and his protégé Heydrich set to watch over the various factions as well as larger sections in Germany which could prove troublesome. Apart from the brownshirt menace under Roehm and his clique, there was a large corps of aristocratic Prussian generals, many of whom were prepared to co-operate with the new government with stiff-necked reserve. They were as a race apart from the Nazi upstarts, of a breed whose families and forefathers had run things across Germany for hundreds of years. In no way could Himmler trust such people.

But it was a happy time for the SD chief. His old pleadings for more funds had always been met by, 'I know, I know. You must be patient, everything is going our way, before long you will have all the money you need'. Such rejoinders from Himmler had been Heydrich's lot for two years, so that more than once he came close to resignation. The crises had been the clamp-down by the government, which had virtually driven the Nazis into bankruptcy. The Party had failed to win the majority it needed in the elections. Indeed, Hitler never did win a landslide victory at the polls, his party simply ended up with more votes than the others, but it was no convincing triumph. Only after gaining power did he contrive against weak opposition to deprive all other parties and the working man's unions of their power. It was the most diabolical and extraordinary process of political rape in Western European history.

In the early days, Heydrich's intelligence had had to be derived from hearsay and gossip, rumours and unsubstantiated tales passed on by part-time informers, some of them SS or even SA men. Everyone knew of the 'disgusting' homosexual circle among the SA leadership, some of them being Roehm's closest collaborators. Edmund Heines was one of them – he was a large man with feminine good looks. It was known the brownshirt chief himself was not averse to a little mixing when it came to sexual activity. To Himmler especially such men were anathema and not fit to hold any kind of office; Roehm and his men were already agitating for the rewards they felt due, but most would gain nothing in return for their years of revolutionary struggle, and many would vanish in the holocaust of war to come.

Himmler, with his rigid principles of racial purity, would tolerate nothing outside the norms of decent family upbringing, their behaviour in that direction had to be beyond reproach. Neither had they been allowed to go the way of the brownshirts and take part in either street or beerhall fighting or even political canvassing. The only 'politicking' the SS man received was by way of a weekly 'teach-in' where the word of the *Führer* was taught.

Heydrich's card indexes grew and grew in number, kept under lock and key, listing every known opponent of the Nazis of any political shade or colour. The indexes were amassed in a remarkably short time, and became so cumbersome Heydrich was obliged to call a halt and reconsider his system. The plain fact was that for the SD there were just too many Germans unsympathetic to the new regime. Well past the days of starvation that

Otto Ohlendorf, one-time lawyer-economist

followed the war, conditions had improved considerably following the great depression of 1929, etc. Also, communist propaganda carried on under the guise of social democracy had won considerable support. It was impossible to mark down everyone who did not vote for the Nazis; Heydrich decided to concentrate on those he considered most dangerous to the regime, and these had to include the SA leadership, certain Army officers and a number of leftist politicians. The rest could wait. This solved his immediate filing problem. But he continued to be short of real agents in the field, and by 1933 he no longer felt it expedient to don a disguise and do a little sleuthing himself, which he had done at first.

It is doubtful if Himmler realised at the time what kind of character he had put in charge of his latest creation. It was as if entry into the *Reichsführer's* élite had released a demon of brainpower and organisational ability. To Heydrich, the SS was quite disorganised, so he set about producing ideas for improvement. It is now supposed, not without reason, that the most far reaching initiatives emanated from the mind of Reinhard Heydrich. It would not be too long before all members of the Nazi Party became increasingly aware of the new *Sicherheitsdienst*, though none could have imagined how far reaching the tentacles of the SD and its parent the SS would become. Heydrich demanded information on everyone and everything, nothing in German life could remain outside his gaze. He knew, even as the young man he still was, that knowledge meant power – power over others, and especially those in positions that could be useful to him later. While his boss spent hours poring over Nordic sagas and history, Heydrich beavered away to build up a real power base, a spy service essential to the expanding power and empire building of the SS.

Despite these efforts, in mid-1933 the SS was still but a small cog in Nazi life. To their chagrin, instead of joining the many other Nazi chieftains who hurried to set up shop in Berlin and grab their share of the spoils, Himmler and Heydrich were in essence sidelined in Munich. Any hopes the faithful 'Heini' had entertained of being offered a post in Hitler's first Cabinet were dashed. Himmler's dream of creating a nationwide secret police force on Soviet lines were crushed, for 'General' Hermann Goering, the *Führer*'s deputy, had easily secured the key post as Prime Minister of Prussia, which automatically gave him the police power in that state's capital – Berlin. Within the Berlin police headquarters lay the old political bureau, the small and allegedly inefficient collection of clerks and detectives supposed to watch over the state's political life. To head this bureau Goering appointed the man who had married his cousin, Rudolf Diels, already a zealous member of the Prussian political police, who had pursued both Reds and Nazis with equal zeal. In fact, Hitler's men had him marked down as an opponent until Diels proved himself by exposing a government minister's alleged dealings with Reds. Goering had no love for Himmler, it was only one of many rivalries among the Nazi leadership which was in reality a very disparate group of somewhat crude opportunists, ready for any double-dealing that went beyond the norms among politicians everywhere.

Himmler, having worked and schemed for many years, now found himself virtually cut off from the main scene of action. Everything was happening in Berlin. His rival Roehm began even greater agitating, and would only be temporarily mollified by being given a seat on the new *Reich Defence Council*. Once there he proved a thorn to all, his real aim being to become chief of one national 'revolutionary' army. It came naturally to Himmler and Heydrich to proceed by stealth: only in Nazi Germany at that time could such events occur. Hitler had taken over the governing of Germany, but the old system of separate state authorities and police remained. For example, the chief minister in the Nazis' own birthplace of Bavaria remained anti-Hitler, and even Himmler's own base town remained under democratic control. Only a telegram from Hitler ordering the old administration out of office effected change, and so enthusiastic was Heydrich to see the wire implemented that he had an SS squad seize the scrap of paper in the city post office, delivering it in person to the city hall and ushering out its governing officials, who were replaced by Nazis.

Heydrich set himself up in the Munich police headquarters. He had hardly ensconced himself in the best office and was in conference with his aides when a visitor was announced. It was one Heinrich Müller, an experienced officer of the Bavarian political police who, like Diels, had done his job and pursued Reds and Nazis. Now, true to form, he was about to offer his services to the new incumbent. Not trusting the man,

Heydrich had his men hide in an outer office and had Müller shown in. All smiles and offering his hand, the man at once confirmed his experience and willingness to co-operate. Heydrich had no difficulty in sizing him up. One later assessment of Müller, as chief of the *Gestapo*, was given by General Dornberger, engineer and director of the V2 rocket programme. Müller struck the general as an: '. . . unobtrusive type of police official who leaves no personal impression in the memory. Later, all I could remember was a pair of piercing blue-grey eyes, fixed on me with an unwavering scrutiny. My first impression was one of cold curiosity and extreme reserve.'

Heydrich knew his visitor was no idiot. He had animal cunning and the abilities expected of policemen, never-ending curiosity about people, a suspicious nature, he was dogged, and had an eye for promotion. It was no great thing for Heydrich to fit him into his scheme of things. Perhaps it can be said the two paired rather well, whatever feelings they harboured for each other; as a policeman Müller could continue, but now concentrating only on the Reds. If he had greater ability to be used later, it would come out under Heydrich's far deeper and more dangerous schemes. They had ruthlessness in common.

The following weeks were marked by two chief developments in Heydrich's career: the first was the natural course forced on Himmler and Heydrich as they waited to move to bigger things; the second was for Heydrich quite unexpected and somewhat dire.

Having secured their power base in Munich, the duo now began the process of absorbing the police apparatus in the German *Länder*, or states, still outside the control of Goering's Prussian administration in Berlin. Whatever Goering's many aspirations, there was nothing he could do to prevent them; indeed, at first he knew nothing of them. It may well be that Hitler himself was so busy trying to organise his first government and get rid of all that remained of the old that he too did not realise the game of stealthy acquisition put into play by the SS. One by one the old state police forces were usurped by Himmler, with SS commanders appointed as police chiefs. Heydrich set about installing SD offices whenever possible, for all regional police headquarters had their own 'special branch' detectives. It is hard to imagine this process, but Himmler felt he had the *Führer*'s authority, whether documented or not. The intimidatory power of armed SS squads acting in Hitler's name was enough to dismiss any police presidents and officials who showed argument.

Himmler had also acted in another direction, taking over the direction and administration of the concentration camps, notably that nearest his own town of Munich-Dachau. To get rid of SA sloppiness, he installed Theodor Eicke, an SS officer of unusual energy and ruthlessness. Eicke would go on to command the *Totenkopf* (Deathshead) SS Division, which committed an appalling act of atrocity in France 1940. The unit, however, developed under his extraordinary leadership into what some consider the most effective of the combat SS divisions. But in 1933 Eicke was only the Inspector of Concentration Camps, then few in number and in no way comparable to the extermination machines of later. Inmates were treated to sharp, shock incarceration with a view to converting the political detainees at least to Hitler's view. Men were released, especially at Christmas-time, which made good propaganda.

The camps had been taken over from the SA, and run by 'swines', according to Heydrich, who had ambitions to take the system over himself. In this he met his match in Eicke, who proved just as determined and cunning; moreover, he was one of Himmler's favourites. Eicke dismissed the disorganised rabble and organised a guard staff corps on professional lines, so that Hitler was able to declare the Deathshead units an essential part of the Party organisation.

But when Eicke began setting up more camps, one of them within Goering's fiefdom of Prussia, Rudolf Diels sat up and tried to intervene. He motored to Osnabrück with a posse of police to investigate the illegality, but was refused entry by the SS guards, who fired shots when Diels persisted. Enraged, Diels rushed back to Berlin to report the incident to Goering, who in turn complained to Hitler. To Himmler and his staff, Diels was simply throwing his weight about and it was decided to get rid of him.

Heydrich was ordered to dig up something damning on the *Gestapo* chief, and sent a squad of SS men to Diels's home. Despite the presence of *Frau* Diels (Goering's cousin), they proceeded to ransack the house in an attempt to find incriminating documents. *Frau* Diels hysterically called her husband

Early SD recruits playing detective

for help, and before long a *Gestapo* squad rushed to the house, where they at once arrested the Heydrich SS team.

This fantastic episode, with *Gestapo* and SS men in confrontation like rival gangsters, brought to a head the serious competition and overlapping responsibilities of these Nazi security forces. The upshot was a furious visit to Goering by Himmler, the scene between them reportedly violent – verbally that is. From this emerged a *Führer* order that they settle their differences. It would take more than that to enable Himmler and Heydrich to get their hands on the Berlin *Gestapo*. Their strategy lay in convincing Hitler that dangerous forces were still at large and threatened the security of the leadership – including the *Führer*. To aid this strategy Heydrich had a small bomb exploded in a street after Hitler's car passed by. The explosion was hardly shattering but was noticed. Himmler argued that it was impossible for Goering to ensure a truly efficient state police force, if only for the fact that for him it was merely a part-time job, one of several he had greedily taken on. After all, Goering was supposed to be chief of the new and as yet still secret *Luftwaffe*, he was also 'Speaker' of the *Reichstag*, and had various other official posts.

One other factor had also got under Himmler's skin – Goering had appointed the *Reichsführer* SS deputy Kurt Daluege as chief of police in Berlin. This was yet another absurd anomaly, as it made the Himmler-Heydrich partnership in far away Munich look foolish. Indeed, Himmler was obliged to send Heydrich to Berlin in an effort to secure Kurt Daluege's co-operation. So far, all they had been allowed to do was to set up a mere SD 'outpost' in Berlin. Especially galling was the fact that Daluege was already well known as *'Dummi-dummi'* (stupid, a 'dummy'), because of his dull character and vanities.

It was not easy for Heydrich to go virtually cap in hand to the large police building and ask to see the chief whom he regarded as by far his inferior. He was asked to wait in an anteroom with others. An hour later he had still not been admitted, and then an aide appeared to say that Daluege was too busy to interview him. Angry, Heydrich telephoned Himmler in Munich, becoming aware of his chief's silent fury. But there was nothing to be done, except wait and bide their time. Curiously, they never did gain revenge for the slight, for Daluege remained in the top echelon of the Nazi police apparatus.

The reason for Daluege's promotion into a top post lay in Goering's use of him as an ally against Roehm, who was now increasingly becoming a liability. The time was fast approaching when Goering would look further afield for allies, no matter if only temporary, to help squash the brownshirt leader and indeed his whole army.

For Heydrich, the setbacks in Berlin followed one far more humbling. The new Hitler government sent a delegation to the Disarmament Conference in Geneva, which began sitting over the early months of 1933. The Nazi dictator had not the slightest intention of disarming. On the contrary, having just won power, his only desire was to set in motion a massive programme of rearmament before plunging into war. The account of German participation is one of obstruction dictated by Hitler, which finally led to their walk-out the next year.

For the first time, Nazi representatives accompanied diplomats of the regular Foreign Service, led by Ambassador Nadolny. Heydrich and an SS officer named Krueger were officially attending as 'security advisers', though in truth they were simply in Geneva to spy on their own official delegation. It proved something of a disaster for Heydrich. He felt ill at ease in diplomatic circles, where socialising, pleasantries and customs produced a kind of crude reaction – he showed himself up by drinking too much and behaving indecorously in the night clubs of the Swiss city. This cast a bad light on the Germans as a whole and led to sour comments from the other foreign delegations and pressmen attending. Matters came to a head after Heydrich discovered the hotel accommodating the Germans was not flying the swastika flag. The manager ignored his complaints, so Heydrich called in some SD agents already working in the city and one night managed to hoist the Nazi flag over the hotel.

Ambassador Nadolny was outraged and ordered his aide to have the flag removed; he also demanded the Nazis pack up and leave. Heydrich reacted with gutter-type 'navy invective', catching the next train home to Munich. Nadolny was summoned to Berlin, where he made the strongest complaint to Hitler on the Heydrich team's behaviour. Nadolny was crafty enough to point out that while in Geneva he was in a sense 'the *Führer*', acting on his behalf. Heydrich's behaviour had therefore been insulting to Hitler. Heydrich now met Hitler in most unfavourable circumstances, receiving a dressing down, even though the dictator cared little for diplomatic protocol and saw the conference in Geneva as merely a temporary expedient for his propaganda. But he referred to 'the less than pleasant incident at Geneva', and certainly saw it as harmful to Germany's prestige.

Though Hitler seemed to rule his roost by permitting rivalries, he had ordered Goering and Himmler to settle their differences. They did so, for the sake of expediency, Goering now regarding Himmler and his SS as very desirable allies against Roehm. For his part, the devious SS chief sent for Rudolf Diels and made him an honorary member of the SS; it had little meaning, as neither Himmler nor Heydrich had any intention of allowing Diels to remain head of the *Gestapo*, even though Bureau 1a was now under Goering's more direct control as Prime Minister of Prussia. In fact, not until Goering took the department directly under his wing did it receive the title '*Gestapo*'. Goering decided to give the bureau the designation GPA, *Geheime Polizei Amt*, but a minor official ordered to produce a rubber stamp for the office supplied one with the simple word '*Gestapo*' – *Geheime Staatspolizei*, or Secret State Police.

Meanwhile, the only result to come from the 'bomb plot' arranged by

Heydrich was an order from Hitler to Sepp Dietrich to enlarge his body-guard unit – the *Leibstandarte* SS.

Behind the power struggles which went on out of public gaze, the Nazis spied on each other; the expanding *Gestapo* spying on the leaders and the SS; the SD spying on everyone, as far as staff shortages would allow, and of course on the *Gestapo* chief Rudolf Diels. It is especially interesting, however, to learn how Heydrich's men were given 'spare time' tasks – spying on the Nazi leadership, or at least, those Heydrich felt might be worth watching. The name Hermann Behrends crops up elsewhere as a member of the SD staff. He used Goering's valet to learn all he could of his master's secrets, the man obviously in a prime position to know about everything. In fact, there was little to learn that was new, since Goering's self-indulgence was well known already – 'It was almost unbelievable', Behrends commented. The valet described all the many luxuries his master had fitted in his palace, including gold-plated bath taps and the like, and a great collection of valuable paintings, begun long before the war. That conflict of course came as a most inconvenient inter-ruption to Goering's preferred lifestyle, though he used it to profitable ends. Behrends was disappointed, however, when no mistresses were appointed, as he felt sure they could have been suitably bribed to work for the SD.

Hitler with the ailing President Hindenburg

Propaganda Minister Goebbels also proved disappointing, the problem being that his weakness for extra-marital affairs was already well known. Actresses would become his preferred prey through his control of the German film industry. His strongest *amour* might have led to divorce, but the *Führer* would not permit that. Goebbels did his best to keep such matters secret; Behrends learned that the *Gestapo* was 'hugely interested', but he kept all he learned for Heydrich's files. It was Behrends's job, and indeed that of all SD agents, to dig the dirt on all the top Nazis, no matter whom, Heydrich believing that all scandal could prove useful in the future. One is reminded of rumours that Britain's MI5 have kept tabs on government politicians and even members of the Royal Family. In the case of Heydrich and the *Gestapo* also, the 'official view' had to be that Nazi leaders needed protection.

Behrends commented on Goebbels's fine speaking voice and his ability to charm beautiful film actresses, despite his slight stature and club foot. Since such women put their careers first, as in Hollywood, they did not seem to mind losing their honour, though a few refused and suffered the consequences (i.e. a sudden stultifying of their career hopes).

Ernst Roehm of course was an even more hopeless case, for much was already known, and there seemed little or nothing new to dig up. However, Behrends succeeded in persuading one of Roehm's staff without difficulty to report on his chief's behaviour and doings. It was easy: this particular gangster in uniform was running a brothel and extortion racket. Hitler, once informed of this latest scandal, was furious and sought a solution. However, the wider, more serious question of eliminating the whole brown-shirt leadership then began to loom and the matter rested. When Behrends sought his SA spy after the 30 June 1934 purge, the man had vanished: like other survivors he had fled for his life.

Of undoubted daring, Hermann Behrends made his own bombshell discovery when he broke into Himmler's personal file system while the SS leader was away on tour. Behrends was astounded to find the Heydrich file with its information on the chief's alleged Jewish background. Amazed, and aware of its import, Behrends decided to keep quiet, but after further thought felt it wiser to tell Heydrich. When he did, his boss said little, commenting he would have been surprised if Himmler had *not* had such a file.

Rudolf Hess, officially Deputy *Führer*, provided nothing new by way of data for SD files. Behrends saw him as a rather naïve adorer of Hitler, though he had real intelligence.

Martin Bormann, suspected to be a womaniser, was hated by Behrends as the most cunning and devious of all those clinging to Hitler. Behrends disclosed this subject believed he was under observation, and Heydrich ordered him left alone. As revealed in *The Bormann Letters*, the man arranged a mistress – with his wife's consent.

Goering's ego and love of power drove him to reach beyond his capabilities. The ex-air ace, now addicted to drugs, was already chief of the still-secret *Luftwaffe*, responsible for a great programme of warplane production, Prime Minister of Prussia, about to become Chief Huntsman of the *Reich* (*Reichsjägermeister*), and involved in various other jobs. But most of all he coveted the post of head of the armed forces, the '*Wehrmacht*' as it was to be called from 1935. With Ernst Roehm installed as a *Reich* minister on the defence committee in December 1933, Goering grew alarmed as he saw the prize slipping through his fingers. In fact, despite long having hitched his star to the Hitler bandwagon, Goering, by virtue of his background, might have made a better *Wehrmacht* chief than Roehm, who had only thoughts of incorporating the German Army into his SA as one huge 'People's Army' of revolution.

The growing division between the Hitler government and the SA became very open at times when men like Karl Ernst, one of the top brown-shirts, openly insulted Goering. It would be Himmler and Heydrich (but mainly the SD chief) who would provide all the ammunition to help Goering and Hitler rid themselves of the SA leadership for good.

A hitherto minor SD agent in Strasbourg discovered a communist plot to assassinate Goering and was sent off to report in person to Heydrich, who seized on it as a grand chance to prove his force was superior to Goering's own *Gestapo*. A secret operation was prepared: the SD, still too small to go it alone, secured the help of the Berlin CID, whose chief was conveniently anti-Diels. The operation was controlled from Munich by Heydrich. The first wave of arrests numbered 160 men and women, and as soon as the final call reached him he departed for Berlin to produce his disclosures in triumph to Goering. At the same time, Himmler saw Hitler to report the assassination plot and the success of his SD, suggesting the plot would probably never have developed had the *Gestapo* been under his control. Yet Hitler hesitated, sending for Goering, who confirmed all he had just heard from Heydrich. Goering now agreed that it would be better if control of the *Gestapo* passed to Himmler – yet the *Führer* still hesitated. The matter went unresolved, much to Himmler's dismay. In fact, judging by one report, Hitler actually sent for Rudolf Diels after his visitors had departed, allegedly making complimentary remarks to the man he seemed to like and assuring him his job was secure. It is also suggested that Hitler showed unease and dislike of this latest Himmler–Heydrich attempt to take over the *Gestapo*. He was no fool, probably suspecting the earlier 'bomb plot' to be an SS tactic, and possibly even dubious of the truth about this latest affair.

However, vacillating seemed to be a Hitler trait at times, though in the event he finally gave in. His change of heart was helped by the added pressure put on him by Interior Minister Wilhelm Frick, who saw no sense in the lack of centralisation in the Hitler government. All Germany should become one *Reich*, under the domination of Prussian Berlin. On 10 April 1934 Goering went to his *Gestapo* offices, assembled the staff and informed them they would henceforth come under the aegis of Himmler's SS. It was a great moment for Himmler and Heydrich who were present. On 20 April Heinrich Himmler was formally made chief of the *Gestapo*, and his protégé Reinhard Heydrich took office as deputy four days later.

Whatever thanks and assertions of fidelity Himmler gave Goering ('I shall always remain faithful to you – you will never have anything to fear from me'), the gross general now began setting up his own, personal protection corps, the *Landespolizeigruppe Goering*. Formed from Berlin police, it was armed and mobile and escorted Goering on his tours and various appointments around Germany. But when Goering decided before war came that he must have *Luftwaffe* soldiers, the unit changed uniforms and were incorporated into the air force. Not long afterwards most were called upon to volunteer for the first German parachute regiment.

During the Nuremberg trial process in 1946 and before being sentenced to death (and cheating the hangman by committing suicide), Goering told the tribunal that in the thirties he had wanted to direct the police himself, but was persuaded by Hitler that the force needed to combat enemies of

Heydrich (turning), with Daluege and Müller during a police visit to Italy

the state should be under one control. 'I placed the *Gestapo* in the hands of Himmler, who put Heydrich at its head.'

With Diels still the *Führer*'s favourite as *Gestapo* executive, Himmler and Heydrich had to tread very carefully, determined as they still were to topple him.

Artur Nebe had risen to the post of Police Commissioner in Berlin. In reality he was a figurehead and the position was a reward for his long-term support of the Hitler cause when head of the CID. Nebe became involved in another plot, this time with a somewhat uncomfortable partner, a young lawyer, Dr Hans Bernd Gisevius. Gisevius was a friend from university days of the 'glass-chewing, lady-killing' Rudolf Diels. Gisevius was another opportunist who got himself a job in the *Gestapo*; he would be one of the few to survive the coming war. The Nebe-Gisevius duo had their own motives for wanting Diels gone, but were unsuccessful – once more it was the machinations of Heydrich which did the job. Heydrich had his SD agents set to work digging out everything on Diels's anti-Nazi activities in the past. In his zeal to ferret out subversives he had done considerable harm to the Nazi cause. Heydrich assembled enough material to fill several fat files, and armed with these Himmler sped to the Munich Braunhaus to convince Rudolf Hess of the need to sack Diels. As it happened, Martin Bormann was present as the faithful secretary in the old Party HQ and 'shrine'.

Himmler of course had a file on Bormann, doubtless filled by Heydrich. The man is said to have been involved in various illicit enterprises before joining the Nazis, one of them a rather respectable brothel. One of his rackets was rumbled by police and Bormann went to prison. After that he joined the Nazis; whatever Hitler did, he would never associate with active criminals. The police file on Bormann's case came to Heydrich's attention in the expected manner, by *Gestapo* inspection of all such records, and was not long in reaching the 'other' secret police department. Heydrich was delighted to make a special mark on that dossier.

When the latest accusations against Diels were shown to Hitler he was finally forced to have Goering remove the man from the *Gestapo*. Obviously, it pained Goering to sack his cousin's husband, so he gave him the post of Deputy Police Commissioner. But Diels was alarmed, and fearing for his life fled to Prague, from where he issued threats to Goering concerning certain questionable deals in his past. It was enough to prompt Goering to persuade the *Führer* to allow Diels to return to his post in the *Gestapo*.

Meantime, unaware of these perambulations, Himmler and Heydrich believed they had won, and were amazed yet again when Hitler deferred permission for them to move their HQ to the capital. Without doubt, by that time Hitler had come to realise that his SS chief nurtured a man to be watched very carefully. Later of course, at least on the surface, he had good reason to be grateful to Heydrich. As a sop he agreed to Himmler's latest advancement, appointment as chief of police in both Lübeck and Mecklenburg, which was announced in the press. Over the following months Himmler succeeded in extending his control to Baden, Hessen-Anstalt, Bremen, and into Saxony, Thuringia, Württemberg and Hamburg; it seemed as if only in Prussia was Himmler denied complete chieftainship. In all these moves he was supported by Heydrich, and it is supposed the whole strategy was planned by him. Furthermore, denied permission to set up a full HQ in Berlin, Heydrich opened a small advance outpost in the Eicher-Allee, placing a former Bavarian detective called Kublinsky in charge.

Needless to say, every police force taken over by Himmler-Heydrich was soon infiltrated by *Gestapo* and SD agents. Hitler's rival, Gregor Strasser, who was coming to the end of his particular road, got wind of this massive extension of SS power, but was quite incapable of doing anything about it.

There remained just one organised body in Nazi Germany detested yet largely unmolested by the Hitler regime – the Church. Heydrich was particularly virulent in his attitude against organised religion. Goering trod more warily; like the SD chief he was a Catholic when young, and always highly conscious of the need to try and mould public opinion. There were no votes to be gained by closing down churches and throwing the clergy into concentration camps. The Nazis sniped at and ridiculed the Church, Heydrich supplying fantasy tales and SD reports to the SS newspaper *Das Schwarze Korps*, which, had it been in a normal society, would have been sued for libel many times. The paper carried campaigns against anyone and anything it disfavoured, without restriction and not under the guiding hand of Dr Goebbels. The aim was to strike, cower and bully its targets into inaction. Its editor, Gunther D'Alquen, let loose his cartoonists, who lampooned nuns and priests. The poisonous columns charged them with a variety of offences, invariably unfounded, but at times followed by *Gestapo* action, such as embezzlement, currency smuggling, rape and homosexuality.

To Himmler and Heydrich the Church constituted a serious threat to Nazi control of the masses. Heydrich was prepared to go to great lengths to destroy religious groupings, even cooking up a hare-brained plot to infiltrate Nazi youths into them as honest, would-be initiates of the priesthood. His aim was that they would gradually sow Nazi ideas and over a period of time transform the Church from within. It was one scheme that came to nothing.

Goebbels was right to move carefully, for he knew the public mood. Even under Nazi coercion the German folk refused to believe Nazi charges against their religious leaders and clung stubbornly to their faiths. But the Himmler-Heydrich duo were of course themselves well informed on public feelings, kept abreast of everything via the *Gestapo* and SD. The latter was charged to submit regular reports on what the people were thinking and their reactions to the government's measures. In 1936, Himmler for example remarked:

> I know there are people in Germany now who become sick when they see these black coats [i.e. of his SS men strutting the streets]. We know the reason, and we do not expect to be loved by too many.

Heydrich himself had this to say about his forces of terror:

> Secret State Police, Criminal Police, and SD are still adorned with the furtive and whispered secrecy of a political detective story. In a mixture of fear and shuddering – and yet, at home, with a certain feeling of security because of their presence – brutality, inhumanity bordering on the sadistic, and ruthlessness, are attributed abroad to men of this profession.

This was later, on German Police Day (February 1941). Heydrich was perfectly aware what kind of people they were and the nature of their doings, and he was certainly fulfilling such a role himself. In the same speech he remarked that, naturally, people did not wish to be involved with the security police 'too much'; '. . . there is no problem down to the smallest egotistical longing which the *Gestapo* cannot solve'. Precisely what he meant by this perhaps only his audience understood. He added:

> Regarded in this way we are, if a joke is permitted, looked upon as a general maid and the dustbin of the *Reich.*

Dr Goebbels made various entries on the SD in his diaries. In March 1942 he referred to an SD report regarding the 'final solution' of the Jewish question, which he viewed involving a 'tremendous number of new angles'. The 'angle' Goebbels had in mind for the approximately eleven million Jews still in Europe was first, to concentrate them in the East, and then (after the war) transport them to an island like Madagascar. As *Gauleiter* of Berlin Goebbels was ever concerned about the city population's feelings as the Nazi authorities tried to clear out the last remaining Jews. He became incensed over SD insensity at arresting and carting them off right after the city had suffered a severe air raid:

> Yet this is the moment that the SD chooses to continue evacuating Jews!

There had, Goebbels admitted in his diary, been some 'regrettable scenes' at a home for aged Jews, when SD police tried to remove them. A large number of non-Jews gathered, some even siding with the unfortunates. Goebbels ordered the SD to cease its activities in that direction, 'We can save it up for a week or two and then resume it all the more thoroughly'.

Again, the SD stepped on Goebbels's toes when it took the Clemens Chapel away from the Berlin Catholics. He ordered it returned to them and delivered a dressing-down to the SD.

During the war the special SD reports monitoring public opinion were circulated to a small circle of Nazi ministers, including of course Dr

Goebbels. But once the tide began to turn irrevocably against Germany, the Propaganda Minister turned sour, insisting in May 1943 that they were far too 'defeatist' and should either be stopped or at most circulated to a far smaller number of readers.

The Minister had already become concerned with sexual problems which certainly involved SD and *Gestapo* reports. He was vexed by the difficulties posed by the thousands of foreign workers, mostly male, who had volunteered or been coerced to Germany. 'The situation in some cases is absolutely grotesque', Goebbels complained, posing the possible solution as a liberal policy of establishing houses of ill-fame. Police raids on houses used by prostitutes in Berlin produced startling figures of VD cases. Once again, Goebbels saw the solution as the setting up of red-light districts, 'as in Hamburg and Nuremberg'. Though the figures were not alarming, the numbers of German women conceiving babies by foreigners (and German males with foreign women) posed a threat, the 'corruption of German blood'. There was little the *Gestapo* or SD could do about such a problem.

The SD spy service had very small beginnings, operating as one of Himmler's side-line brainchilds. It progressed in the thirties to employ some 3,000 employees and perhaps 100,000 informers (estimates vary). Like the *Gestapo*, it came to take into its ranks both 'intellectuals' (that is, men of above-average intelligence) and brutes. Like the *Gestapo* it managed to infiltrate every facet of German life under the laws charging it with protecting the Nazi State. The SD violated privacy of the ballot box in order to identify waverers and anti-Nazis by simply apportioning a number to every name on the voting list.

From its early days both SD and *Gestapo* aimed to ride roughshod over all previous laws regulating police powers. The first indications of this came during the early days of Nazi power, when Goering issued a Prussian Ministerial Ordinance authorising the police to ignore paragraphs 14 and 41 of the existing Police Law. The Nazi aim was to remove the police and security forces (*Gestapo* and SD) from the civil administration which had hitherto controlled them. As soon as practical the newly constituted *Gestapo* moved into the former headquarters of the German Communist Party in Prinz-Albrecht-Strasse.

Political tasks had been the job of the Land Criminal Police Office, local offices of the 'Special Branch'; on 26 April 1933 all such regional offices were replaced by *Gestapo* offices. The SD followed, Heydrich ensuring his agents infiltrated both *Gestapo* and local police departments. However, until the end of November 1933 the *Gestapo* offices were still subservient to the local police commissioners. On 30 November they became completely independent, though not until March 1934 was the last vestige of civil and normal police authority removed and the *Gestapo* became answerable to nobody but its leaders. Another significant date was 9 June 1934, not long before the elimination of the SA leadership, when Deputy *Führer*

Rudolf Hess decreed the Foreign Political Intelligence Service of the Nazi Party was to be transferred to the Security Service of the *Reichsführer* SS (RFSS). There would henceforth be no other intelligence service whatever, for either foreign or domestic usage. This declaration did not of course apply to the *Abwehr*.

One authority has stated that, eventually, the SD became superfluous, though this can hardly be the case. True, it was absorbed into the SIPO, or Security Police, with its men often carrying out purely police tasks. Through various reorganisations, command of the SD passed to the chief of the Security Police, his title becoming *Chef der Sicherheitspolizei und des SD* (CSSD).

The notion that the SD became superfluous probably stemmed from ignorance of its work as a counter-intelligence and foreign spy service. Among examples (some given elsewhere) of this work is the famous 'Cicero' affair, in which an audacious and cool-headed Turkish valet employed by the British Ambassador in Ankara managed to steal a succession of highly secret documents from the diplomat's safe. Following the receipt of photographs of the documents in Berlin, SS officers were sent to Turkey to supervise liaison and operation of the agent, whom they rewarded with several thousand English fivers, which were part of the great consignment of forgeries printed by the SS.

Unfortunately for those few apprehended after the war, and of course the many victims, the SD, as part of the Security Police, became involved in many actions involving the expulsion and elimination of Jewish populations. The history of such events is not within the bounds of this work. Of interest is the mentality of men like Otto Ohlendorf, the ex-lawyer/economist who forsook his SD desk in Berlin and, as a Major-General, admitted commanding one of the Action Groups in Russia responsible for the killing of 90,000 men, women and children. At Nuremberg Ohlendorf stated that it would have been inconceivable to refuse to carry out such orders since they were given by the legal authority above him, and how concerned he had been at the somewhat inefficient, 'inhumane' methods used to execute the victims. He was also concerned the mass killings should not place too great a spiritual and psychological burden on the men under his command.

4

'THE NIGHT OF THE
LONG KNIVES'

Two episodes in the thirties marked Heydrich's SD as a force to be reckoned with.

The evidence gathered on Ernst Roehm's mob of drunken, sexual revellers became compelling, giving Himmler the chance to persuade Hitler he must act to clean up the problem. Though Himmler knew the Army chiefs were even more alarmed about the threat of Roehm and his brownshirt army of over three million, he saw it prudent to seek out allies in other quarters, men who had been and to an extent still were his rivals. Foremost among these was Hermann Goering, whose secret police department Himmler had filched; the other was Joseph Goebbels, the club-footed propaganda genius whose work Hitler would later quote as worth many divisions. Goering, who had himself for expediency worn the brownshirt outfit, became a willing plotter in the scheme to get rid of Roehm and his entourage. But Goebbels was, as in his earlier days, less avid, at least at first. He maintained ties with Roehm, just as he had done with opponents of Hitler before 1933. Goebbels played a waiting game, keeping a foot in each camp for as long as possible, until it became crystal clear which side would win in the battle to persuade the *Führer* to take action.

Sexual deviation was insufficient reason to remove Roehm, whose men believed that having been the major force in Hitler's success they deserved greater reward. Roehm himself, given a chair in the defence council, was ever at odds with Minister von Blomberg and others. He was a fire-cracker who despised the Army chiefs and saw his men as the heirs apparent to become Germany's 'People's Army'. Roehm would, despite his avowed allegiance to Hitler, use violence to gain his ends, even initiating a second revolution in which his force would be matched against the *Reichswehr* and those more loyal to Hitler.

Himmler played cleverly on Hitler's fears, and no matter how reluctant the *Führer* was to act against old comrades who had done so much to help him win power, he was in the end forced to cede to the pressures from the Himmler clique of plotters and of course the urgings emanating from the Army staff. But among the most telling 'facts' given Hitler was evidence

SA Stabschef Ernst Roehm, executed June 1934

of a plot against him personally by Roehm. That 'evidence' was largely supplied by Heydrich.

The atmosphere in Nazi circles in Germany in the early summer of 1934 was electric, to some degree reflected throughout the land. The people as a whole felt they were undergoing great change, and overall this was seen as exciting, promising much for their country. The new Chancellor was making himself more comfortable in the saddle of power; the Nazified 'parliament', the *Reichstag*, would continue to meet, the deputies merely attending to cheer on their *Führer* and rubber stamp his decisions, which were rapidly executed via a series of 'enabling' acts. By these means Hitler planned to appropriate sole power for himself, including very shortly complete command of the armed forces, all of whose officers (and later all other ranks) would have to swear a personal oath of allegiance to Hitler. This would bring them great difficulty in the moral and legal sense later.

Despite great progress in the months since taking office, Hitler had some way to go before achieving total control of the German nation and all its assets. In 1934 the *Führer*'s most pressing task was to clear the air of the continuing conflict between Roehm and the Army. It is possible that without the kind of men it had in command, the SA might have gradually subsided into an army of impotence, allowed to wither on the vine. However, with Roehm, Heines and others in command this was impossible. Hitler was coerced by Himmler's evidence into action.

At 9 a.m. on 28 June 1934, Hitler's personal Junkers 52 transport stood waiting on the tarmac at Tempelhof Airport in Berlin. An SS guard of honour waited at ease nearby, drawn up in three rows in their black uniforms, white gloves and belts, weapons grounded. As Hitler arrived in his limousine heavy rain was falling; alighting from the car, hat in hand, he made for the waiting plane, his pilot Baur already in the cockpit. Behind the *Führer* strode Goering, who had yet to announce his new air force, and was consequently still clad in a brown uniform. Then came Hitler's ADC, ex-soldier Brückner, and old comrade Schaub, who wore his usual SS uniform. Lastly, also clad in black, strode press attaché, Dr Otto Dietrich.

On a shouted word of command, the SS guard snapped to the 'present' as Hitler marched past them, to climb the short ladder into the aircraft, his entourage following. Baur waved to the mechanics, starting up the three engines. The single-blade props spun and the assembled watchers, including the guard, moved off. The Junkers's destination was the big and important Ruhr city of Essen, foremost among the steel towns and the location of the all-important, giant Krupp arms complex.

Despite the rainstorms sweeping Germany, crowds had gathered around the airport and along the ten-kilometre highway as Hitler's plane touched down at Essen-Mulheim Airport. The swastika banners hanging limp in the rain had already been hoisted to display the mourning decreed by the *Führer* marking the eighteenth anniversary of the cursed Treaty of Versailles. But Hitler's visit was, ostensibly, to attend the wedding of the newly installed *Gauleiter* of the Rhineland, Josef Terboven. This Nazi stood waiting under cover with his bride-to-be. When Hitler stepped from his plane Terboven hurried forward, his brown Party outfit with its swastika armband and red-gold tabs quickly staining with raindrops as he shot up one arm in salute. His beloved was already garbed for the ceremony in a white wedding gown and head-dress. Clutching a bouquet of red roses, she curtseyed and offered her hand to the *Führer*, her eyes betokening the kind of adoring feelings displayed by many German women, who looked on Hitler as the Messiah.

Of greater significance was the attendance of the Berlin SA chief, Karl Ernst, who sat among the congregation at the church. His own nuptials had been most recent, and his honeymoon postponed in order to be at the wedding in Essen. When the ceremony was over, SS General Zeck made a speech in which he celebrated 'the companionship which unites SS and SA to the manual and intellectual workers of Germany'. This utterance provoked loud applause.

That afternoon, Hitler was whisked away to tour the Krupp factories – Karl Ernst flew back to Berlin to pack and leave for a South American honeymoon. By the time Hitler returned to the Hotel Kaiserhof the anti-Roehm conspirators had everything sewn up; Goering would do most of the persuading, armed with a mass of documents provided by Himmler and Heydrich which proved the SA chief's perfidy. Hitler turned pale as

Goering recited the latest catalogue of brownshirt crimes and plots. Roehm and his henchmen had drawn up a hit list of Army generals to be liquidated. Then, a report was passed to aide Brückner on the telephone. Hitler became infuriated when informed that a foreign diplomat had been assaulted by SA men in Cologne, a report emanating from the SD in that city.

'The SA has become a danger to the *Reich!*' Hitler exploded. He asked that Roehm be contacted by telephone at once at his suite in the hotel he and his entourage were occupying at Bad Wiessee.

Goering was delighted, now things were really moving against the brownshirt mob. He looked suitably grim as the *Führer* ordered him back to Berlin to assess the situation, adding in his rough brogue that the brownshirt lunatics must be arrested as an example to the rest. However, when Roehm was contacted Hitler told him they must meet to iron out the problems with the Army. Hitler asked Roehm to call in all his principal officers to Bad Wiessee – he would meet them there.

Hitler kept his promise, but hardly in the manner Roehm and his men expected. Two days after Goering had begun his presentation, the brownshirt leadership had been murdered – or circumscribed. Roehm had in reality connived no plans, no anti-Army or anti-Hitler *Putsch* was planned, despite his frustrations and grievances; he was content for the moment to see how things developed. They had not done too badly, they lived the good life and really had nothing to gain by pushing Hitler.

On the afternoon following his *Führer*'s call, Roehm told his confidant von Epp he would receive Hitler royally, laying on a big banquet, including a vegetarian menu for their leader. Elsewhere, at the Hotel Kaiserhof in Essen, a certain young SS junior officer was attending as a security guard to Hitler.

Walter Schellenberg was an ex-Jesuit and trainee lawyer who had, on his university professor's advice, joined the Nazi Party and SS solely to get ahead. In other words, he was yet another who, though seeing in Hitler the answer to Germany's problems, was anxious to jump on the Nazi bandwagon to carve out a career. His star would rise very rapidly once he came to Heydrich's notice. But on Friday 29 June 1934, he was only one of many SS officers and men guarding the *Führer*, who had left the hotel once more to fulfil another engagement. He toured RAD labour corps camps around Buddenburg Castle near Lunen, but seemed preoccupied and cut short his afternoon, returning in the rain to his hotel at Bad Godesberg. In the restrained rooms of the Hotel Dreesen, Hitler was bombarded by a stream of messages over the telephone and even by special couriers who arrived by air. Much of this activity was witnessed by Schellenberg, who for much of the time was stationed in the grounds of the hotel, conveniently near the French windows of Hitler's room. He was able to see the increasingly nervous and scowling *Führer* as he received various visitors, among them Dr Dietrich and the SA General Viktor Lutze, who had become more attached to Hitler than his supposed boss Roehm; he had, however, been won over by being appointed *Gau* (district) leader in Hanover.

Among the leaders attending was Dr Goebbels, now up to his neck in the plot, having decided it healthier to side with Hitler. The reports passed by Heydrich's SD agents and other sources seemed to confirm without doubt that an SA uprising was imminent – probably before Hitler could address them at Bad Wiessee. Schellenberg, possibly the cleverest and craftiest of the later SD chiefs, embellished his account of these dramatic hours when he came to write his memoirs.

> Suddenly, the sky darkened. The air became suffocating. With astonishing violence the storm broke.

When the deluge of rain came, Schellenberg tried to press himself against a window for shelter. Brilliant, jagged lightning flashed across the leaden sky, and he was aware that from time to time the *Führer* went to the window to gaze out at the spectacle, '. . . his eyes lost in reverie'.

Goering now told Hitler that the newly wed Karl Ernst had, on returning to Berlin, neglected to take his bride on honeymoon, instead going to his headquarters to put his quarter-of-a-million brownshirt troops on alert. Ernst, the ex-hotel porter and former café waiter, was now dressed up in grand style as one of the powers of the new Germany, but marked down by Himmler as a criminal sadist. Ernst was Roehm's right-hand man, and so to strike at him was akin to hitting Roehm himself.

To the soaked but still-attendant Schellenberg came feelings of awe and admiration as he observed the man who held the fate of so many in his hands. 'The tranquility of Germany and the fate of those men who had until so recently been his intimates.' Word had soon spread among the guards of unusual and possible shattering events. The storm raged until eight in the evening, then the weather began to improve: '. . . the massed clouds drifted away and little by little all became quite serene, as if pacified by magic.' After going off duty and having a meal, Schellenberg was on hand again to see the one man Hitler could rely upon, his old comrade and body-guard, Sepp Dietrich, who had arrived by plane from Berlin. Dietrich, an ex-World War One sergeant and tankman, had forsaken his family in the late twenties to be with Hitler. He had soon graduated to become head of the *Führer*'s special SS escort squad which had now become the *Leibstandarte SS Adolf Hitler* (LSSAH), a 'palace bodyguard' unit of picked SS soldiers. Schellenberg was close enough to overhear Hitler's orders – Dietrich must fly to Munich and stand by for further instructions. The instructions arrived before midnight, Dietrich was to proceed at once to Kaufering with two companies of armed SS to await Hitler's arrival. They would then go on to Bad Wiessee.

Hitler had decided to act, decisively. There was no more talk of sorting things out with Roehm, the whole bunch had to be got rid of – permanently. The alarming reports had continued to arrive, each fresh jot of evidence being served up by Himmler and Goebbels to convince the *Führer* he must act without further delay. Adolf Wagner, the Nazi governor of Bavaria, who had also become Minister of the Interior, reported that SA brownshirt louts had marched through the streets of Munich bawling anti-Hitler slogans, singing lines such as, 'Sharpen your long knives on the kerbstones!' This was nonsense, the line quoted was merely taken from one of the brownshirts' old marching songs. But seized on and embellished by fictions from the *Gauleiter* and his ally Himmler, they added fuel to the smouldering fire. Hitler needed no more bidding; he would himself lead the reckoning with Roehm.

Yet even this was not enough for Himmler, who now played his trump card. The SA in Berlin would, he reported, swing into action at 5 p.m. next evening, when they would seize the government and other important buildings. Obviously, it seemed to Hitler, Ernst the traitor had orders to capture the capital and so paralyse the *Reich.* In fact, as Goebbels knew very well from his spies, Ernst had indeed picked up his bride and was about to depart for his sea voyage to Tenerife and Madeira. But Goebbels was the supreme opportunist, and knowing Ernst had left for Bremen he said nothing. Once more he had played a dangerous game, opting for the man

Lloyd George – favourably impressed

he believed held the better hand. At 2 a.m. on 30 June, Goebbels was at Hitler's side as their plane took off from Hangelar Airport near Bonn. Meanwhile, Roehm and his officers slept peacefully in their beds in the Hanslbauer Hotel at Bad Wiessee on the shores of Lake Tegernsee. Goebbels had studied psychology – his art had become that of manipulating minds by propaganda, using his skills with language and oration to greater effect than any other Nazi.

The bloody events of the rightly termed 'Night of the Long Knives' were to extend well into the following days as the chief conspirators checked through their personal hit lists for those who had offended, opposed them, or were inconveniently in the way of vengeance. The lancing of the brownshirt boil grew into a greater bloodletting that in the end even Hitler had to halt.

Karl Ernst was intercepted by armed SS men as his car neared Bremen. He was roughly handled and taken back to Berlin to face 'trial' and immediate execution.

Though Roehm and Ernst were guiltless in so far as they had plotted nothing, Defence Minister von Blomberg had complained that the brownshirts were arming with machine-guns and planned to take over the Army – which hardly seems feasible. It is true the SA had been arriving in column at local Army barracks to demand with apparent higher authority that they be given instruction on the rifle ranges, for not all were veterans by any means. They carried their own weapons and did in fact receive drill and shooting practice, locking up their weapons afterwards and having the nerve to eat in the soldiers' messes. Hitler had already spent several hours in talks with Roehm earlier in June, in which he claimed he said, 'Conscienceless elements are preparing a national Bolshevist-style action that could bring nothing but untold misery to Germany'. But this admission came later, when he was trying to justify the murders. 'I implored Roehm to put things right, and for his part he promised to do all in his power to do so.'

Hitler was under pressure from several directions, especially from the Army generals, to do something about the SA rabble. Without the Army his plans could not mature, and his position in Germany was not yet fully secure. President Hindenburg was still in office, though his time was short; he had never liked the 'Bohemian corporal'. Only a few days earlier, on his way to see the President, General von Blomberg had intercepted Hitler, telling him that unless he 'settled the SA's hash' the President would declare martial law and allow the German Army to do the necessary. This ultimatum was confirmed by Hindenburg a few minutes later.

Where then, in this atmosphere of menace and intrigue, stood Heydrich and his SD? In view of all the existing pressures on Hitler, was it really necessary for Himmler's Secret Service to cook up anything at all? The answer, from the conspirators' point of view, has to be 'yes'. Goering, Himmler, Goebbels and several other top Nazis leapt in to confirm all

Hitler's worst fears, by whatever means came to hand – and Heydrich saw to that. By colourful interpretation and pure invention, he provided the plotters with the means to rid themselves of a nuisance rival for power. To the SD's masterly web of lies these spoilers applied their own lists of people undesirable from their positions as patricians in the still forming Nazi senate. These were not lists of rivals and suspects to be resigned – but humans to be killed off. Some were themselves rascals, others not, even totally innocent. That was the measure of Nazi politics, violent squabbling between rival gangs.

On the other hand, leaving aside for the moment those destined to die whose only crime was to utter opinions contrary to those of the Nazis, as Sepp Dietrich once remarked in his own defence, in dealing with men like Ernst Roehm, one simply could not go to them and ask for their resignation. The answer could well be a bullet. For they were truly gangsters in uniform, although in their minds they were tough revolutionaries used to violence. They expected it and dealt it out. It was how they had lived and made their mark. Indeed, some were felons, guilty of murder and other crimes – aside from the perverted sexual aspects with which some were tainted.

Having received Himmler's orders, Heydrich had set to work with a will. In the SD offices there already existed cards on many of the leading SA brownshirt personalities. The cards detailed every whim and weakness of Roehm and his lieutenants, whether it was wine or women, and their various activities including jobs if they had them – and many did not. These cards were properly collated, the men at the top justifying much fatter files which had been greatly added to in recent times. Edmund Heines's affair with a young chauffeur was well known. He had been quite open about it, so was perhaps not wide open to blackmail. Roehm and his closer friends were prone to drinking bouts and womanising; it was comparatively easy to fill page after page on their activities and indiscretions. In more than one case SA men had committed criminal offences, rape and burglary among them. It was not surprising that among this huge army, many of them unemployed, there should be a few bad hats. These offences had been hushed up by their officers, for the SA was a brotherhood, a vast group of 'comrades'. There could never be any question of bringing brownshirt miscreants before the civil courts. In this respect, while allowing that SS men were bound to behave correctly, Himmler would himself never have permitted the name of his movement to be besmirched in that fashion.

Heydrich therefore had no problem producing a collection of known facts and fantasies documented in precise fashion, rather like terse lines, which he knew the *Führer* could take in at a glance. But Heydrich guessed Hitler would not be too jolted by such tales, even though believing them; so he re-invented all the little plots and facets, adding various nuances which made it appear the *Führer* himself as well as the State were in im-

Himmler, poultry farmer and believer in herbal remedies

mediate danger. It only needed a secretary to type into one of the routine SD report forms whatever he dictated: 'Agent Z15 reports hearing the following in such and such a bar or café or brothel frequented by the local SA troop.' At least a dozen such reports were played up and added to by the results of wire taps carried out by SD and *Gestapo* agents which further ensnared Roehm and his gang. The results of Heydrich's labours were either sent by courier or delivered personally by him to Himmler, the documents minus any further comments or interpretation by Heydrich.

Walter Schellenberg was, like Goebbels, a man who preferred to use his brains rather than his fists. When Hitler's aide Lieutenant Brückner told him to arrange security for Hitler's passage to Bonn Airport he reported to his superior, and presently saw the *Führer* depart with Goebbels under close escort. With them went Brückner, Viktor Lutze, Dr Dietrich, SS Adjutant Schaub and Hitler's old comrade in SS uniform, Julius Schreck. The latter was to die by natural causes within three years. From Bonn, the *Führer's* party flew in his Junkers to Munich, landing at 4 a.m.

Meanwhile, satisfied their work was bearing fruit, Himmler and Heydrich took their positions in their offices in Berlin, waiting from 11 p.m. until 3.45 a.m., going over the lists of men to be eliminated. They were assisted by ADC Karl Wolff, destined to become an SS general and to negotiate the German surrender in Italy in 1945. *Gauleiter* Wagner had also been astir all night in Munich, and he telephoned Himmler to advise that as soon as the *Führer* arrived in that city he would pass orders to the SS in the capital. On hearing this, Heydrich is alleged to have said, 'The *Führer* will be obeyed beyond his hopes'.

At the lakeside hotel complex at Tegernsee outside Munich, the SA bosses had enjoyed an evening of drinking and singing. Roehm and his men were completely unaware of the terrible fate about to overtake them, oblivious to the fact that some of their allies had already been arrested in nearby Munich, as Hitler had found on his arrival. The men involved with the arrests included Adolf Wagner, aided by the chief of the Nazi Party court (USCHLA – the Committee for Examination and Adjustment), Major Walter Buch; Emil Maurice, one of Hitler's oldest comrades and alleged lover of the *Führer*'s cousin Geli Raubel who had committed suicide; Christian Weber, ex-convict, horse dealer and club bouncer. This group, aided by more SS men, grabbed the local SA officers, including *Gruppenführer* Schneidhuber, who was chief of police in the city. All figured in Heydrich's SD files, and all were thrown into jail. When told of these arrests, Hitler went to see them, apparently worked up into a passion and hysteria, to berate Schneidhuber as a traitor, ripping off his insignia before storming out in a rage.

Shortly after dawn, Hitler sped off in a vehicle convoy, accompanied by Sepp Dietrich and a posse of hand-picked SS commandos to deal with the sleeping brownshirts at Tegernsee. When they reached the Hotel Hanslbauer all seemed quiet. The snoring brownshirts were about to suffer

Himmler salutes the tomb of King Henry

76

the rudest of awakenings; the arrests and killings would be carried out regardless of the civil police or Army. In fact, the Hitler convoy had already met an officer and troops *en route* who had been alerted by their general to assure security cordons around the area so that the work could proceed undisturbed. Hitler had stopped to confer with the officer and assure him he need not be involved more directly. There was another reason for this short discussion; Hitler wanted some greater muscle on hand should his comparatively small SS force be faced with a gun battle.

Heines, reported to have the body of an athlete, was found asleep, entwined in the arms of his chauffeur, the 'homosexual boy', as Dr Dietrich described the scene. This and others the Hitler group saw as 'disgusting and defying description'. According to Konrad Heiden, who later wrote copiously on *Der Führer* and his followers, it was Edmund Heines, the ex-adjutant of General Rossbach in the Freecorps, who had lured Roehm into the lewd practices which in part led to their destruction. 'The secret army of murderers and mercenaries were breeding grounds for perversion.' Hitler himself had once rounded on them as 'a bunch of fairies!' They tried (as in *The Banquet*) to present themselves as above other men, a breed capable of great things, far removed from the perverts and murderers they were. As for their chief Roehm, he had declared his contempt for a world where the man-woman relationship entailed democracy – which could never thrive in Germany. One of their favourite Nazi philosophers wrote of a world dominated by homosexuals.

During their earlier, sometimes stormy, days Hitler had thrown Heines out of the Party, partly to insult Roehm; yet it was Heines who had brought the pair together again. Heines had been prosecuted in 1928 for cold-bloodedly shooting a man in the face, which occurred some eight years before. Given five years in jail, he was released after eighteen months, whining that he should have been acquitted with honour. Heines went on to be made SA boss in Silesia and police chief in Breslau, where he insti-tuted a reign of terror.

Even Goering had been affronted by the excesses committed by both SA and SS men after he declared them auxiliary police. He had ordered them to stand down. But rumours the brownshirts were to be held down perma-nently led to various angry utterances from Roehm; any who believed his army was a spent force were much mistaken, '. . . they will be given suit-able answer in due time and in whatever form is necessary. The SA IS and remains Germany's destiny.'

Having largely rid Germany of the Red menace, Hitler felt a potentially greater one in his midst. However, Roehm had sent his men on leave while sojourning and receiving treatment at Bad Wiessee with his 'all-male harem'. The Hotel Hanselbauer had physicians of some kind on its staff, and Heines's health was reputedly unsound. There was no question of an SA coup. Roehm had left his personal guards behind in Munich, and he had devoted the last sober moments of the day planning the reception for

Hitler and how he would present him with a bookplate specially designed by an artist in Munich.

Heines and his lover were shaken out of their slumbers as Brückner and Maurice broke into their bedroom. They were seized at gunpoint. Hitler rushed in, ordering Major Buch to 'ruthlessly exterminate the pestilential tumour!' One account describes how the pair were thrust outside and shot in a car; another claims they were put up against a wall and executed, before being buried in mud.

Count Spreti, another of Roehm's generals, was dragged out of bed and into the corridor; when the luckless man made a gesture, Hitler thought he was reaching for a gun and struck him over the head with the iron top of his whip until he collapsed to the floor. Then Hitler hurried into Roehm's room, delivering a thundering tirade before handing him a pistol and leaving. Hitler then left the building and returned to Munich. But shortly afterwards, when Sepp Dietrich investigated, he found Roehm had not shot himself. He was then removed to Stadelheim Prison where from a cell he heard the endless volleys of rifle fire as the SS death squad worked in the yard to get rid of those to be executed. For Roehm it was simpler. Dietrich and Michael Lippert simply opened his cell door and shot him.

In Berlin, Himmler's and Heydrich's SS squads had swung into action, and by midday 150 SA officers were incarcerated in the barracks at Lichterfelde, from where only one man escaped alive to tell the tale. Over the following hours and days many more Germans perished, politicians, Reds, policemen and innocents, as the SS commandos went about their work. Errors were made, confusions arose, but in the end the old scores had been settled. The 'Night of the Long Knives' marked a major turning point in German, or rather, Nazi politics, and incidentally, of Heydrich's SD. By the time the *Führer* ordered the killings to stop, the SD had performed a most useful exercise in cunning and deceit which proved excellent grounding for its next triumph two years later.

5

FOREIGN OPERATIONS – 1

On Sunday afternoon, 1 July 1934, Hitler held a tea party in the *Reichs Chancellery*, which was attended by many Nazi leaders. However, Heydrich did not attend, as he was even then still busily engaged in overseeing the round-ups and executions. Not until the next morning did Hitler decide these must stop. He had by then been told of Roehm's death, apparently turning pale on receiving the news. He sobered considerably. Hitler had received a congratulatory telegram from President Hindenburg which stated:

> You have delivered the German people from a great danger. I offer you my profound gratitude and sincere regards.

These sentiments contrasted greatly with the kind of attitude shown Hitler by the old man earlier.

Hitler's next move was to consolidate his position *vis-à-vis* the SA by issuing an Order of the Day in which he demanded 'the most perfect discipline, loyalty and fidelity without reserve to the army of the *Reich*'. His relief was great, for in one night of bloody action he had succeeded in removing the potentially worst threat to his position as *Führer*. From then on the huge brown army would prove docile, and they were in any case progressively cut down by two-thirds through various means. Viktor Lutze was appointed Roehm's successor. He confirmed they should continue on leave for a month, and either destroy all 'honour daggers' bearing Roehm's dedication or have the blade inscriptions removed. A few have survived to become rare collectors' items today.

One French historian referred to the new SA as 'former militiamen', new 'minor priests' – the SS being the 'major priests'. It was the SS and SD who gained most from the bloodletting. In Essen, *Gauleiter* Terboven (who would later rule in Norway), celebrated the 'lancing of an abscess . . . what matters is to know how to react to gangrene'. As to the German people, and to a lesser extent the world outside, Goebbels made sure his *Führer* was well briefed in the right phrases to use when explaining in public the necessity for such action.

The veteran American journalist William Shirer called Heydrich 'a young man of diabolical caste, an arrogant, icy, ruthless character'. Shirer's observations and anecdotes carry weight since he was actually present in Berlin during these events and saw many of the leading participants.

It is doubtful if Heydrich devoted any time to self-analysis, he was far too busy congratulating himself and his helpers and scheming anew. He had found and taken on some very promising pupils, namely Hermann Behrends and Alfred Naujocks. The former had proved useful as a recruiting officer, scouting for talent to be interviewed by his chief. Behrends was a one-time brownshirt turned stool pigeon who had informed on many of his former friends. He had maintained contacts among them, an arrangement which proved greatly advantageous to Heydrich. Heydrich suggested Behrends feign a stomach complaint to excuse himself from SA duty, while he made the rounds of his chums, gathering gossip to pass back to Heydrich. Behrends fell from favour later, as indeed did Naujocks, being called into the Army and killed in Russia.

Alfred Naujocks was a very different character. How he came to be recruited into Heydrich's Secret Service will be told later. Handy with his fists, he proved himself to be a counter-spy *par excellence.*

Can Heydrich's recruits be compared with those in MI6, the veteran spy service looked upon with great respect by their chief enemy? Though astute enough to appoint men like the lawyer types Schellenberg and Ohlendorf, Heydrich also had use for the tougher types like Naujocks. In time even more brutish men with little or no guile whatever who would follow base, inhuman orders without question were used. Such men did, however, work 'in the field' with Ohlendorf and other cleverer types who bent their brains for Hitler.

On a wider level, one account states that the SD 'field force' expanded rapidly into an army of some 100,000 informers. This huge spy net was quite independent of the *Gestapo* and other intelligence agencies, such as those run by Goering, von Ribbentrop and Goebbels. This army was administered by 3,000 full-time SD agent-overseers. The figures are nebulous, as are those for the *Gestapo*, which have been given as a 'few hundred' to some thousands. Heydrich was very careful in his search for the brainy types whose characters included not merely initiative, but deviousness; people such as university and college drop-outs, as they would be termed today – but not duds of course. He searched for men – or women – who had the right talents but for various reasons had been stymied in finding proper employment.

One character who fulfilled the criteria was Walter Schellenberg, who as shown had been wasting his time and brains as an SS guard. 'Fascinated' by the sight of Hitler at Bad Godesberg, immediately following the Roehm purge he found himself ordered to report to his superior, who told him he was transferred to the SD in Berlin. His officer seemed as baffled as he was, but Schellenberg wasted no time complying with the order. He was fully committed to the Nazi cause and never questioned the *Führer*'s right to get rid of undesirables. He swallowed all the propaganda, and became aware of Deputy *Führer* Rudolf Hess's statement that the SD was the Party's sole intelligence service. To an intelligent young man like Schellenberg the brownshirts had been mere street rabble. He had been encouraged by the insistence of the SS officers that they were something very different, an élite apart, no matter what was said about comradeship with SA brothers.

Despite Heydrich's habit of interviewing every new employee, in the case of Schellenberg he adopted a different approach. Exactly why is hard to fathom. He had of course seen the record and been struck by Schellenberg's alleged profession of 'lawyer'. As an academic he seemed an obvious choice for the SD to be seen by an officer below Heydrich, and if they gave wrong signals they got no further. Schellenberg, still wary and mystified, was surprised to be told almost at once he had been accepted into the SD and would begin training. Later, not only Schellenberg, but those whose hands he passed through, felt there was a guiding hand over him, that in fact of Heydrich, who proceeded to groom him by having him study in the various departments of the SD and *Gestapo* in Berlin. Only much later did the pupil finally meet his mentor, and then he became one of Heydrich's most trusted lieutenants.

Himmler once outlined the function of the SD as 'the ideological information service of the Party and State'. Its struggle was against the Jews, communists, Freemasons, reactionaries and 'confessional and politicising groups'. In fact, such struggles were mere routine for Heydrich, who looked to wider horizons, not forgetting the 'front' unmentioned by Himmler – the dissidents within the Army.

Less than three weeks after the Roehm affair, Austrian SS men tried to stage a coup in Vienna. Though it failed, they succeeded in assassinating the Austrian Chancellor, Dr Engelbert Dollfuss. Severe repercussions followed, which was embarrassing for Hitler, who received condemnation from abroad for interfering in Austrian affairs. Hitler was not directly guilty; the 89th SS 'regiment' of Austrian Nazis had been solely responsible, and were broken up by Austrian police. Seven men were arrested, tried and hanged. A furious Hitler, suspecting Himmler and Heydrich for complicity, served them with a severe memorandum forbidding them to ever repeat such an exercise. Sobered and irritated as they were, the pair of SS leaders knew the Austrian Nazis had only been premature.

Himmler tried to explain to Hitler that none of his organisations were involved in the fiasco in Vienna. The *Führer* was doubly embarrassed, as his ally and fellow dictator Mussolini had been alarmed enough to order Italian troops to rush to the frontier. Himmler felt the 'good name' of his SS had been dragged through the mud; whatever tricks the *Gestapo* and SD were to get up to, they would never be allowed to act in such blatantly open fashion as the fools in Austria had done.

Then, Defence Minister General von Blomberg announced rather prematurely that the two offices of President and Chancellor were to be combined. This was to take effect on the passing away of von Hindenberg, who obliged by dying the next day, 2 August 1934. Hitler wasted no time, becoming both President and Chancellor in one, though both titles soon lost their original meaning under his leadership. Hitler then called on all officers of the German Army to swear an oath of allegiance to him personally – which the vast majority did without argument. When conscription was implemented the following year every member of the new '*Wehrmacht*' was obliged to follow suit.

Meanwhile, Heydrich directed his new pupil Schellenberg to begin 'classes' in Bonn, where he ensconced himself in the Nazi Secret Service offices, a course lasting several weeks. He was then posted to Frankfurt to begin the next stage of his schooling – the functions of the police force. During this time, reports of the pupil's progress were forwarded directly to Heydrich in Berlin, the chief satisfied he had chosen well. Schellenberg recorded later how he felt his 'acts and doings were ruled by some invisible hand'. It is well to bear in mind the man's salient characteristics: Schellenberg had an easy charm and natural ability to get along with people, especially those he wished or was obliged to cultivate for 'business' reasons. His cunning, intuition and instinct for self-preservation made him an excellent spy.

Schellenberg advanced rapidly under his unseen master's guidance, with Heydrich now convinced he had found a star recruit and determined to further things by giving him a field assignment. Classwork suspended, Schellenberg was despatched to Paris on the first mission carried out by the SD outside Germany. His job was to trace a certain professor at the Sorbonne University in order to ascertain his political allegiances. This was not merely an exercise to test Schellenberg's mettle, Heydrich was already thinking beyond his usual brief, probing into espionage and subversion in the West – and without Himmler's knowledge. The Frenchman has not been named, but he had paid a visit to Germany some time before, and since all foreign visitors above a certain stamp were noted, his name had entered the SD files. It is possible that the professor, like a few other visitors, had been given the treatment by the Nazis, shown a few pet projects and left with a few complimentary comments. Celebrities and even royalty, such as Lloyd George, the Duke of Windsor, as well as the gullible leading journalist Ward Price of the *Daily Mail,* all went to Germany to see things for themselves. Ward Price was impressed enough to write a book which he called *I Know These Dictators* (the other being Mussolini). Such visits made good propaganda for the Nazis, and the guests were suitably noted in the secret police indexes.

Schellenberg's first assignment lasted less than a month. It was a very pleasant stay in Paris, resulting in a satisfactory report submitted through the appropriate channels after he returned to Frankfurt. He was then sent to Berlin and Prinz-Albrecht-Strasse for more studying, about the organisation of the SD and *Gestapo* headquarters, and how their work intertwined. During these weeks he was tutored by Dr Oswald Schaefer, a former

Walter Schellenberg exuded cunning and oily charm

director of Criminal Police and *Gestapo* boss in Munich. Once again Schellenberg, a newcomer of no rank, found everyone at all levels most agreeable and co-operative ('All doors opened before me') as he progressed through the complexities of the 'gigantic machine'. This was hardly an exaggeration, as in the year or two following Hitler's 'accession' both SD and *Gestapo* had expanded enormously, their various offices overflowing with files and indexes and the staff to fuss over them. Schellenberg met Dr Werner Best, Himmler's right-hand man overseeing the *Gestapo*, who spent an hour with him, ostensibly going over a technical dossier. On leaving, the pupil was told, 'I don't know what Heydrich has in mind for you, probably he will explain it to you one day'.

Schellenberg was mystified and a little uneasy, having no idea what lay ahead; he had yet to meet his mentor. As for Dr Best, the brain behind the *Gestapo*, his own future was to be clouded by his behaviour in Denmark.

Having chosen the police for his career, Best became chief in Hesse in 1933, clashing with the local *Gauleiter* before his talent was recognised by Himmler and he was given the post of SD boss in Bavaria. Expansion meant promotion to Berlin, where he was for a time Heydrich's superior of the SD while acting as 'Superior Councillor' of the judicial and administrative side of the *Gestapo*. Despite their lack of scruples and use of terror tactics, the Nazi security services tried to maintain some aura of legality, at least, under Nazi laws which were designed to ensure the State remained supreme in all matters of life and death. Through his SD connections, Best became involved in subversion abroad.

Something of a culture shock hit Schellenberg when he met Heinrich Müller. Dr Best he had found 'cultivated – intellectual'. He saw Müller as small and brutish, 'with the skull of a peasant', a protruding forehead, thin lips and penetrating brown eyes. He had thick, massive fingers. It was, probably to the new man's relief, a brief meeting. Müller told him he would work in the SD's central office, adding this was a pity, as he could have used him in his *Gestapo*. Only later did Schellenberg discover Müller's true feelings of great distrust towards Heydrich and the SD. He also learned at last that the SD chief was himself responsible for the months of grooming, that his good progress had at last warranted promotion to the heart of the security services in Berlin.

He met then Herbert Mehlhorn, who impressed him with 'extraordinary intelligence'. Mehlhorn was to become for a time chief of the SD 'inland', the home front intelligence service, under the direction of another Nazified intellectual, Otto Ohlendorf. Son of a rich, industrial family, Mehlhorn was much like Schellenberg. He too had studied law and practised in Saxony, but he had become a dyed-in-the-wool Nazi and willingly accepted the post Heydrich offered him. Yet he remained clear in his mind on one thing: perhaps unique among Nazis he took the long view of German history and had the nerve to inform the recruit that the Nazi regime was but one more passing phase. This was close to treason – in view of the leadership's assertion that their *Reich* would last a thousand years. In fact, as Mehlhorn said: 'Talk of a thousand-year *Reich* is an absurdity!'

It is likely that Heydrich and others capable of wider consideration took the same view, though few within the Nazi edifice would have bothered to consider such matters. The more intelligent simply assimilated the short-term advantages and worked with the regime in power, without being hoodwinked by claptrap ideology. It was an unparalleled opportunity to carve out a career via the 'talents' needed to be successful in a totalitarian regime. Men like Mehlhorn walked a tightrope, for whatever his chosen calling, his deeper feelings were little different to those of the opposition. In any case, whatever finer susceptibilities he had, if they were that, Mehlhorn had a weakness. He believed he was of greater brainpower and cunning and schemed against Heydrich. Underestimating his enemy, his ideas backfired and he was unseated. He was, as events proved, quite

FOREIGN OPERATIONS – 1

unsuited to 'field work', whatever his intelligence. Like Schellenberg he could not tackle the kind of dirtier work Alfred Naujocks proved so adept at.

But in welcoming Schellenberg under his wing, Mehlhorn disclosed that the chief had thoroughly recommended him. Actually, alike as they were and though great comradeship developed, Mehlhorn had his doubts about the newcomer – as indeed did Naujocks, who soon met Schellenberg and disliked him from the start. For one thing, the rougher, more direct Naujocks recoiled instinctively from the somewhat oily charm displayed by the all-smiling Schellenberg. There was also of course the barrier that always made itself felt between the working-class type and the brainbox – an uneasy relationship faltered along. Craftiness and naked ambition seemed to Naujocks to be Schellenberg's chief traits – 'a master of the art of deceit' was how he put it later. He would never trust him, yet had the brains to realise the recruit could prove useful to the team. Naujocks had a secure feeling he was valued by Heydrich, though his real testing time lay ahead. By then he had seen all the files, including those dealing with foreign agents working in Germany, and in particular Soviet subversion. It pleased Naujocks to feel a comparative veteran in such things, compared to the sly Schellenberg, who for his part had found Naujocks crude and boastful of his boxing prowess.

One name cropped up frequently in the SD reports of foreign suspects – Anton Horvath. Ostensibly a major in the Czech Army, Horvath was in fact a spy and an expert on the Soviet Union, with several friendly contacts in the Red Army. Czechoslovakia leaned more to the left, President Benes's feelings continually turning towards Moscow. Major Horvath was posted to the military attaché's office in his country's embassy in Berlin, and naturally immediately came to the notice of the German counter-spy services, including the *Abwehr*. Horvath was tailed and his telephone tapped by the *Gestapo*. German Military Intelligence, the *Abwehr*, was at the time still commanded by Captain Patzig, no lover of the new regime and openly critical of the Nazis. As a result of his views he would be removed, his place taken by a far wilier opponent of Hitler – none other than Heydrich's old commander and friend – the now Admiral Canaris.

Despite their suspicions, the German security agencies could pin nothing on Major Horvath, whose service in Germany ended rather soon. He gave a farewell party in the Czech Embassy. During his time in the *Reich* he had been received by General von Blomberg, the Minister of Defence, and other leading military figures, which was routine. But in this post-Roehm period Alfred Naujocks himself became involved in his chief's first counter-espionage case and all that was to flow from it.

Naujocks made a habit of frequenting the more elegant and stylish Berlin cafés and restaurants used by foreign dignitaries, military staff, and others less easy to define. His task was to pick up any gossip or useful information for the SD. This was how he met Joseph Borg.

After some general conversation Borg made it clear he was acquainted with various German and Soviet military men. He posed as an author, or at least a commentator on military affairs. Naujocks's interest was thoroughly aroused, though he remained cautious, as he thought Borg could well be a spy. He knew from Heydrich's tutelage that it paid to be very wary when dealing with foreigners in Germany, secret agents lurked among them. Naujocks reckoned Borg must be working for the Soviets, and the fact that he seemed well acquainted with some high German staff officers seemed dangerous. A few days later, as the pair drank in a better-class bar, Borg confided that he believed the liaisons practised between Soviet and German staff officers had gone further. Naujocks pricked up his ears, already convinced by what Heydrich had told him that traitors existed among the *Reichswehr* staff. But he decided to wait and see what else his contact divulged before reporting to Heydrich. Sure enough, soon afterwards he received what seemed confirmation – Soviet officers were privy to information from the German military.

A man and woman previously spurned by the *Gestapo* as 'adventurers' arrived in Naujocks's own little office. They told him they were White Russians, just two of the many who had fled the bloody Bolshevik revolution of 1917, to settle in western Europe, especially in Paris and Berlin. The pair claimed they were personally acquainted with several White Russian generals who were themselves now allied to Stalin; in other words, they had turned coat and were actually working for Soviet Intelligence, penetrating White Russian, anti-Stalin circles abroad, and with ease. Naujocks listened with interest, but only really perked up when the couple mentioned 'Horvath'; at once alert, Naujocks suspected a Soviet trap. Suppose all this was all part of an elaborate Russian plot, with the name 'Horvath' used to gain Nazi interest? He decided to test the couple, inviting them out to lunch in a restaurant where they could point out various faces they could identify as agents of one sort or another.

No sooner had the three been shown to a table in the restaurant than the two Russians pointed to Joseph Borg, whom they identified as working for Stalin – he always had been. This seemed to confirm what Naujocks had suspected, but when the pair laughingly asked if Borg was also working for the Germans he simply grinned and shook his head.

Not long after learning the restrictive but not ungenerous clauses of the Allied-dictated Treaty of Versailles which permitted them an army of 100,000 men, the German staff began scheming to circumvent them. Having forced the Russians into terms to end their part in the war, the German military then curried favour with them and arranged for certain mutually advantageous liaisons. For example they arranged the clandestine use of Russian territory for the training of new German air force and *Panzer* units. The new Red Army staff officers were invited to Germany to liaise and watch manoeuvres, these friendly contacts continuing after Hitler came to power.

All this was pertinent when Naujocks presented his updated file on Major Horvath, Joseph Borg and the White Russian couple to Heydrich. His chief was delighted, not only because it enabled his SD to become more involved in espionage, but it also furthered his leverage into the machinations of some German staff officers. Heydrich shared his *Führer*'s distrust and dislike of the military caste, especially the more conservative, hidebound Prussian types who had their counterparts in England. Both men, and many in Nazi circles, looked on such men as representing the old order. They were perfectly aware that despite swearing allegiance to Adolf Hitler, such men looked down on and despised him. Nevertheless, it would be Hitler who was to afford them the greatest opportunities to practise their chosen craft. The honourable and aristocratic gentlemen in field grey and red tabs would generally follow orders and assiduously practise their professional skills. Most fell into line, men like Rommel becoming used to shooting up their right arms in the Nazi salute and extolling Hitler. Some believed they could outwit and circumvent him, but in this they were much mistaken, since the dictator proved time and time again his superior will, cunning and ability to play them in the game.

The plot that sprang from the early meetings between Borg and Naujocks may have originated with the Soviets, as there is evidence enough pointing

Alfred Naujocks – Heydrich's 'James Bond'

to their greater cunning. The truth is probably that while in part it was Stalin-inspired, a subplot developed quite unexpectedly from Heydrich, which proved in the long run to be disastrous for the USSR. The notion that the idea commenced at *Führer* level seems very unlikely, though Hitler certainly gave his approval.

Heydrich's scheme was breathtaking: it was the undermining of the Red Army's officer corps. It was a subtle plot of great potential and advantage to Nazi Germany that would indeed bring dividends at a later date.

But first there were preliminary experiences for Heydrich and his agents to undergo which proved their growing expertise in matters of counter-espionage.

Heydrich became convinced that a Soviet agent had extracted information from the German military. This view was gained from various sources: the spurious, shadowy characters who dabbled in such gossip for gain of one kind or another, and not only in Berlin, but from Vienna and Prague. Heydrich and Naujocks concluded the 'Soviet spy' and Major Horvath were one and the same. Since the Czech had returned to Prague, Heydrich ordered Naujocks to go there, but to act very carefully. No 'incidents' were permitted. The Czech counter-spy system was one of the best.

As already indicated, Alfred Naujocks was far from the kind of rough diamond depicted in some quarters, his thinking and initiative were precise and to the point. He realised he would have to liaise with his prime informer, Joseph Borg, who was also in the Czech capital. It would be risky, as Naujocks felt he himself could well come under surveillance the moment he crossed the border. Nevertheless, he travelled to Prague, with nothing occurring to rouse his suspicions. Once he had booked into the Central Hotel he called Borg on the telephone. The agent suggested they meet in a certain bar at noon. Naujocks watched him arrive: smallish, Borg was well built and a snappy dresser. Naujocks greeted him, and over a drink asked at once to meet Major Horvath. Borg was startled, but then asked curiously what guise the German proposed to use if such a meeting could be arranged. Naujocks suggested he pose as 'a representative from Moscow'. Borg looking dubious, but then remarked that Horvath was not a professional so it might work. The German had to be content with that.

Returning to his room, Naujocks saw at once that his belongings had been interfered with. He had left his suitcase and neatly folded raincoat on the bed. They had obviously been gone over, his small kit lying over the bed covers and on the bedside table. His mind in a whirl, he tried to guess who could have entered his room – a Czech or Soviet agent? No common burglar would have left useful, saleable loot lying around. Someone had searched his belongings for clues, and been rather careless about it; unless they didn't care if he knew it or not. He blamed himself for his carelessness in not locking the door unless, perhaps, it had been one of the hotel staff?

That evening Naujocks took a walk in the rain before taking tea in his room, impatiently waiting for Borg to call. When he did call at seven,

Naujocks learned he should be at the same bar in thirty minutes. Shortly afterwards the German went downstairs, had a stiff whisky in the hotel bar and left for the rendezvous. As he walked along the wet Prague streets his nerves tingled with excitement. He, a complete amateur, was now involved in the real thing – the world of spies. He wondered what he would report to Heydrich in Berlin, or if there would be anything to report. He realised too that he trusted no one beyond his own chief, certainly not Borg.

When he reached the bar a surprise awaited him. Borg was in the street outside, and with him were two others, a smartly turned out Czech major who had to be Horvath and a beautiful girl. Naujocks felt a fresh tingle of alarm and excitement, all kinds of thoughts racing through his head as Borg made the introductions. The major, speaking perfect German, remarked that since the visitor was a stranger in town they would be happy to show him round. The girl, Paula, was the major's sister; Naujocks' interest quickened as she smiled winningly, seeming to favour him with her fullest attention, her glances promising much. At his suggestion they went for a meal, Borg taking them into the old town quarter, but when they selected a restaurant he excused himself to attend a business meeting and left them to talk.

Once the meal was over, Paula excused herself. Her brother, well aware of the German's interest, grinned as he remarked on it. The major then startled Naujocks by expressing regret that his sister had 'become mixed up in it', so it seemed she too was in the pay of the Soviets.

It is hard to imagine even the crafty Schellenberg handling this tricky meeting any better. Naujocks parried Paula's questions with guile, putting forward some of his own, but letting nothing slip. 'Did he need anything from them?' she asked. No, Naujocks told her, he had only wanted to meet them to be assured they were satisfied and had no complaints. Then the major stunned the SD agent by asking for money to help secure a *Luftwaffe* man who was working on secret projects near Lübeck. The German had a Czech mother. Naujocks, trying to appear calm, assured Horvath that finance was no problem. Trying to maintain his alias as an emissary from Moscow, he chatted with them and presently, to his great satisfaction, extracted the name of the *Luftwaffe* traitor near Lübeck. Moreover, his hosts gave him the names of three more 'Sovietised' Germans and that of their contact man. Naujocks realised the gorgeous Paula was in the business up to her pretty neck and working as a courier between Prague and Berlin. When they left the restaurant the major suggested they return to his apartment for a drink. Naujocks then walked Paula back to her flat where she at once offered herself to him, hugging and kissing him before inviting him to spend the night with her. Though greatly excited by the offer, Naujocks allowed caution to dampen his ardour, wary lest she worm secrets out of him in weak moments.

Delighted with his progress, Naujocks hastened back to Berlin the next day. He had succeeded far beyond his hopes. Going immediately to his office, late as it was, he began to make out his report, adding various interpretative notes and comments. The job took him all night. Next morning, he reported to his immediate boss, Hermann Behrends, an old friend of Heydrich from their earlier days in the SS. Behrends owed his job in the Nazi Secret Service to the downfall of an ex-Bavarian detective who had been recruited by Heydrich to set up shop in Berlin – almost literally, for the first SD premises in the capital had been a former shop at 16 Eicherallee. As expansion came, so did Kublinsky, inasmuch as he tried, like Mehlhorn later, to outwit his chief and mentor Heydrich by allying himself with the then head of Goering's new *Gestapo*, Rudolf Diels. Kublinsky promised to pass on everything of interest emanating from Heydrich in Munich – Heydrich chanced on this dangerous information by chance.

Enter Alfred Naujocks, who had become embroiled with the Nazi brownshirts even in his early 'teens. He had been involved in street battles in his native Kiel, where his comrades soon saw his usefulness as a mauler. Naujocks had been 'brought up' into Nazism by a man called Groethe, who went on to help man the new SD office in Berlin. Naujocks worked as a welder in a loco factory in Kiel, but went to Berlin, where his old friend Groethe again took him under his wing, introducing him to his chief, Kurt Kublinsky, who agreed to enlist him in the SD. In doing so he delivered a stern lecture on what was involved in joining the SS Secret Service, emphasising that once in he stayed – 'One does not leave the service of the SD alive'.

Impressed, the young Naujocks envisaged becoming a spy, and all kinds of adventures rushed into his agile mind. However, he was to be greatly disappointed. Maintained solely as a chauffeur and general duties man, Naujocks never entered into spying or secret activities of any kind. When the big chief Heydrich visited from Munich it was Naujocks who was sent to fetch him from the station. During the drive to the SD headquarters he boldly entered into conversation with the general, mentioning that he too hailed from Kiel. If Naujocks knew of Heydrich's unhappy parting from the Navy he gave no hint of it, but instead he chatted amiably of people and places in their home town, the passenger in the rear seat proving perfectly amiable. When Heydrich dined with Kublinsky it was Naujocks who served the meal, aware from the tense atmosphere and outbursts he had heard from outside the room that the pair were at odds. Then, as he was leaving, Heydrich advised a trembling Kublinsky he was in need of a holiday. This utterance was delivered with the icy, unsmiling tones of a Mafia gangster hinting it was time for a rival to vanish.

Naujocks drove Heydrich back to the station, again involved in conversation, but of a different kind. The general asked if he was happy with his job. Naujocks became alerted, as if he were being probed as to opinions. Responding boldly, he complained of the menial nature of his duties, and how his kind never seemed to be trusted to do any of the real work – i.e.

spying, etc. He went further, wondering later if he had made a grievous error. Allowing himself to talk freely, he mentioned a meeting at the SD office between Rudolf Diels and Kublinsky, at which he had as usual acted as butler, overhearing certain things which he repeated to his passenger. Heydrich remained icy calm as he learned his deputy in Berlin had agreed to betray him to the *Gestapo* boss.

A week later a high-ranking SS officer arrived quite suddenly in Berlin and without warning; a few minutes later Kublinsky was led out, mumbling to his staff he was taking a holiday. The SD chief of Russo-Polish origins was never seen again. His position was filled the next day by Hermann Behrends.

After receiving Naujock's report on Horvath, Behrends took him to see Heydrich, who began scanning the report's salient points, his expression disclosing his amazement and appreciation. After receiving the heartiest of congratulations, Naujocks was allowed to return home for a meal and some sleep.

Over the following days the wheels of the German security police began to turn, but it was some three weeks before Naujocks saw a document listing six people arrested and charged with treason and espionage. Among those held were German Army officers and the *Luftwaffe* man, but the name which hit Naujocks most was that of Paula Horvath, who had been taken from a train *en route* to Prague. In her possession was found a microfilm destined for the Soviets. Naujocks wondered who had ordered her arrest, and he suspected Walter Schellenberg. He was sad she had been taken, yet knew her guilt and what lay ahead.

Schellenberg had now been permitted into the most secret documentation of the SD HQ, and interviewed at last by Heydrich. The latter surprised him by chatting about general topics, including music, before going into the urgent task awaiting the SD. At last, after some ninety minutes, he told Schellenberg he would work under the direction of Dr Best, principally on counter-espionage.

The case of the Polish Major Jurik von Sosnowski must rank among the best of true spy stories. It is more like fiction in some aspects.

It first came to the attention of Walter Schellenberg early in 1935, after it had been closed. Heydrich had given him the file in case one or two of the defendants could be of use to the SD. The case had actually begun six years before, in 1929, when a Lieutenant Colonel Bender of the *Reichswehr* employed as secretary a pretty young divorcee called Benita. She had been married to Count von Falkenhayn, who had been one of the Kaiser's field marshals. Benita's father, who had also served as a high-ranking officer in the Imperial Army, had just died, leaving his wife and daughter a miserly pension to live on – which was why Benita had taken the poorly paid job in the *Reichswehr* building in Berlin's Bendlerstrasse. A keen horsewoman, she attended equestrian shows, and at one of them met the keen rider Major

Sosnowski. Benita fell in love with him; his skill as a horseman, and his grace and charm proved irresistable. Naturally, things would look rather different in the light of later events, after he had professed his own love and entered into a passionate affair with her – even insisting on clearing the debts incurred by Benita and her mother, who was as charmed by the Pole as her daughter. For one thing, he was titled, and so, though an *Auslander,* he fell into their class. His cards pronounced him to be Major Jurik von Sosnowski, Chevalier von Nalecz.

The night life in Berlin, and particularly in the famous Kurfurstendamm, was lively, and the worst excesses and decadences of the twenties had slipped away. The smart, fashionable cafés, restaurants and night spots were attended by German officers and their womenfolk. Major Sosnowski and his attractive mistress mixed in this gay and carefree atmosphere with officers of the new *Luftwaffe.* After one entertaining evening the couple returned to their apartment, where the Pole disrobed before going to the bathroom. The major's shirt was carelessly thrown on the bed, and Benita saw the cuffs were covered in scribble; curious, she looked more closely, realising at once what the marks signified. Her lover had been taking notes in the night spot after chatting with the German officers – he was a spy!

However, in the scene that followed she confessed to not caring what he did, her love for him was too great. Yet they argued and discussed the issue far into the night, the major unsure of her. Would she betray him? With his persuasive charm and command over her it proved easy to have Benita sign a written receipt for all the money he had given her and her mother. It was a form of blackmail, though whether the girl realised this is uncertain. Should she give him away to the German police, Sosnowski would make sure she too became implicated. She had received cash from the Polish spy – the inference obvious once they discovered her employer.

All this Walter Schellenberg learned on reading the file passed to him by Heydrich. By early 1935 Major Sosnowski had been arrested, along with his mistress Benita von Falkenhayn – who told all.

It was the Sosnowski affair which brought to a head the clash of interests between SD and *Gestapo,* or rather, the fact that both agencies were now engaged in counter-espionage. In fact, Heydrich had got wind of the Sosnowski business from one of his spies inside the *Gestapo.* It was the SD's remit to investigate such activities, not the *Gestapo,* so Heydrich was quick to initiate his own sleuthing of the Pole. The absurdity of both departments working independently on the same case, in Müller's ignorance, led to his protest to Himmler when the case came to a head through the arrests. Himmler called both department chiefs to a meeting, at which Heydrich assured his boss (quite untruthfully) that the Pole had been under investigation by his men for some time. Obviously, as Himmler declared, this kind of situation was no good at all, therefore steps had to be taken to eliminate any recurrence of such wasted effort. He ordered both chiefs to liaise in future on all counter-espionage cases and report to him. Heydrich agreed, but secretly ordered his agents to step up all surveillance on foreign diplomatic and military staff in order to get ahead of the *Gestapo* – should any leads appear. Heydrich was hungry for power in several directions, but especially in the matter of espionage; if he could, he would prevent the *Gestapo* from having any say in such affairs.

He went further, instructing the SD agent who had the friend in 'the other camp' to cultivate the association very, very carefully in order to gain a better insight into *Gestapo* dealings, cases and investigations. The very idea of one spy organisation spying on one of its fellow agencies may seem ludicrous, but it also happened elsewhere. Wherever similar agencies exist, rivalries develop, as between the American FBI and CIA, and MI6 and SOE in wartime. But apart from rivalries, many top Nazis were anxious to impress their *Führer* in order to advance themselves further, and none more than Heydrich, who may even have been confident enough of his growing power to by-pass him.

While the SS became a growing power unto itself in those times, Reinhard Heydrich was rapidly becoming the most dangerous man in the *Reich*. In this respect it has been hinted, but never proved, that in his personal safe he even maintained files on Himmler and Hitler, which is more than likely no more than an intriguing idea. It is extremely unlikely that Heydrich would have risked investigating the Geli Raubel affair, for example. The suggestion Hitler himself shot the cousin he loved might, if proved, have enabled Heydrich to add the greatest and most dangerous piece of evidence ever to his files. Then again, there were, as with Heydrich, the poisonous snippets circulated by those gossips and others with something to gain concerning the *Führer*'s antecedents. As in the case of Heydrich, no trace of Jewishness was ever found. There were also scurrilous tales spread about to discredit Hitler by way of his sex life, the most degrading and somewhat absurd concocted and published by two ex-BBC employees.

Run-of-the-mill police work held no interest for Heydrich, as his colleagues discovered. There were more than enough policemen of one kind or another in Nazi Germany, men in a great variety of uniforms to oversee every facet of German life, as well as the many in plain clothes or pure civilians employed as informers. Espionage and counter-espionage became Heydrich's main interest as the thirties saw Hitler's Germany steered towards war, an event which in reality proved a turning point for the career Heydrich had carved for himself. In fact, however, it was a disaster in that as 'spy chief' he became deflected completely.

Returning to Major Sosnowski, the Germans soon discovered and relished no doubt the scandalous trail left behind their prisoner. His insatiable appetite for women had landed him in hot water long before he left Poland. Sosnowski had seduced the wife of his commanding officer, but though disgraced was saved from dismissal by the chief of Polish Intelligence, Colonel Lipitsk. Enrolled into spying, the major succeeded in his task in Germany, but even after corralling Benita von Falkenhayn he widened his sexual activities, actually exchanging her for a friend's mistress. This took place following Benita's introduction to the Pole's erotic parties, which usually degenerated into orgies. It was the carelessness of one mistress which led to, not the SD or *Gestapo*'s interest, but that of the *Abwehr*, yet a third agency involved in counter-espionage. The *Abwehr* collected the evidence, but was obliged to allow the *Gestapo* to make the arrests. Sosnowski was seized in a wild and highly dramatic fashion by *Gestapo* agents posing as waiters and other staff for one of the Pole's disgraceful parties. The major had by then become the talk of Berlin. He had somewhat absurdly drawn attention to himself by his flamboyant lifestyle among the capital's night life, and was even mentioned in the gossip columns.

The SD's involvement was marginal, but how Heydrich's men were so late on the scene is not known. The Secret Service chief was chagrined and forced to chew over the leavings, the files passed to him by Müller. He felt, however, that two of the prisoners could be useful to the SD, and sent Schellenberg to interview them. These were the two women betrayed in the case, who had suffered all the indignity of being thrown into jail and being interrogated by *Abwehr* and *Gestapo*. In the trial, Benita was sentenced to death, as was Renate von Natzmer, who had also worked in the *Reichswehr* Ministry. The third woman trapped by the Pole, also a military secretary, received like her master penal servitude for life.

It transpired the major was Austrian-born, in territory once owned by Poland; this saved him from death, though he never served his full sentence. In May 1935 a German spy was arrested while trying to infiltrate Polish frontier fortifications; he was exchanged the following year for Sosnowski, reportedly because he was an intimate friend of a high-ranking German officer.

However, the Polish major had been broken by the *Gestapo* and returned to his country an old man, with white hair and trembling hands. By 1942 he was back in a German concentration camp, where he died of dysentery.

Despite hopes by Heydrich to make use of the two principal female witnesses and prisoners, on 18 February 1935 Benita and Renate were beheaded in the courtyard of Blockensee Prison, in Berlin's Charlottenburg. In his memoirs, and in typical fashion, Walter Schellenberg tried to claim total credit for the Sosnowski case ('from beginning to end'). In fact, the *Abwehr* agent Captain Protze had begun investigating the Pole as early as 1933, the SD entering the picture late in 1934. Schellenberg played no part in the sleuthing or interrogations that followed the round-up. What Schellenberg did achieve was small by comparison, as he managed to persuade (without difficulty) one Katie Berberian to save her head by working as a counter-spy for the SD. The woman was Persian by origin, and the mistress of Sosnowski's friend Joseph von Berg. She had been exchanged by him for Benita. After release from prison, Katie

Berberian was eventually allowed by the Poles to work for them as a spy, and despite being watched by her new employers succeeded in trapping ten Polish agents. Katie, the one-time ballerina called Niako, who had performed near-pornographic dances at Major Sosnowski's parties, then vanished.

6

FOREIGN OPERATIONS – 2

It is possible that men like Alfred Naujocks may have been employed in certain circumstances on dirty jobs by MI6, but it is extremely unlikely he would ever have been taken on as a full-time agent. However, Reinhard Heydrich discovered to his great satisfaction that Naujocks, the former roughneck of the street battles, had astute qualities which enabled him to successfully carry out dangerous assignments in the James Bond manner. He had an appeal for women, toughness and ruthlessness, and an ability to keep his mouth shut when it suited; add to that an easy ability to befog adversaries with verbal camouflage and we have the ideal secret agent. All the named qualities came to the fore when, in January 1935, his chief sent him on another mission into foreign territory.

By that time Naujocks had found himself a mistress called Tania, an attractive brunette aged twenty-four who seemed inconveniently keen on marriage. On 19 January he called at her flat, but found Tania absent and only her flatmate Edith there, washing the dishes. Surprised, Naujocks enquired about Tania's whereabouts. He had arranged to combine business with pleasure, a job in Czechoslovakia, and it seemed expedient to take the girl with him. Edith explained that Tania had been called away for duty at 'the Ministry', and would not be free for some days. She then amazed Naujocks by offering herself as available for the trip. Edith was blonde and attractive, so he quickly adjusted to the new situation and accepted, especially as she already had her bags packed and seemed eager to get started.

They drove off into the night, heading for the frontier, Naujocks going over in his mind the points Heydrich had hammered out for him. His target was a man called Rudolf Formis, who was making anti-Nazi broadcasts from inside Czechoslovakia on behalf of the exiled leader of the Black Front, Otto Strasser. Strasser, socialist and ex-Nazi brother of Gregor, had fled following their split with Hitler. With Gregor murdered, Otto played his anti-Hitler game from a safe hiding place outside the *Reich*. Unlike others who had fallen out with Hitler and left hurriedly, Otto Strasser could not be forgotten, as his insidious anti-Nazi propaganda broadcast by Formis was beamed over a wide area of southern Germany.

Radio detection had pinpointed the Black Front transmissions as emanating from about thirty-five miles south-west of Prague. Heydrich's

Otto Strasser, leader of the Black Front

radio team had placed the transmitter in or near the little town of Pribram; the broadcasts began at 8 p.m. and lasted two hours – and the *Führer* wanted them stopped. The Strassers were well known to Himmler, as he had acted as political runabout for Gregor in the early days, using a motorcycle combination while canvassing support for the Nazi cause in Bavaria. During that period Otto directed the Nazi press, aided by a promising young man with a deformed foot – Joseph Goebbels. Goebbels abandoned his employer once he saw which way the wind was blowing, nailing his colours to Hitler's flagpole, and abandoning all allegiance to the Strassers. When Hitler gained power, Otto Strasser fled to Austria, guessing that haven as too dangerous and going on to Prague, using an alias. The *Gestapo* had failed to kidnap him, and now it was up to the SD to silence his propaganda.

The lead to the source of Strasser's radio game had come from two of his own collaborators bribed by the *Gestapo*. The key man and sole operator of the transmitter was Richard Formis; remove him and destroy the set was the order given to Naujocks, who had confided in his Tania, disappointed when her interest suddenly waned. She began to realise there would be more to their vacation than sunning and skiing. Tania had backed out, suggesting he take Edith, but though he had been persuaded, he never really expected to find her ready to leave with him. As for his boss, Heydrich was enthusiastic; taking a woman along seemed a good ploy. Naujocks was equipped with skis, clothing, a Mercedes and a passport made out to 'Alfred Gerber', a businessman.

Naujocks had studied the maps carefully, and gone over the possible contingencies. There would, so Heydrich told him, be no shooting, and no blowing up of the transmitter – if he managed to find it. All he had to do was locate Formis and his set-up and report to Berlin. Heydrich explained the risk of being caught on such a reconnaissance carrying explosives. He wanted no embarrassing incidents in Czechoslovakia. As to funds, his colleague Groethe provided bundles of 100-mark notes which were hidden about the car. If a nosy Czech customs man found the money, Naujocks would jokingly assert his female was a big spender.

They stopped off in Dresden, intending to continue the journey the following morning. As they ate supper in a hotel Edith chattered away, seeming to have no idea of her companion's real line of work. Tania had not confided in her that much. On the other hand, Naujocks knew all about Edith's business – she ran a massage parlour for tired businessmen. When he put one or two innocent but pointed questions to her she soon tried her best to disabuse him of any ideas he might have had on that score. No, Edith insisted, it was a respectable salon, her clients were carefully chosen, as were her female staff, who were watched; they were well paid and received good tips from clients who derived pleasure and satisfaction at their hands. The salon had already been inspected by the criminal police and nothing untoward found, though the dangers to security with regard to confidential and government matters were obvious. Naujocks knew about the security checks made on Madame Edith's Salon, but said nothing.

They slept in separate rooms, driving off after breakfast. They stopped at a little café in Attenberg for coffee, where Naujocks took the opportunity to warn Edith he was travelling under the name of 'Gerber', just in case any query arose during the frontier check. She reacted with surprise, wondering no doubt what he was up to.

When they reached the German-Czech border they found it necessary for drivers to leave their vehicles and report with documents to a control building. The Czechs were thorough, an armed guard accompanying Naujocks into the office while another checked the Mercedes for contraband and noted its licence plate. But they were passed through without trouble and were soon driving along an icy road under leaden skies, the hills and mountains white with snow.

They lunched at a village inn before driving on to Prague, where the snow also lay quite thick in the streets. Naujock was of course no stranger to the Czech capital and took Edith for a stroll around the well-lit shopping precincts. They bought a few items, she seemed happy and it was all good cover in case the Czechs had them under surveillance. But these were early days, and the Czech spymaster, Lieutenant-Colonel Moravec had barely had time to try his desk for size since his appointment the previous March to head the investigative section of the Czech Army. It takes time to build up a spy and counter-spy network. Czechoslovakia was a new nation surrounded by enemies – real and potential – composed of a strip of land 800 miles long and varying in width from 150 miles in Bohemia, 120 miles in Moravia, and as little as 80 miles in Slovakia. The people had not had enough time to meld together into real nationhood, though legions from these lands had fought on various fronts under Allied officers, notably against the Bolsheviks in Russia. Now, they had over a million Germans living within their borders, and neighbouring nations (Poland and Hungary), laying claim to their territory, fascist Italy siding with the last named in its disputes with Prague.

Colonel Moravec would later be referred to as a 'master of spies', because of his great success in handling German attempts to infiltrate agents and his own triumphs in ferreting out secrets from within the *Reich* itself. Not that this could prevent his country falling into Hitler's hands, the land where Heydrich's career reached its apogee and end.

Despite Moravec's precautions, 'Alfred Gerber' penetrated the Czech countryside in January 1935, driving south-west with his lady companion until nearing the town of Pribram. A few miles short of that spot Naujocks pulled to a halt before a signpost which indicated Pribram lay to the right, Dubenec dead ahead, and a third place called Obory was a few miles on to the left. Somehow, he felt drawn to the latter, and on arrival discovered it to be no more than a rather placid-looking village near the River Moldau. The whole scene presented a picture card landscape of snowy fields divided by black hedgerows and little woods. Small as it was, the village boasted a hotel, but it looked most unwelcoming, and the two Germans guessed it was no popular tourist spot. This was confirmed when an old crone reluctantly admitted them into the hotel, where they signed the visitors' book. The woman's scraggy husband then led them upstairs into two unheated bedrooms.

After a chilled and restless night they recovered the following morning, finding bright sunshine and glorious mountain views. Even their female host seemed changed, greeting them cordially and serving a large breakfast. Naujocks then persuaded Edith to take a walk by the river, but then decided to tour the valley by car. He took snapshots of Edith, making sure various buildings appeared in the background; he planned to use the photographs later in his mission. As they drove on Naujocks wondered about the other guests mentioned by their hosts also staying in their billet. After an hour's drive, however, they came across another hotel, and now sheer luck entered the equation.

Set in an even more picturesque setting, this hotel employed a maid who showed the couple into the dining room, where they saw a man sitting before a log fire sipping coffee. Naujocks was startled, unable to believe his good fortune as he recognised Rudolf Formis. Heydrich had shown him a photograph – there was no mistaking him. The man turned to look at them, his interest obviously quickening as he saw Edith; Naujocks was thankful he had brought her along. Unwittingly, she was playing her part perfectly, tidying her hair before a mirror, Formis smiling silently as he looked her over. And, as Naujocks moved to a chair, Formis stood up, asking if they were German, as he was, and invited them to join him for some coffee. Curbing his excitement, Naujocks tried to appear cool. As the couple sat down, as if on cue, the maid appeared again to enquire if 'Herr Formis' would like another coffee. It seemed incredible to Naujocks, that in all the many square miles of Czech territory he had considered searching, his quarry should fall right into his lap – almost immediately.

The SD agent could not know the true character of Rudolf Formis. He was in fact a brilliant engineer, who had fought in the war and then become a fanatically dedicated anti-Nazi. It is said that Formis actually cut the transmission cable during an important speech Hitler made in Stuttgart. But his enemies were not stupid, and when he felt the net closing he fled from Germany. It was Otto Strasser who revealed such facts later, also disclosing that Formis had been a long-time member of the Black Front. It was Strasser who persuaded Formis to use his skills to construct and operate a pirate radio station to broadcast anti-Hitler propaganda from a remote spot in Czechoslovakia, but close enough to Germany to be heard by a sizeable audience.

During their conversation the newcomers learnt that Formis was a keen skier, although he alleged he was clumsy. He was, he told them, an electrical engineer. Naujocks knew he had found his target. Formis assumed them to be a married couple, and at his suggestion they agreed to move into the vacant room next to his own. Indeed, the jovial proprietor had concluded they were honeymooning and gladly showed them up to the room. Once alone, Naujocks felt obliged to tell Edith some of the truth, her face showing astonishment when he explained their new friend was a traitor to Germany. Then, accepting the situation, much to his relief, Edith rearranged the ring on her finger so that it appeared they really were man and wife. Naujocks let her into more of the truth, and despite her shock, she agreed to help him.

Continuing in the vein of spy fiction, 'Alfred Gerber' said he must now return to Berlin to receive further orders. Edith would have to remain in the hotel – to play up to Formis. The first priority was to get a key made to enter the man's room, where he strongly believed the transmitter was kept. At one point Naujocks had gone outside for some air, glancing up he had seen Edith waving gaily, and as he returned her greeting he was startled to see a thin cylinder poking out from the dormer window of Formis's room; obviously, this contained a radio antenna. This clinched it, and Naujocks could now report with certainty to Heydrich.

They lunched amicably with Formis, who seemed very open, charming and innocent, so much so that Edith began to doubt the tale her 'husband' had told her. Was Alfred really an SD agent? It all seemed so fantastic and far-fetched, certainly quite unlike the skiing holiday she had expected. Yet, that afternoon when the three went out into the snow she proved herself expert at the sport, while the two males were no more than amateurs. Edith tried to give them a few tips; Formis seemed to topple over frequently, always conveniently close to Edith, clutching at her for support. Naujocks recognised his feelings of jealousy, but knew all was proceeding splendidly, and he sped back to Berlin in good fettle. He reported to an amazed Heydrich, who remained cool enough to remind Naujocks their man was wanted back in Berlin for questioning. Heydrich had been even more impressed when Naujocks showed him the impression he had made with ski wax of the key to Formis's room. He had managed this while Edith kept the man chatting in the hotel lounge.

When Naujocks returned to Prague he was accompanied by Gert Groethe, who travelled with a passport made out in the name of 'Gert Schubert'. They had equipped themselves with phosphorus, chloroform and pistols. After landing at the Czech capital via a Lufthansa flight they passed through the usual formalities without bother. Naujocks drove his Mercedes straight to the first village hotel he had visited, leaving Gert to book in. But in his absence things had gone awry, as Naujocks soon discovered when he arrived at his billet. He met Formis on the stairs, surprised and alerted when the man brushed past with barely an acknowledgement. In their room Edith gave him disturbing news – Formis seemed to know the truth, they had been unmasked. She seemed upset, and Naujocks tried to assure her all would be well, though his mind was now in some turmoil.

All was in fact far from well. The hotel staff, especially the chambermaid, had looked on askance while Edith, a 'married' woman, had made up to *Herr* Formis while her new husband was away in Prague on business. Worse, as was disclosed by Strasser much later, Formis had become highly suspicious of the couple and had gone to Prague to meet his chief to report the bogus 'honeymoon couple' who had arrived unexpectedly at his hideaway. But, though Strasser warned him to be extra-careful, Formis had returned to the village and started to behave oddly, absenting himself from the hotel dining room. This was enough to warn Edith things had gone wrong.

Naujocks decided that in view of the rough stuff planned by Groethe he must remove Edith back to Prague – he had developed real feelings for her. After the evening meal they went to the bar for a drink and saw Formis, who left hurriedly, wishing them a brief '*Guten abend*'. Back in their room, Edith's state deteriorated into one of nervous fear; Naujocks tried to calm her tenderly, before resorting to love-making until they fell asleep.

The following morning he strolled alone by the river, going over the plan he had formed; Naujocks was determined to snatch Formis that evening, in his broadcasting period, between eight and ten. He realised he needed at least three hours to carry out the first part of his plan.

The couple left in their car to pick up Groethe, Edith a bundle of nerves. They had passed Formis in the hotel entrance, receiving only a brief greeting. Naujocks was now uneasy, baffled as to how he had been rumbled, if indeed he had been. Why else would Formis suddenly start behaving so coldly? Edith remarked she felt sure their room would be searched while they were away, and by the time they met Groethe her fears had turned to anger as she decided Naujocks had after all only been using her as cover for his dirty work. Later on, she would refer to him as 'exquisite' in the love role, but 'hard as steel and ruthless in action' – a real James Bond type. Yet he also terrified her.

The three returned to Prague, to the railway station, where Naujocks bought a ticket for Edith before they dropped Groethe off at his village hotel. Then they returned to their own hotel, noting the target's car parked in the garage. It had now turned colder, the temperature near zero. Back in their room, Edith packed her bag in silence: for her the vacation had turned to ruin. Naujocks appeared calm, reclining in an armchair and reading a crime novel. Then they heard something – Formis was leaving his room, creeping along the hall to clamber into the attic. Naujocks glanced at his watch: it was obvious, Formis was getting ready to broadcast.

It was after nine o'clock when Naujocks decided the time had come to act. Going to the window, he opened and closed it three times: Groethe had arrived outside and saw the signal. In a moment Naujocks had lowered their suitcases out of the window on a rope, Groethe loading them into the car before hauling himself up into their room. The plan was to grab Formis when he climbed back into the attic to make his last broadcast at ten o'clock. They waited and waited, a chloroform pad ready for use and the bottle of phosphorus to hand for destroying the radio transmitter. Naujocks opened the bedroom door, leaving it pushed to; they listened intently.

At last they heard footsteps. Naujocks glanced round at Edith who sat shaking on the bed. At that moment he realised Formis was in fact coming upstairs from the dining room; he was not yet in the hall and was making for his attic 'studio'. Formis went back to his room, so Naujocks slipped out into the hall and rapped on the door. He heard Formis respond, asking who was there. Naujocks, suppressing a grin and his excitement, told him he needed to borrow some soap, at the same time easing his duplicate key into the keyhole – but finding it jammed against a key on the other side.

The door was then opened slightly by Formis who handed out a small bar of soap without a word. At once Naujocks threw all his weight against the door, grabbing at the man's throat as he fell backwards. They fell to the floor, and the bottle of chloroform in Naujock's hand went flying and broke. Formis broke free, grabbed his dressing gown and pulled out a pistol. Before Naujocks could dodge Formis had fired. A sharp pain hit the agent's shoulder, quickly followed by another in the foot as Formis fired a second shot. Almost at once came a third loud report and Formis tumbled over Naujocks – shot through the head by Groethe. Edith rushed into the room and promptly fainted. There on the bed lay an open suitcase, the transmitter plain to see. As Naujocks tried to struggle to his feet in great pain, Groethe leapt across the room, opened the bottle of phosphorus and poured it over the radio. His attention was abruptly diverted from the resulting spectacle as the transmitter burned up by the sound of rushing feet on the stairs as the staff hurried to investigate.

With great presence of mind, Groethe ran outside to head them off – just as Naujocks managed to haul himself and Edith out of the room. Behind them the stench of chloroform and phosphorus was now punctuated by flames and an explosion. Groethe ushered the staff downstairs, waving his pistol and locking them in the cellar. Even though it was only a hotel in a large village, the manager had installed an alarm system which had already been switched on for the night. The Germans now heard a bell ringing loudly, and fearing a police presence, began scrambling down the rope from their room window. Groethe helped Edith to descend, then turned to assist his moaning comrade. But Naujocks was tough and somehow managed to drive them away from the scene. It was an ordeal, and they eventually arrived back in Prague with a few minutes to spare before Edith's train departed for Berlin. The two men then drove to the frontier, a nightmare journey for Naujocks, whose wounds seeped blood over the car seat. Stopping well short of the border control post, they abandoned the Mercedes, donned ski clothing and surprisingly, considering the state of the wounded man, managed to cross into Germany without problem. Finding the nearest hotel, they told staff they had been involved in an accident with their car over the border and needed a doctor. When he arrived and examined Naujocks's wounds he insisted on calling the police. This seems to have been smoothed over, as the pair travelled on to Berlin next day while their car was recovered.

Heydrich congratulated them on the destruction of the transmitter, but seemed muted and then gave vent to his anger over the way they had dealt with Formis. What could he tell the *Führer* when the diplomatic repercussions came?

The news media broadcast brief details of the incident in which a German national had been killed on Czech territory by German suspects. Dr Goebbels made sure further reports were hushed up, while Hitler actually sent his congratulations. The Czech authorities made their investigation, arresting the hotel proprietor for complicity, though unable to identify the culprits. Naujocks never saw his Tania or Edith again.

7

A MASTER FORGERY

In mid-June 1936, Heinrich Himmler was appointed *Reichsführer* SS and Chief of the German Police. This order from Hitler merely confirmed the process Himmler had first begun when he entered the *Gestapo*. Meanwhile, Heydrich had already taken short leave from his SD at Himmler's request to reorganise the *Gestapo* (in January 1933). Next, in terms of organisation, the *Sicherheitsamt*, or Security Office, was re-titled Main Security Office (*Sicherheitshauptamt*), one more step towards Himmler's goal to organise one large police apparatus. It was also Heydrich's goal – a single Nazi State Security Corps. This aim was never realised, the war and Heydrich's diversion into politics saw to that.

It has been said that with the huge burgeoning of the *Gestapo* across Germany, which Heydrich helped to organise, the need for a 'Secret Service' vanished, and that the SD as such became superfluous, but was retained because of Himmler's wishes as the Party's only true intelligence service. The SD was small by comparison. By the end of January 1938 its staff of full-time and 'honorary' members numbered only 5,050, though this number climbed quite rapidly to 7,230 by December. As already described, the *Gestapo* agent was basically a detective, a policeman in plain clothes. Heydrich did not recruit detectives, even though the work of his outside agents was often much the same; the inside men were more akin to middle-class intellectuals. Whether the *Gestapo* could have pulled off the kind of operations undertaken by Alfred Naujocks and the second great triumph of Heydrich in the thirties is questionable.

Heydrich was therefore permitted to retain his Secret Service as a small, quite independent force, which he felt free to use in matters of espionage and counter-espionage as he saw fit. His model was the British SIS, the Secret Intelligence Service (MI6), which then operated under a blanket of total secrecy, unlike today when its operations, methods and recruitment come under public scrutiny. Heydrich's knowledge of the SIS was hardly based on fact, at least not in the mid-thirties, more on what he had read and surmised through novels and perhaps a few anecdotes from Captain Canaris. The success of the British Empire was due, so Heydrich believed, to the SIS, which treated spying as a profession fit only for gentlemen, a view coinciding neatly with the old *Abwehr* view. Heydrich believed that every decent Englishman was ready to aid the SIS if called upon; it was how the British operated, both in war and business, by calling in every snippet of information about the other chap's methods and capabilities. British secret agents were an élite, creamed off from the gentlemen's establishment. These were Heydrich's beliefs. Neither Heydrich nor those in charge of these 'gentlemen' in London's Broadway had any notion that a few were of a new breed, not dedicated to Britain's causes, but to a foreign ideology completely alien to both their homeland and indeed Germany.

The usual method of recruitment had permitted weak links to enter the SIS. Although men of the right class, there were university types who had, in a wave of student sympathy for the workers of the world, allowed themselves to be subverted by Moscow. Personal weaknesses such as drink and homosexual practices made them easy targets for the Soviet espionage masters. Men like Philby, Burgess, Maclean and Anthony Blunt did the jobs they had been trained to do in MI6, but were controlled by Moscow. Not that their efforts really affected operations against Nazi Germany. Kim Philby, the super-spy at the heart of Britain's spy establishment, would operate the 'Soviet desk'; whatever MI6 planned affecting the USSR became known in Moscow.

Ironically, Heydrich's SD, the *Gestapo*, and indeed the entire Hitler police apparatus were engaged in a struggle against the same enemy as Britain – the Soviet 'Comintern', the Communist International. This movement spread subversive propaganda directly or through its various front organisations around the world, in conjunction with its vast spy network. The sole objective of the propaganda was the undermining of every independent and sovereign nation everywhere – including of course that of the 'Nazified' capitalist state of Germany. It transpires the gentlemen in London also operated against Red subversion and had done so for decades and in some ways more successfully than the Nazis. Rather than throw the communists into camps, the British infiltrated their organisations, keeping abreast of the pay and orders received from Moscow. There was nothing the likes of Kim Philby could do about that during his earlier career in MI6.

Such problems were never encountered in the SD, whose personnel in general never defected until the last.

Only in the smallest way possible can Heydrich's Intelligence Service be compared to Britain's SIS: its operations abroad were almost exclusively confined to the European continent. The useful exercise which ended with the fall of the Ernst Roehm clique was for Heydrich an excellent result; the SD's role in the Sosnowski case was peripheral, and though Naujocks had done remarkably well in expunging the Black Front broadcasting service, the death of Richard Formis counted against him. At this time Himmler and Heydrich's dream of a *Staats Schutz Korps*, a totally integrated police and security force – a State Protection Corps – with the virtual disappearance of the old civil police organisation, was very far from fruition. Above all, both men wished the SS to absorb the *Abwehr*, they were content to work alongside it for the time being while missing no opportunity to circumvent and nibble away at it. If Heydrich was aware of the old *Abwehr* chief's dictum, then he ignored it. Colonel Nicolai said:

The Intelligence Service is the appanage of gentlemen; if it is entrusted to others it will collapse.

Colonel Nicolai's successor Captain Patzig irritated Heydrich and other Nazi chiefs until co-operation became impossible. The appointment of Canaris and his reunion with Heydrich in a Berlin restaurant was intended to mark a new beginning between the rival services. Heydrich was genuinely pleased to see his old commander again and chat over old times, enquiring after *Frau* Canaris's cello playing and the family. As for 'Old Whitehead', whatever pleasure he derived did not prevent him from making derogatory entries in his diary that night. He saw their path of intended co-operation strewn with obstacles, not least because of the 'fanaticism' he read in the eyes of the younger man. How right he was is proved by the fact that it took almost two years for an agreement to be finally hammered out, this document being signed by Canaris and Dr Best on 21 December 1936. The ambiguities between duties would continue, and in fact neither Heydrich nor Admiral (as he became) Canaris had any real intention of implementing the concord. Both services continued as before, prying into both political and military matters at home and further afield.

Yet, whatever machinations they got up to at work, in their private lives the two families developed an easy rapport, residing in the sedate Zehlendorf district, as did other Nazi chieftains. The Berlin chief of police, Count Helldorf, who would fall foul of Hitler following the Bomb Plot in 1944 (as would the chief of Criminal Police, Artur Nebe); Colonel Oster, one of the *Abwehr* department heads; and the government counsellor, Hans-Bernd Gisevius, whose name is much quoted in histories of those times, all kept homes within easy walking distance of each other. Sunday evenings were reserved for socialising, sometimes at the Heydrich villa, on other occasions at the Admiral's home.

It seems bizarre that so much lay behind these friendly family gatherings, at least for the two men. Lina Heydrich later reported that the menfolk never talked shop, rather their conversations were given over to philosophy and the arts, and amusing anecdotes were told. Heydrich would engage in earnest talk with Erika Canaris about music, especially Mozart. Lina further remarked that her husband seemed to work twenty-four hours a day, and that their evenings with the Admiral and his family were his only relaxation – plus of course his other off-duty activities, such as fencing and flying. His tuition in the latter pastime had come via instruction with the Nazi Party Air Corps, the NSFK. It was an occupation that, when taken further, would bring him into conflict with Hitler.

It was also a period when 'the Archangel of Death' (as one historian has called him) permitted the still career-climbing Walter Schellenberg to enter his private life. Here too, both men enjoyed a curious mixture of regard and distrust. Heydrich confided to his wife that Schellenberg had considerable potential but needed to be more frank with his chief – if he wished to advance further. Heydrich also realised that his junior would be quite useless in difficult or tough situations; this was proved later.

Schellenberg began accompanying the Heydrichs as they enjoyed the Berlin night life, and when Lina stayed at home there was much girl chasing. None of this tallies with *Frau* Heydrich's assertion that her husband only had time for work. 'Yes, there were always girls', she told a British journalist in 1961. Schellenberg discovered his boss had an apparently insatiable appetite for women, and that he had become a well-known face in the night scene. One witness commented that the number of females had by Heydrich was 'incalculable' – and not all German at that. It was not always Schellenberg, other colleagues including Naujocks and even the dull *Gestapo* chief Heinrich Müller were also towed along; it was in the latter's presence that an unusual incident took place.

Heydrich had acquired a vacation cottage on the Baltic island of Fehmarn, a most agreeable spot for family visits, and he could also show off his expertise in small boat handling. Schellenberg accompanied the Heydrichs for one weekend trip, but his boss excused himself, saying he had to attend a further conference with SD and *Gestapo* chiefs on the island. He asked Schellenberg to stay behind and keep his wife company. Lina loved the thatched cottage, often staying on longer with their two children, sometimes until autumn. Schellenberg was very personable, with dark hair and flashing eyes. He was also married but never presented with his own family. He seemed excellent company to Lina, and Heydrich had no qualms about leaving the pair together.

Later, in the Frida bar and in company with Heydrich and Müller, Schellenberg was startled when his boss solemnly informed him the drink he was imbibing contained poison. Heydrich said that unless he was told the truth concerning Walter's afternoon with Lina on Fehmarn the antidote to the poison would be withheld. As Schellenberg related later, he indignantly refuted any allegation of impropriety with *Frau* Heydrich. Heydrich forced him to recount every move on the afternoon in question. At this point, as Schellenberg struggled to protest his innocence, Müller intervened, hinting broadly that more had taken place. Amazed, Schellenberg admitted he had taken a dip with Lina, realising the *Gestapo* must have been watching them. At last, Heydrich put on a show of reluctantly accepting his innocence, and called a waiter, who stood ready with a glass which proved to be a dry martini which Schellenberg drank hastily, though believing it had an unusual flavour.

Schellenberg never knew whether he really had been drinking poison, though his boss made it clear elsewhere it had been a jape. Schellenberg saw Heydrich as a jealous man and even more dangerous.

Schellenberg was also admitted into the Canaris family circle, thoroughly enjoying himself and, like the Heydrichs, playing croquet on the lawn. He found Canaris an inspiration and loved to hear the older man's tales of worldly travel and adventure. Schellenberg had travelled far since his earlier, rather insignificant days as a security guard outside Hitler's hotel. He had in fact done very little for such rewards, mixing freely with the mighty, men whose names would go down in history, and for varying reasons. But he knew the outwardly cosy relationship between his boss and the *Abwehr* chief concealed deep divisions and distrust. At Heydrich's prodding, Schellenberg had taken up horse-riding, and sometimes encountered the admiral out on his own steed in the Berlin equivalent of Hyde Park's Rotten Row. On such occasions, and despite his real feelings of friendship and regard for Canaris, Schellenberg did his best to sound out the other man's intentions, which Canaris no doubt realised and put down to Heydrich's instructions.

In fact, the two men had a common feeling for religion, whatever their devious occupations, both coming from Catholic backgrounds. Schellenberg never disclosed this side of his make-up, while Canaris had a profound respect for the Pope and his Church.

Canaris then became involved in the Spanish Civil War, when General Franco fought the Red and Socialist revolutionaries. It was a bitter struggle that would last three years and see Italian and German assistance for Franco, and covert Soviet help for the other side, which included in its ranks a so-called 'International Brigade' containing, among others, British socialist volunteers. It is unlikely that Canaris's love of Spain and his friendship with Franco blinded him to events at home – in no way could he get Heydrich out of his mind for long. But Canaris certainly remained unaware of the SD's latest scheme, the second of its thirties triumphs. It was a daring plan, and to Heydrich's ignorance, triggered by Moscow. It is thus one of the most amazing twists of all time in the long history of espionage.

While the Kaiser's spy chief had wanted closer ties with Russia, his eventual successor had little interest in Eastern Europe. Canaris had feelings only, it seems, for Spain and the Mediterranean zone, though suggestions he himself derived from Greece have not been substantiated. In any case, the bloody Bolshevik actions in Germany itself precluded any ideas of co-operation with Moscow. This was not so to some generals, who as previously mentioned had found it agreeable and expedient to use territory in the new Soviet republic for the training of new air force and *Panzer* units. This liaison, continued into the thirties, was curtailed by Hitler, perhaps to the disappointment of the said generals, whose fledgling units had enjoyed full co-operation across land cleared specially of all population between Moscow and Voronezh, and at Kazan by the River Volga. It had been especially necessary for Stalin to evacuate the villagers from their hovels, for his troops engaged with the German guests in poison gas experiments. By 1930 this co-operation had extended to joint war games, the Germans imparting their expertise to the Russian generals, some of whom made

*Josef Stalin, a dictator of
unparalleled distrust*

visits to Germany. Among those taking part in the eleven-year cooperation were Generals von Blomberg and Köstring on the German side, with Marshals Voroshilov and Tukachevsky for the Soviets.

The Soviet co-operation, ironically, enabled the Germans to experiment and advance their ideas on land and air blitz warfare, which smashed into the USSR in 1941. Hitler recognised Stalin had been most useful, but now such liaison came to an abrupt halt.

During his chats with Canaris, Schellenberg discovered the admiral had heard of the Soviet Marshal Tukachevsky, through some of the German staff who had co-operated with him. The Russian seemed to know Germany well, visiting the country five times over seven years; he had made a very good impression on General von Blomberg, which contrasted sharply with some of the Russian's comrades.

Heydrich then invited Canaris out to lunch, apparently a semi-social occasion. However, after a while Heydrich steered the conversation to the Soviet Union, admitting ignorance on Stalin's state, and asking Canaris for an informal briefing. In fact, Canaris of course knew little himself, and when Heydrich casually asked if he might borrow a few *Abwehr* and military files on the Soviets and its military staff the admiral pricked up his ears. He was at once suspicious as to what might lie behind the request. Moreover, Heydrich seemed especially interested in documents signed by the Russian generals, and hinted that Hitler himself lay behind it all. Heydrich throughout this conversation made his interest appear to be part of his general curiosity to improve his knowledge of the USSR; but obviously, to ask for signed papers signified much more. Heydrich knew perfectly well that Canaris had access to Army files in the Bendlerstrasse ministry. Some accounts have referred to Heydrich's requests as 'demands'; authors have tried to further the already black picture of a ruthless SD boss turning a friendly meeting into a frosty occasion, which is incorrect, as that would have been quite counter-productive. In any event, Canaris politely refused, laughing as he suggested Heydrich 'try the Gestapo'.

So that was that. If Canaris had known what was afoot he might have been more co-operative; as it was, the question of a joint operation between Abwehr and SD never arose. Heydrich was disappointed, but had to accept it. As a military man of the 'other camp' the admiral would not filch papers from his Army comrades; quite apart from other considerations, there was the mistrust between them. Not that Heydrich had any intention of giving up, quite the contrary. If he could not obtain the papers he needed through channels then they would have to be stolen.

But where lay the origins of what came to be called 'The Tukachevsky Affair'?

At first glance it would seem the answer lies in the prodigious energy and imagination of Reinhard Heydrich. When not in his office studying the endless flow of SD reports, or out engaged in sports of one kind or another, he used his mind for plotting. In fact, Heydrich was not as ignorant of the USSR as he tried to have Canaris believe, and certainly had some insight into the nature of Stalin, in particular his innate and psychopathic distrust of everyone. Was it conceivable that a little, poisonous worm inserted into the dictator's brain by devious means could grow into a darker result and cause favourable repercussions for Germany? A notion formed in Heydrich's mind to initiate another, more devastating, Stalin purge that would decimate his Red Army hierarchy. This was the cunning plot developed by Heydrich from a smaller worm which had been floated the Germans' way by the crafty Soviets themselves.

Though Heydrich parted after his meeting with Canaris on amiable terms, both he and the admiral were put out, the SD chief by the older man's refusal to co-operate, while the Abwehr head was prickled into great and irritating curiosity. Canaris guessed that Heydrich had subversion in mind, and on returning to his office he sent for his two chief officers, Pieckenbrock and Oster, but no firm conclusion was reached after their discussion to try and figure out Heydrich's motives. Only one thing was obvious: the SD was expanding its sphere of operations; beyond that the Abwehr chiefs were unable to throw any light on the mystery. Colonel Oster's spies could come up with nothing; it would be some weeks before the light dawned on the Abwehr, and then only following the sensational news from Moscow which the whole world shared.

A few days after the spy chiefs' luncheon, a burglary and fire took place in both the Abwehr and German Army headquarters of the ministry in the

*Marshal Tukachevsky, destroyed
by Stalin and Heydrich*

Bendlerstrasse. An investigation soon revealed to Canaris that the records most affected were those relating to German–Soviet co-operation; despite the fire and general disruption, Canaris found that documents were missing. Obviously, the felons had started a fire to try and cover it up. Canaris was in no doubt who was responsible, concluding there was nothing he could do about it but await developments.

The idea of sowing poison into the Soviet system was, Heydrich thought, his alone; in fact, the real inspiration behind it had come following a second meeting Heydrich arranged with a White Russian general called Nicholas Skoblin, apparently a fiercely anti-Stalinist *émigré* and assistant to General Miller. The latter had replaced General Kutiepov, kidnapped by Red agents in 1930. It was Skoblin who had requested the meeting which took place in conditions of security in the well-known Hotel Adlon in Berlin. Heydrich realised how useful it could be to find trusted allies among those Russians willing to cooperate with anyone against Stalin – and the SD paid well for information. The Russians had been cut off from their old sources of income, and made a living in their domiciles as best they could, even inventing tales to earn a sou – or marks in this case. However, Heydrich was convinced of Skoblin's sincerity, though never abandoning his customary caution.

111

What the Russian general told him was explosive and set Heydrich's mind racing: the two groups of Russian and German staff officers who had liaised for so long were now actually plotting to overthrow the two dictators – Hitler and Stalin. Heydrich believed the story to be true for two reasons: it fitted in with his own suspicions, and also because he knew there were those among the Red Army staff who had reservations about Stalin.

Heydrich went to work, summoning his 'Eastern expert', Hermann Behrends, and Erich Jahnke, who specialised in international affairs. After disclosing his news, Heydrich announced his decision to hit both enemy camps: to split Stalin's General Staff and get rid of the dissidents in Germany's own Army command. To this Jahnke voiced the suspicion that the Soviets themselves could well be behind it all, that in fact it was they who were intent on wrecking the German staff by sowing suspicions with Hitler. That would also give Stalin the chance to be rid of Tukachevsky, with whom he had old scores to settle from the time of the First World War. Heydrich countered that in any case the end result would be the same. But Jahnke persisted with his arguments, so much so that eventually Heydrich became incensed by his uncooperative attitude and dismissed him under three months' house arrest.

Behrends had only listened. Heydrich told him they would put the matter to Himmler, who could consult with the *Führer*. When this meeting took place, on Christmas Eve 1936, Heydrich was in attendance, as were Rudolf Hess and Martin Bormann. Heydrich explained his scheme, to produce sufficient documentary evidence to convince Marshal Stalin of traitorous activities among his generals. Much later, after the war in fact, Walter Schellenberg reported that Hitler was enthusiastic, but canny enough to order the German General Staff kept in ignorance – 'he did not wish to tempt Providence'.

Hitler was at the time hesitating between East and West, nowhere near ready to begin his drive eastwards. But however contemptuous he was of the Western allies, he much preferred to have them quiescent, needing to placate them by various ploys and bluffs. There was also a chance the plot might misfire and produce unintended effects, such as an outbreak of war. After deliberating, Hitler decided against Tukachevsky and in favour of Stalin, as it suited him at the time. It eventually ended (so Schellenberg added later), with Hitler concluding a convenient pact with Stalin and attacking the West (1939–40).

At this stage, Heydrich had no real method to implement his scheme, which was no more than that; the *modus operandi* was entirely lacking. He called in Schellenberg, Naujocks and Behrends, explaining that though the *Führer* had agreed they could proceed with the operation, he had expressly ordered them to keep the General Staff in ignorance, for the valid reason that one or more of his own generals might tip off Tukachevsky to the danger. Heydrich told his men they needed the documents relevant to past

German–Russian co-operation – plus a first-class forger capable of producing likely-looking documents. Some of these had to appear as if stolen from the *Abwehr* offices, the intention to slip them by some means to the Soviet secret police, the NKVD. Papers obtained by such means would convince Stalin and he would act.

After this meeting broke up, Naujocks expressed the fear to Behrends that General von Blomberg could prove a weak link and spill the beans. Behrends found this idea amusing and impossible. The SD, Behrends said, already held a thick file on von Blomberg, who would certainly be toppled when the time was ripe. As events proved, that time was not far off. However, von Blomberg was kept in the dark; despite all his fawning on Hitler, the dictator had no intention of disclosing such plots to any of the military.

The break-in at the *Abwehr* and Army offices therefore went ahead. The right man for the job was Gert Groethe, who, once he had recovered from the shock of being given the task, organised a commando split into three groups, each accompanied by an expert safe cracker from the CID. The resemblance to Watergate is there, only the motives are different. In the operation, the fire-raisers, charged to obliterate traces, let the small fire get out of hand, and the fire brigade tackled a blaze that practically gutted one of the *Abwehr* offices. One floor almost caved in and the walls were cracked by the heat. But the burglars escaped with all they needed and delighted Heydrich with their haul.

The fat dossier Himmler and Heydrich were eventually able to present to Hitler contained thirty-two documents, most of which were originals stolen from the *Abwehr* and Army files. To these had been added forgeries, materpieces of deception, cunningly contrived to link the whole and prove a conspiracy between the Soviet and German General Staffs. In fact, the original papers dealt only with the earlier military co-operation and were not in themselves incriminating. It was the additional material which proved explosive.

Heydrich had decided to add a few bits and pieces of his own concoction (just as he had done to scupper Roehm), such as Secret Service reports on further contacts between the generals which proved events over and beyond mere military co-operation in the field. The items manufactured by Heydrich included supposed transcripts of telephone taps, intercepted letters and notes, etc. The final 'proof' was a signed letter from Tukachevsky himself which alluded to earlier, secret correspondence. These pieces of 'evidence' Heydrich contrived to have appear as stolen from *Abwehr* and SD files. He wanted to include a note signed by Canaris, but did not pursue the idea. The dossier would have to be offered by one of his men to the NKVD through an intermediary, the motive being money.

The real problem had lain in forging signatures, for which task a master craftsman was needed. A few German officers were already languishing in jail for anti-Nazi talk, so there was no problem getting their signatures.

Others, such as men still working in the Bendlerstrasse, were not so easy to obtain; those of their main target and several more Russian generals had come to hand through the break-in. More was needed: official seals and stamps to make the papers look authentic, plus a typewriter bearing Russian characters. Naujocks was given this task, plus the all-important one of finding a suitable forger. Neither SD nor *Gestapo* files turned up one of these, but a typewriter was found at a firm which had manufactured machines for export to the USSR. The firm sold one to the SD.

Still stuck for a forger, Naujocks tried the Nazi Party records as a last resort, surprised and delighted to find such tradesmen listed. Of the five noted, four proved useless as no longer in business; the fifth man proved eminently suitable, though at first uncooperative. The man was elderly and lived in Heydrich's own manor of Zehlendorf, his equipment small but serviceable. Not until Naujocks produced his SS card did Franz Putzig enquire what was needed of him; with thirty years' experience behind him as an engraver-printer he seemed the ideal candidate. Yet he continued to hesitate, as if wary of some trap, only agreeing to take on the work on receipt of a written order from both the local Party and SD stating he would receive no payment. Once he had these papers he would do his best.

Three of the SD staff worked night and day, dreaming up the necessary texts to be set up in type by Putzig on suitable papers, the engraver having to create seals and stamps to be used on the fakes. Naujocks visited the printer's premises every night to monitor progress, astonished by the results. The man seemed a genius.

Lastly, came the Tukachevsky letter, and when Heydrich had this and all the other forgeries on his desk he was suitably impressed, peering closely at apparent scrawled pencil notes in the margins put there by 'Russian generals'. Even the special Russian watermark on the paper had not been overlooked. And all of this fantastic faking had been provided free.

The actual documents were not stolen by Naujocks, only photocopies. Heydrich had agreed with the reinstated Behrends that the package of documents should be passed to the Soviet secret police by Czech Intelligence. He looked forward to profiting from the operation financially, for obviously the Soviets would have to pay for the find. Heydrich quipped that the cash roubles earned would help to pay for his agents in Russia. This hope proved illusory.

At this point it is necessary to throw light on another aspect of the manoeuvres. General Skoblin was not quite the dedicated anti-Soviet he claimed to be. He had married a Russian ballerina who, unknown to her new husband, was a long-time employee of the Soviet NKVD. Worse, and despite Heydrich knowing of Skoblin's contacts among Soviet officers, the man himself worked on both sides; in fact, he was a double agent. This had become obvious to the French security service when, following a period of poverty common to such survivors of the Bolshevik revolution, Skoblin and his wife suddenly bought a comfortable cottage in the French countryside and began pursuing a gay social life in Paris. The couple were arrested, the police finding documentary proof they were abusing French hospitality by engaging in espionage. *Madame* Skoblin confessed to being a Soviet agent and dragging her husband into the game. Skoblin had become twisted: having once been the youngest general in the Tsar's Army, he had been displaced on that score by Tukachevksy, and become his sworn enemy. Yet, despite betraying his own *émigré* comrades to the Soviet secret police, he continued to be a bitter enemy of the Stalin regime. His motives were therefore even more powerful than Heydrich's, and based on personal jealousy and revenge. Skoblin's hopes that Britain and France would take aggressive action against Stalin proved ill founded. He therefore turned to the Nazis in his quest. Moreover, Skoblin desired to take over

An early picture of General Skoblin

from General Miller, who headed the so-called 'Organisation of Russian Soldiers in Exile'.

If it had not been for the plot by Skoblin against Marshal Tukachevsky, the entire Russian military community in the West, already penetrated by the NKVD, would have been seen as a useless bunch of flotsam which would eventually disappear, leaving very little trace. This displaced rump of the Tsar's Army, infiltrated and losing an occasional member kidnapped back to the USSR, nevertheless continued to dream of a grand return to their homeland at the head of a great army of liberation. Even Hitler's war on Stalin in 1941 did not enable this dream to be realised, though muddled attempts were made by the Germans, who did not use these ageing *émigrés*, but men like the fresh renegade Red Army General Vlassov and various brigades numbering up to a million men (the exact figure is nebulous).

As it happened, and unknown to Heydrich, the Soviet dictator already had his suspicions which went hand in hand with the normal Soviet paranoia, which at times amounted to near insanity. Stalin was already concerned about loyalty among his military staffs, loyalty to his Red Revolution, that is. He had already had millions killed off, either by executions (which never stopped in the USSR), or the widespread deaths through starvation which came about through his enforced 'collectivisation' policy throughout Russian farmlands. His secret police boss Beria employed executioners who worked routine days in the cells of the Lubianka Prison; some were family men who despatched enemies or suspected deviants by pistol shot. In the end, years of such grisly work became too much for some who had breakdowns and retired, most certainly themselves executed in turn, for they knew too much. Beria too would find a similar end in the fifties, reportedly shot in the Kremlin by one of Stalin's closest. It has long been known that the ruler affectionately seen as 'Uncle Joe' by innocents in the West far outstripped even Hitler in his bid to keep the peoples of his empire loyal. The number of Stalin's victims will never be known. As his predecessor Lenin made clear, it mattered little how many hundreds were shot, so long as the 'Soviet paradise' was attained. That the end always justified the means was the communist maxim everywhere.

The path of the Russian Army had not been that of the Communist Party – the parallel with Hitler and his own army is striking. Neither dictator trusted his generals. Whether Hitler realised it or not, Stalin looked on Nazi Germany as one more capitalist state he would deal with in due course. Hitler would, Stalin hoped, involve Germany in another disastrous war which would enable the USSR to step in and gather the pieces. In any case, the capitalist world was doomed to extinction due to its inherently rotten foundations; it was likely the Soviets would inherit the world with little effort. This was the same theme continued by a still-bellicose Nikita Kruschev later when he bawled 'We will bury you!'

Stalin, however, did expect Hitler to drive eastwards, but no further than Poland, by which time Britain and France would have intervened. Through the march-in of the Red Army after the capitalists had fought themselves to a standstill would fall the much prized riches of the West. Stalin's strategy in the thirties was designed to ensure this scenario came about. But he needed to ensure the absolute obedience of his generals, exactly as did Hitler. They were two tyrannical dictators, both gambling on similar lines.

Tukachevsky was born of lesser nobility which aped French culture; he gained prominence as an officer in the First World War, but was captured by the Germans and by coincidence was imprisoned in Bavaria in the same camp as Charles de Gaulle. Despite his better background, he embraced the Leninist-Bolshevik revolution, and by the age of twenty-five had risen to command the First Army, the first unit of size to be termed a 'Red' army. Tukachevsky's rise continued until he became Assistant Minister for Defence and Armaments, well known for his publications extolling Stalin and the dogma of a USSR surrounded by capitalist enemies, a theme very similar to that used by Hitler. Tukachevsky's mistake was to become too big, and his fame began to worry Stalin, who brooked no prima donnas in his state. He also erred by having secret discussions with British leaders while attending the state funeral of King George V, which took place in London in June 1936. The talks were the result of a belief among some Soviet generals that the Western powers should join them in a preventative war to stop Hitler before it was too late – which was counter to Stalin's strategy. Tukachevsky laid all his cards on the table in London, including facts and figures concerning Soviet military potential, only to be given the cold shoulder by the British. The figures produced by the visitors did not coincide with those already available through British and French Intelligence.

Early in 1937, Tukachevsky put forward similar proposals to the French, this time receiving the thumbs down from General Gamelin; the French had no intention of making war with Germany. Back in Moscow, Tukachevksy made a speech denouncing Hitler, quoting from *Mein Kampf* to prove the dictator's intention to march East. He was expressing the opinion of most of the Russian military, but Stalin read things otherwise. He smelt a conspiracy, suspecting the Red Army marshals were trying to win over their staffs against him. However, Stalin waited until September before ordering his new secret police chief Iezhov to 'get the goods' on Tukachevsky, to 'collect evidence' (i.e. fabricate), making it damning enough to see the marshal condemned.

Thus, without Heydrich realising it, the double agent Skoblin was used to feed the idea to the SD; the very cunning Soviets actually manufactured their own dossier for Stalin to put before his Politburo and other marshals in order to trap his quarry. There were more twists to the tale, for the name Tukachevsky had come up much earlier in a plot allegedly hatched by the *Abwehr* chief Colonel Nicolai. There were also more instances later which Stalin noted. More bizarrely, certainly surpassing the realms of fiction, both the Soviet secret police and Heydrich's SD decided to slip their 'evidence'

SS Gruppenführer *Heydrich worked unceasingly to gain power*

through the Czech office of Dr Benes. The latter passed the news to Stalin, who must have been astounded to learn he now had two pistols to point at Tukachevsky. The NKVD chief Iezhov paid three million roubles for Heydrich's dossier; the SD would later find the banknotes useless. The cunning Soviets were a step ahead once more; they numbered all the notes, and German spies trying to use them in Russia were promptly arrested.

It was not at all unusual for show trials to take place in Russia, the accused invariably pleading guilty to all charges. Marshal Tukachevsky knew that something boding ill for him was in the wind when his journey to London to attend the coronation of King George VI was cancelled. In the month before that event, on 12 April 1937, Voroshilov informed him he was relieved of duties as Minister for Defence and Armaments. Also, when the annual May Day parade took place, his fellow marshals 'put the freeze' on him, and he was not saluted but given the cold shoulder. On the same day the new King was crowned in London, Stalin took charge of the NKVD and SD files on Tukachevsky. The marshal was not, however, the first to be arrested; General Eideman was removed during a Communist Party conference in Moscow. This was followed by a terse announcement that 'Y.B. Gamarnik' had committed suicide after 'compromising himself with anti-Soviet elements'. Before May was out, Stalin's purge was getting under way: eight prominent generals and marshals were named and imprisoned, including Tukachevsky. The charges were as usual fabricated: 'breaches of military duty, treason to the country, treason to the peoples of the USSR, treason to the Red Army of workers and peasants'; the accused had 'colluded with a foreign power hostile to the USSR'. By 12 June all eight military leaders had been executed.

This was only the beginning of Stalin's great military bloodletting. When it was all over the mad dictator had not only executed the original eight (all of whom were innocent) but seven of the nine *judges* at the first trial; plus eleven deputy Defence Commissars; three out of five more Red Army marshals; 75 of the 80 members of the Supreme War Council; thirteen out of fifteen Army commanders; 57 of 85 corps commanders; 110 of 195 divisional commanders; 200 of 406 brigade commanders – the lists of those executed seem endless. The total number killed off through Stalin's paranoia has been quoted at somewhere between 30,000 and 50,000. In one estimate, half the Red Army's specialist officer corps and field commanders were eliminated.

No one outside, or perhaps even inside, the madhouse of Stalin's court could have imagined such a bloodbath from such small beginnings, the three dozen or so pieces of paper contrived by the Soviet secret police to remove one suspected marshal. The Red Army was grievously weakened, almost fatally, virtually beheaded. This became painfully apparent when Hitler launched his invasion of the USSR in 1941. The lack of leadership in the field was an enormous boon to the Germans. Most Red Army generals in the combat proved amateurish, and in any case for the rest of the war relied on the use of massed infantry to win battles, rather than military skills. They relied too (apart from Allied aid) on the police troops stationed in strength behind the front to deter defections or wavering. Did Stalin finally wake up to the irreparable damage he was doing to his army? Not technically insane, he was nevertheless a ruthless killer, driven by suspicions that made him paranoid.

The NKVD chief Iezhov had no idea that the Heydrich file he had bought would be used by Stalin to doubly convince his judges and marshals of his case. In the official Soviet trials the Nazi dossier was not produced, only the NKVD fakes. It may never be known if Heydrich and his team were really responsible for having the heart torn out of the Red Army.

8

THE SD IN BRITAIN

Meanwhile, on the international scene Hitler had not been idle; he had in fact kept his neighbours on edge, creating one alarm after another. He had withdrawn his team from the disarmament talks at the League of Nations; announced a new German *Wehrmacht* based on conscription; re-occupied the dimilitarised Rhineland, and congratulated his 'specialist' on Britain who had just pulled off a coup – the Anglo-German Naval Agreement. He ordered Goebbels to ensure that the controlled media never again mentioned a German General Staff, any publishing of such lists were forbidden. In fact, the official Rank List of the German Army was not published after 1932, solely to hide its great increase in numbers from foreign intelligence. General Keitel, newly appointed as chairman of the *Reich* Defence Council, admonished every member not to misplace or lose a single document – 'otherwise enemy propaganda will make use of it'. Grand Admiral Raeder was instructed to keep quiet about ships of 26,000 tons displacement, and only allowed mention of 'improved ships of 10,000 tons', a reference to the new design of 'pocket battleships'. When Raeder told Hitler there were insufficient funds for the huge new warship-building programme he was assured he need not worry about it, the money would be forthcoming, if need be from the Labour Front organisation run by Dr Ley. The new and only 'union' forced on the workers by the Nazis would, if needed, have to cough up 120–150 million marks. The German workers would never know their compulsory union subs would end up being used to pay shipyards for warship construction – not for their welfare.

In March 1935 Hitler announced a new military conscription programme, the first eligible class to be called in November. This would provide an army of half-a-million men, clearly breaking the Treaty of Versailles, the military clauses of which Hitler brazenly declared were null and void since they placed Germany in a straitjacket. Other clauses, such as the reparations to France, which had suffered most from the German Kaiser's invasion in 1914, had already been to a large extent circumvented by pre-Hitler governments which had by various ploys managed to avoid the worst of them. American aid and British sympathy had helped ensure Germany's economic recovery. Hitler built on propaganda myths, such as that of the wicked Allies, of the 'stab in the back' on the home front (and in the Fleet) which had fatally undermined the Army in the field, and of course the Jewish-Bolshevik menace. Britain and France did nothing following Hitler's bellicose speech announcing a greatly increased Army for which a peacetime Germany had no possible need. Indeed, the British hastened to enquire if *Herr* Hitler was still prepared to receive Foreign Secretary Anthony Eden, Hitler 'graciously' agreeing to this at once.

Naturally, the German people were jubilant that the perceived shackles of Versailles had at last been thrown off; in truth, it had only been a matter of face-saving, rather than economic reality. Hitler was believed to be responsible for the upturn in the German economy, whereas it had already been on the up, once the nasty hiccup of the 1931–3 world depression was over. The placing of hundreds of thousands of young men into compulsory labour service ensured many were taken off the unemployment roll. The unemployement figures were also improved by the increasing number of workers needed in the burgeoning war industries and grand civil construction schemes such as the *Autobahnen*. These programmes, plus of course the induction of great numbers into the *Wehrmacht*, were paid for by the German people in taxes and contributions to the many funds set up by the Party. It would, however, be wrong to ignore the fact that the already existing state welfare and health schemes were improved by the Nazis.

While bamboozled by constant Goebbels propaganda and shows of pageant, the German people were being sewn up tight by the *Gestapo*, SS and SD, who infiltrated every facet of civil life. The 100,000-strong police force and the army of informers were not yet unified by Himmler and Heydrich, but they were all under central Nazi control. And, as seen, Heydrich and in fact the *Gestapo* sent agents outside Germany on various missions.

Long before the war, in fact following von Ribbentrop's successful negotiation of the naval treaty with Britain, Heydrich had managed to insert two of his agents into the Minister's London staff. Seen by the *Führer* as the one man capable of fawning upon and grooming the English politicians into a lasting understanding with Germany, von Ribbentrop had entered into London life and its circles, using his existing contacts as a former wine salesman to try and further his aim. While von Ribbentrop bungled his mission, causing offence by his vain stupidity, such as raising his arm in the Nazi salute when meeting the King, Heydrich's agents were busy touring Britain, spying on military and civil installations. Indeed, von Ribbentrop was filmed with his civilian staff in London, the photographers having no idea that two of the men in plain, dark suits were Nazi Secret Service agents foisted on von Ribbentrop. He had no control over them at all, even though they were ostensibly part of his diplomatic staff in Carlton Gardens. Under Heydrich's orders, these two agents travelled unhindered by the British, apparently finding out everything their chief wanted. If MI5 knew anything about it, no action was taken to bring such behaviour to a halt. The two spies, never identified, had a good time into the bargain, one of them meeting and almost becoming engaged to an English girl in the North.

German tourists were fairly common in Britain in the pre-war days, and friendships were made which in some cases were renewed after the war. The author's attractive cousin met two young German holiday-makers in London while out with her equally attractive chum. The Germans took snapshots in the West End and sent copies with friendly greetings after returning home to Berlin. Any notion that the pair were Heydrich's men cannot be verified. Naturally, the British SIS was engaged in similar activities in Germany.

Heydrich's men sent innocent-looking postcards home to a cover address in Germany. The messages written on them were code phrases. The real intelligence data gathered by them went home in total security via the diplomatic bag; if, as Heydrich chose to believe, the British authorities carefully scrutinised the picture cards, then they would learn nothing from them.

Yet, despite all the information gathered from the potential enemy land by the SD, not one piece was ever passed on to the *Wehrmacht*, and certainly not the *Abwehr*. It is doubtful if Canaris ever knew how his service had been scooped by the SD in that avenue of spying. The *Military Geographia* books issued to the *Wehrmacht* listing basic (chiefly economic) data on every British town and city were not based on anything collected by Heydrich. The activities of his two spies in Britain continued until the von Ribbentrop mission was wound up, and he and his staff, including the two spies, returned to Germany. Their stay had lasted the better part of two years, from 1937 to 1939. Their mission had been a success, while the Minister had failed utterly. Hitler never relied on von Ribbentrop again, whereas Heydrich had every reason to be delighted once again with the men who worked for him. This satisfaction was to continue.

Heydrich's man Boemelberg was sent to Paris. It seemed too good a chance to miss. The official reason for the SS officer's stay in France was to assist the French to track down German Bolshevik terrorists. His real activities were subversive, a fact the hosts caught on to; when Boemelberg was seen by the French police official dealing with his case the meeting was short and curt. The Frenchman could not have imagined that before long the same SD spy would march triumphantly into his office as a conqueror, which is what Boemelberg did after the French collapse in June 1940.

Before that time came the SD was instrumental in setting up spy cells in Scandinavia, operated under the guise of 'goodwill' missions. These often included Hitler Youth groups whose adult overseers acted as spies, as indeed they are alleged to have done in Britain. Heydrich's spies were very busy in those countries, but Sweden was forbidden territory due to its special relationship with Germany. Nazi subversion in Holland was not dependent on that country's comparatively large fascist movement, and Heydrich kept his spies aloof from them, fearing traps and general unreliability and probable British penetration. Other Nazi organisations paid the Dutch traitors money and suborned them during paid vacations in Germany. Heydrich did none of that, though he certainly did not refuse to use the odd Dutch civilian or military man when reliability such as German ancestry could be proved. He had no idea at that time of any plan of Hitler's to invade the Low Countries; his activities in these lands were simply part of his expansion. Holland, Belgium, Luxembourg and France were all penetrated with comparative ease by SD agents, who gathered any data needed.

Why did Heydrich not pass his intelligence on to German Military Intelligence? The answer is complex. In the first place, the situation *vis-à-vis* the *Wehrmacht* intelligence departments was that the SD had no remit to collaborate with them at all in such matters, as that was the job of the *Abwehr*. Did Heydrich simply collect the data for his own sake? In a sense yes, he was anxious at the time to establish himself as a spymaster on all levels, and by 1939 he had done just that; he was ready to provide the *Führer* with anything he asked for – up to a point. For example, with the outbreak of war all intelligence from Britain virtually ceased for the SD; it did not attempt to set up permanent espionage bases or agents, though this might have been possible via friendly embassies. Hitler rarely requested special intelligence from abroad, though in one area he was kept well informed, and that was of the various tales and rumours that circulated among spy and other circles via the neutral capitals such as Lisbon and Stockholm. Apart from this, even though he had never been abroad, Hitler prided himself on being an 'expert' on other nations. It is true that in some ways he did have accurate insight into the nature and character of some, but in other ways he was very ignorant. His feelings about the French proved correct, while on Britain his perceptions were based on his front experience in the war, his meetings with diplomats and what people like von Ribbentrop and Goebbels fed him. He would have done better to listen to Canaris.

Heydrich filled several filing cabinets with 'England' data, paperwork and photographs, undoubtedly a valuable collection, which went up in smoke during the war through air raids.

The Soviet Union proved difficult to penetrate, as did Czechoslovakia to a lesser extent; the Poles were also on the alert against German agents. But Heydrich had his successes, as always, in competition with the *Abwehr*. German agents caught in the above countries faced no show trials and were invariably released when the *Wehrmacht* invaded. However, the Soviets were paranoid about all foreigners, even friendly delegations who were shown around the achievement zones but always monitored. The Soviets had a mania about spying, suspecting that even the groups sent by foreign communist parties would contain spies, simply because it was their own practice. It seemed inconceivable to the Soviet security agents that spies were not accompanying every group of tourists. Heydrich tried to insert agents into the diplomatic staffs in Moscow and Leningrad and other large cities. However, the traditional-type German diplomats caused difficulties, even though they indulged in a little mild spying themselves now and again. But, like their British counterparts, they usually looked askance at real spies in their midst who were trying to use embassies and legations as cover. Overall, Heydrich's attempts to place agents in Russia failed. Nevertheless, he did not give up, proceeding to use other methods, such as bribing foreigners to do the work, especially Bulgarians, who were quite close to the Russians in type. However, such people were also watched by the NKVD. Some small successes were made, but not enough to be seen as a breakthrough.

Strangely, it was through a few co-operative Frenchmen that better success was achieved. These people were shown much by their Soviet hosts, as they were regarded as apparently sympathetic to and greatly interested in the great socialist experiment. Unfortunately, in the long run, Heydrich found them unreliable; a few reports were passed on in Berlin or Paris, but thereafter the Frenchmen refused further missions.

One brainwave Heydrich had was in the comparatively new field of wireless surveillance. This was something both the Kaiser's Navy and that of Britain had developed during the First World War – a listening watch on each other's signals. Heydrich's short term as a naval communications officer had given him clues into the possibilities inherent in such spying. Crude though the available equipment was by comparison with that of today, Heydrich acquired the necessary gear and organised a surveillance of all foreign diplomatic and military wireless traffic. It took time, as the equipment had to be found, usually ordered through manufacturers; and at first he had no specialist personnel. He had his staff comb through the SS records until they found a few with experience of such matters. These men had to be prised out of their parent units, which was not difficult. Heydrich then contacted an old friend in the Navy who agreed to try and get him the right manuals for copying, specifically, the instruction books dealing with radio monitoring. Naturally, such information was not available through the usual type of manuals on wireless telegraphy.

This part of the operation proved tricky, as such data was kept in a safe at naval HQ. It took some time before Heydrich got his hands on the necessary manuals for copying. From then on his course was easier, only restricted by the quality and range of his radio equipment. Owing to the ever increasing amount of wireless traffic in Berlin, his SD unit was set up well outside the city. As is now known, most of the German Enigma code traffic was eventually read by the British, from high-level exchanges to the most trivial routine matters. But this aspect had no relevance for Heydrich's surveillance operation.

Both SD and *Gestapo* resorted to telephone tapping in peacetime, all foreign diplomatic lines being 'overseen' by the Nazi security services. The experience of one young woman in this area is relevant (as told in *Under*

Hitler's Banner (Airlife 1996)). Gerda Klinger had been chosen as a most promising girls' league (BDM) leader to be promoted to the Hitler Youth HQ in Berlin. But, bored with sitting behind a desk and only occasionally showing round foreign youth delegations, she agitated until she was moved to what she believed was a better position in the SS building not far away. This at first proved interesting, for having been transferred to the SS and re-uniformed (partly at her expense), sworn an oath of allegiance and secrecy, Gerda found herself handling secret material in the SD offices. This comprised both routine and sensitive messages which needed to be filed; some were mere trivia, concerned with pay, promotions and the like, but there were also the results of 'phone taps on foreign embassies and other places, from SD and *Gestapo* agents. Yet, monitored by a sour-faced supervisor who refused to allow personal photographs to adorn her desk and no make-up, Gerda Klinger soon became bored again and had the temerity to ask the SS commander of the establishment for a change.

This was at once made, for by chance the officer happened to have with him one of Heydrich's lesser known but important operatives. Masquerading as a *Luftwaffe* officer, the man took Gerda under his wing, instructing her to hereafter act as his wife when they attended receptions and other functions in foreign embassies. Her mentor would act as a *Luftwaffe* liaison officer, although in reality he was an SD spy trying to gather intelligence. His ward was instructed to report to her boss all snippets of more interesting conversation. Their main line of enquiry was aviation matters. Gerda was outfitted for her role in a smart Berlin salon, and was appealing enough to attract the interest of foreign functionaries, which was all to the Germans' advantage. Greater adventures came during the early part of the war when her boss took her on trips abroad – into Romania, for example. They booked into a hotel in Bucharest and went shopping, Gerda's chief leaving her to browse and spend a little while he went off on business. They wore civilian clothes during this trip, and it was at their hotel that an extraordinary incident took place.

The two Germans used separate bedrooms, and one morning Gerda went downstairs to join her boss for breakfast, finding him already seated at a table and in conversation with another man. As she reached the table Gerda was surprised to realise the pair were conversing in English; she had learned enough at school to recognise the language. Her chief then introduced his companion as an old friend, and their conversation resumed – in English. Amazed, Gerda surmised that the man was in fact one of their now enemies. After he had said his polite farewells her boss confirmed that the man was indeed English and an old friend from pre-war days. He smiled as he remarked that he saw no reason why a war should end such friendship. The bizarre fact, however, was that both men were engaged in the same game – and knew it. At the time (1940), the British were trying both diplomatically and by agents to persuade the Romanians to at least remain neutral. The Nazi security agencies were doing their best to prevent their enemy from making progress in these endeavours. Eventually, Hitler won the game, and Romanian oil from the great fields at Ploesti fed the *Wehrmacht.*

British attempts to try and persuade the Romanians to opt for the Allied side were not confined to mere diplomatic skills. One ex-employee of MI6 told later how he had taken a trip with his mistress in a small boat along the River Danube, pretending to be an innocent tourist. In reality his orders were to sabotage lock gates and other bottlenecks in order to disrupt German barge traffic. He did not succeed. Interruptions to Hitler's oil supplies from Ploesti did not occur until 1943, when American Liberator bombers made two costly raids on the installations.

9

BLACKMAIL

In 1935 Hitler as usual attended the old Party fighters' anniversary meeting to 'celebrate' the attempted *Putsch* of 9 November 1923. In his speech he referred to his having transformed the old *Reichswehr* Army into a 'new, popular German Army with which all can co-operate who might otherwise have become our enemies'.

Was he dropping a hint to the Army generals who still opposed him? Or the now subdued brownshirts – or both? Hitler then rubbed home the Nazi leadership's view: 'The Party is the guarantor of the nation. Our army its protection.'

Hitler was trying to do two things: he was restoring the German Army's confidence in itself, while trying to elevate it to its former level of national esteem. In this way he was also wooing his generals, and telling the people of the honour he was bestowing on the Army, as the rightful head of society. Service in the *Wehrmacht* was not an 'exaction', it was an honour. But if Hitler thought he had by such words brought the Army into the Nazi pen and ensured its loyalty for the tasks ahead, Himmler and Heydrich thought otherwise. They still believed the generals needed bringing to heel; something had to be done to shackle them to the Nazi cause once and for all – and eventually ensure the dominance of the SS.

As in other states, the armed forces were deemed apolitical, and no serving member of the *Wehrmacht* was permitted to engage in political activity, even if he or she had been involved before. Even membership of the Nazi Party was suspended while a German served in the forces. This clause enabled those potential officers opposed to Hitler to escape into non-political life which could at their choice continue indefinitely, at least, in peacetime.

The chiefs of the SS and SD were determined to bring the despised and untrustworthy military gentlemen to heel by laying plots and traps which when sprung would expose selected generals to Hitler's scorn and prove to him what kind of men they really were, or rather, what Himmler and Heydrich wished to portray them as.

On 26 January 1938 the brilliant Colonel Alfred Jodl wrote in his diary: 'What influence a woman, even without realising it, can exert on the history of a country and thereby the world!' He added: 'One has the feeling of living in a fateful hour for the German people.'

One might imagine Jodl was referring to some Mata Hari. Jodl was chronicling events engineered by Heydrich and the *Gestapo* to ensnare and disgrace some of the generals they despised. Jodl himself was completely compliant to Hitler's will, content to pursue a military career and become the *Führer's* Chief of Operations at OKH (*Oberkommando des Heeres*), and as such was deemed by the victorious Allies after 1945 as a war criminal and hanged at Nuremberg.

The woman Jodl referred to was quite lowly, not a spy or seductress bent on worming secrets from her general; *Fraulein* Gruhn worked as secretary to General von Blomberg, top man in the German Army, who had chosen to co-operate quite fully with Hitler. By late 1937 the general had grown tired of widowhood; his first wife, whom he had married in 1904, had borne five children, but had died in 1932. The youngest child, a daughter, had married General Wilhelm Keitel, another candidate for the Allied hangman at Nuremberg. Keitel was ambitious and fast becoming Hitler's lackey. Von Blomberg decided to marry *Fraulein* Gruhn; she was willing, the only problem being her status as a commoner. The highly conservative officer corps would look askance at such a match.

Von Blomberg consulted Goering, who laughed at the other man's timidity. Why should he not marry the girl? After all, he himself had lost a wife and re-married – an actress and a divorced one at that. Goering berated the old-fashioned notions of the officer corps which he said had no place in a National Socialist state. Of course, the *Führer* was himself rather on the conservative side in such matters, so Goering offered to help smooth von Blomberg's path in that direction and try to help in other ways.

There was, however, another potentially more serious problem: *Fraulein* Gruhn had another man friend. No problem at all, was Goering's response. There were ways in such cases; the nuisance fellow could be re-moved to 'a camp' – even to South America (which is apparently what happened).

> The General Field Marshal in a high state of excitement. Reason not known
> . . . he retired for eight days to an unknown place.

The above was Jodl's further diary entry on the von Blomberg affair on 15 December 1937, recording the unease felt by the general, who did, however, show up in time to deliver the funeral oration following the passing away of General Ludendorff. Ludendorff was the First World War hero who had joined Hitler in the abortive march in Munich in November 1923 and fled when police opened fire. Hitler also attended the service, after which von Blomberg spoke to him of his proposed wedding; he received the *Führer's* approval, which brought great relief.

The wedding took place on 12 January 1938, both Hitler and Goering attending.

Not long before, a group of staff officers had approached von Blomberg to express their uneasiness over Hitler's policies, which they believed

Hitler with (left) General von Blomberg and General von Fritsch, both framed by Heydrich

entailed grave risks for Germany. Von Blomberg dismissed them gruffly, telling them to stick to their duties and not dabble in politics.

Immediately after von Blomberg and his new bride departed on their honeymoon, the storm prepared by Himmler and Heydrich was released. Their timing was perfect. The *Reichsführer* SS had touched on the problem of lukewarm National Socialist generals months before. It was, Himmler told his closest aides, impossible to lance the officer corps in the way Stalin had done his Red Army. But there was an alternative.

No pictures and very little copy appeared in the German Press concerning the von Blomberg wedding, but somehow news of the nuptials spread. Rumours began to circulate, humorous tales and, of all things, telephone calls to stiff-necked generals from giggling girls congratulating the Army for taking in one of their own. The inference was clear, the *Generalfeldmarschall* had married a whore. Worse was to come, as the SS plot to discredit the army staff took shape.

One version of the story says that a Berlin police inspector decided to check on the rumours, as such a juicy piece of gossip needed looking into, if only to satisfy his own curiosity. The policeman was horrified to find a file in his own department listing Eva Gruhn as a prostitute, well known to the police, who had posed for pornographic photographs. The file was quite thick; Gruhn had a long record. Indeed, the file detailed how the girl had grown up in an atmosphere of sexual corruption; her mother ran a brothel masquerading as a massage parlour. The inspector took the file to his chief, Count von Helldorf, an old Nazi who would, however, fall from grace and life in 1944. Von Helldorf was an ex-Army man, so instead of showing the file to the head of criminal police, Artur Nebe, he took it to General Keitel, realising what the Nazis would make of the material. He had no idea that the file he held had originated from Himmler, cooked up by Heydrich's SD. It was a blunder: von Helldorf erred in believing that von Blomberg's son-in-law would, through family loyalty, have the matter handled discreetly, if not hushed up. On the contrary, the vain and ambitious Keitel proved betrayer of his father-in-law. However, he moved carefully, saying nothing to the Army chief General von Fritsch (who happened to be next on Himmler's list). Instead, he sent von Helldorf to see Goering, who, despite the advice he had given and attending von Blomberg's wedding, decided at once the general had to go. Goering, an opportunist like Goebbels, coveted the post of *Wehrmacht* C-in-C. He waited until von Blomberg had returned from his Italian honeymoon and attended his mother's funeral before resuming his duties on 20 January.

Goering then presented the file to Hitler, who had just returned from Berchtesgarden. Hitler was furious, believing von Blomberg had misled him completely, and above all made him look a fool – having him attend the wedding of a prostitute. Goering completely agreed with him, and volunteered to break the news to the unsuspecting general. When this happened von Blomberg appeared devastated, offering to divorce his wife at once. This was no good: the *Führer* demanded his resignation immediately, as indeed did his Army colleagues. As Jodl wrote in his diary, noting the view of everyone as expressed by General Beck: 'One cannot tolerate the highest-ranking soldier marrying a whore!'

General von Blomberg was dismissed by Hitler on 25 January, and the sixty-year-old soldier left at once to rejoin his bride in Capri. But that was not the end of the affair. Admiral Canaris intervened (and this is perhaps also revealing of the man), despatching a mere Lieutenant to chase von Blomberg and demand that 'for the sake of the officer corps' he must divorce *Frau* von Blomberg. A 'von' himself, the junior officer acted arrogantly, actually presenting von Blomberg with a pistol and suggesting he do the honourable thing. But von Blomberg was not to be intimidated, and he sent the Lieutenant packing. He still believed in his wife, and sent a letter of complaint to Keitel.

Surprisingly, as von Blomberg himself disclosed much later in his unpublished memoirs, Hitler had put on a show of sympathy during the dismissal interview. He had promised faithfully that 'as soon as Germany's hour comes, you will be by my side'. He also promised von Blomberg command of the Army as soon as war came. In fact, von Blomberg was never employed again, despite offering his services in September 1939. He stayed with his wife Eva in the Bavarian village of Wiesee until the war was over, when he was arraigned by the Allies to give evidence for the prosecution in the Nuremberg trials.

The downfall of the Minister of Defence was entirely due to the machinations of Himmler and Heydrich, principally SD work, with a modicum of help from the *Gestapo*. Eva Gruhn had indeed come from a poor background, her mother did manage a massage salon and had been visited by police, who found nothing improper going on. This had occurred years earlier. By 1938 the police notes on the unconvicted *Frau* Gruhn had been replaced by a full dossier giving the 'facts' stated earlier. The tarts who made the malicious calls to generals had been paid by the *Gestapo* and SD, as had the usual informers, who had done their work well and made sure the gossip reached the ears of the police. From then on things had taken their course, though Himmler and Heydrich had no control over events once the file reached higher quarters.

Satisfied, the conspirators now turned their attention to the next general on their list, the Army chief. Although this time things did not quite go as planned, the result still counted.

The obvious replacement for the disgraced von Blomberg was General Freiherr Werner von Fritsch, another officer of the old school. His path, however, was blocked by Goering, and it was the corpulent ex-air ace who had surprisingly been recommended for the job of Defence Minister by von Blomberg. However, this did not suit Hitler, who knew Goering's indulgent habits and greed for titles well. Yet, neither did the *Führer* want von Fritsch, who was critical of his plans and the Party and especially hostile to the SS; his indiscretions had reached the ears of Himmler. When von Fritsch stood on the reviewing stand as a German battalion reoccupied the rich coal area of the Saar on 1 March 1935, he was near an American correspondent who heard the general's vociferous complaints delivered in sarcastic tones about the SS and various Nazi leaders – including Hitler.

Heydrich, on Himmler's orders, arranged a frame-up designed to utterly disgrace von Fritsch, and it was clumsily done. Even so, a bungle somewhere in the SD machine turned out to be an even greater bomb under the German officer corps.

Heydrich's team had prepared a second dossier, concurrent with that against von Blomberg, which was also shown to Hitler on 25 January. Obviously, it rattled the *Führer* and provoked an outburst of hysteria. File No. 2 was designed to prove General von Fritsch guilty of homosexual offences, contrary to section 175 of the German penal code, and that he was being blackmailed by an ex-convict over his activities. Von Blomberg had been shown the convincing police file, remarking that von Fritsch did not seem to have been a man for the ladies. He was a lifelong bachelor, 'who might well have succumbed to weakness'.

The *Führer's* Army adjutant, Colonel Hossbach, had been present at these scenes, and without telling Hitler went straight to von Fritsch to report

131

the charges. 'A lot of stinking lies!' he exploded, swearing he had never been guilty of such conduct. Hossbach would lose his job because of his action. He reported his findings to Hitler, who agreed to see von Fritsch.

When the meeting took place the following evening in Hitler's chancellery, von Fritsch found Himmler and Goering also in attendance. He proceeded to swear on his honour as an Army officer that he was totally innocent. Hitler seemed to waver, but then Himmler ushered in a pathetic-looking civilian introduced as Hans Schmidt, whose prison record had begun as a boy in reform school. Prompted by Himmler, Schmidt identi-fied von Fritsch as the man he had seen involved in a homosexual act with a well-known degenerate known as 'Bavarian Joe', in a dark alley near the Potsdam railway station.

General von Fritsch went red with speechless rage; he was too stupefied to speak, and this convinced Hitler of his guilt. After Schmidt was removed, von Fritsch demanded an Army court of honour to clear his name. However, Hitler seized on the chance to get rid of him, sending the general on indefinite leave. The following day he summoned Keitel to try and find a successor to von Blomberg and von Fritsch, while the latter conferred urgently with General Beck. The next few days were dramatic, producing results neither Himmler or Heydrich expected.

Beck's efforts to intercede with Hitler proved fruitless. In fact, Hitler's opinion of Beck himself was lowered, so that following the Bomb Plot of 1944 he too was executed. Von Fritsch, growing desperate, now contem-plated an Army *Putsch* against Hitler, but soon abandoned the idea; no matter how much he and his colleagues detested the Hitler gang, that kind of action would only bring dissension in the *Wehrmacht*. It could lead to civil war, resurrection of the SA brownshirts, and chaos. The generals were not bold, resolute or courageous enough to take such a risk, and were rightly uncertain of *Luftwaffe* and naval support.

However, the pendulum then swung in favour of von Fritsch, who succeeded in having an Army judicial investigation set up, which soon discovered that Hans Schmidt had in fact caught another Army officer in the said act and blackmailed him for years. The plot against the general really fell apart when the victim's name was found to be *Frisch*, not *Fritsch*. The man in question was a retired cavalry captain, now bedridden. The *Gestapo* had known this, and the frame-up became obvious. The crotchety cavalryman was already under arrest, and Schmidt threatened with death unless he collaborated. Surprisingly, the Army managed to secure the release of both men to serve as witnesses to clear General von Fritsch.

At the end of January 1938, Berlin seethed with rumours of fresh drama in Hitler's camp: a new *Putsch* by Army generals had taken place; two top men had been sacked for no known reason; the French ambassador's dinner date with von Fritsch was suddenly cancelled; the *Reichstag* session was postponed – the Army was about to take over the capital and government.

All conjecture ended on 4 February, when it was announced that the *Führer* had himself taken personal command of the *Wehrmacht*; the War Ministry was abolished. As new Commander-in-Chief Hitler headed a new command staff called *Oberkommando der Wehrmacht* (OKW). His deputy was General Keitel. Both men had got what they wanted, with Goering placated by promotion to Field Marshal. Officially, von Blomberg and von Fritsch had resigned for health reasons. Sixteen generals resigned in disgust; forty-four others were pushed out into dead-end jobs because of their anti-Nazi views. However, Hitler's problems with his generals were not over, for the successor to von Fritsch was himself in need of a divorce, which, as Jodl noted, had to be approved by his mother. The general in question was von Brauchitsch, who remarried, to a rabid, committed Nazi supporter. The bonus results of the SS plot included Hitler's removal of various officials of the diplomatic staff. The reasons were unclear, but it was in this period that Joachim von Ribbentrop became Hitler's top foreign policy adviser.

On 5 February Goebbels's principal mouthpiece in the German Press, the *Völkischer Beobachter* (People's Observer), announced in banner headlines, the 'Strongest concentration of all powers in the *Führer*'s hands!'

Hitler had finally secured a firm grip on Germany and its armed forces; the Army officer corps had missed its chance to unseat him. There would be more opportunities, all of them missed or fudged. The fact that Heydrich's anti-von Fritsch plot had misfired was irrelevant: the dice, as that general remarked, were cast. Germany was stuck with its '*Führer*' for good or ill. 'He will drag us all down with him. There is nothing we can do!' von Fritsch wailed.

10

'ACTION GROUPS'

It had become obvious to Heydrich through his conversations with Himmler that Hitler was determined to achieve his aims through war. This would if possible be directed eastwards and exclude any action against the Western powers; but should it become necessary, the *Wehrmacht* would strike at France and England, if the latter intervened. Once the strength of the Allies was gone, Hitler would concentrate everything on his drive to the East and secure vast new living space for the German people, principally at the expense of western Russia.

Heydrich was indifferent to such dreams, and did not dwell on the morality of them, only on what problems any results would bring in terms of security. To this end he entered into various 'case studies' with his officers, concerning the implications of Hitler's plans. These dreams of conquest included the wholesale removal of undesirable elements, including of course the Jews. Heydrich had long accepted such ideas, that the Jews were an infection to be eradicated from German life; whether he believed in wild tales of a world-wide Jewish plot to take over all nations is another matter. There certainly existed a hard core of Jewish leaders and Zionists who firmly believed in pursuing the so-called 'Balfour Declaration' made by the British politician of that name, in which the setting up of a Jewish state was promoted in Palestine.

The 'trial' of General von Fritsch, which he and his supporters felt sure would be a mere formality and exonerate him completely, in fact went on for hours. It took place on 10 March 1938, and the witness Schmidt, doubtless more interested in preserving his life than his honour, maintained it was the general he had seen in the alley at Potsdam, the defence lawyer failing to shake him. Suddenly, the proceedings were suspended by Goering as chairman of the court, who announced an adjournment – 'For important reasons concerning the interests of the *Reich*'. The reason was the German occupation of Austria, which Hitler had ordered to go ahead.

Austria was incorporated into the *Reich* by a device called the '*Anschluss*', a supposed plebiscite, which today would be termed a referendum. The nation was permitted to vote on its fate: did it want to be part of Hitler's *Reich* – or not? Heydrich saw to it that the answer was an unequivocal '*Ja!*' It has been said that the occupation of Austria without a shot being fired

134

was a personal triumph for Heydrich; he had laid the ground so well that the opposition were undermined and reduced to helplessness. A programme of terror and subversion had been laid through his agents and Austrian Nazis. Bombings, demonstrations and constant harassment of Chancellor von Schussnigg's government went on throughout 1937. Hardly a day passed without some new outrage, all of it financed from Berlin. The various Nazi organisations set up in Austria to promote 'friendship' and other ties all played their part. Finally, on 25 January 1938, Austrian police raided the headquarters of the Committee of Seven, an SD front organisation pretending to promote Austro-German peace. In reality it was a terrorist centre. Documents were found signed by the *Führer*'s deputy, Rudolf Hess, outlining a revolt to take place by Austrian Nazis which would have to be put down by troops. This would be the excuse Hitler needed to send in his own army to restore order and prevent further bloodshed 'between Germans and Germans'. One of those to be marked down in the plot as a victim of Austrian murder was Hitler's own plenipotentiary, Franz von Papen, who had himself been very active trying to pressure the Austrian Chancellor into bowing to the inevitable – a German occupation. His death would provide another excuse for Hitler to march in.

Hitler had ordered Hess to take over the three Nazi organisations charged with looking after the interests of Germans abroad. Hess created the *Volksdeutsche Mittelstelle* (VOMI) under Otto Kursell, who proved useless, and following an appeal to Himmler for a replacement, a former aviation officer called Werner Lorenz took over the VOMI office in January 1937. Heydrich was quick to install his own agents in its staff, who were directed from Berlin by Heinz Jost. Heydrich even had Hermann Behrends installed as right-hand man to Lorenz.

As Schellenberg recorded later, many Austrian Nazis fled when the police of that country cracked down on them and their activities. From these people the SD received a great deal of useful information, especially contact addresses which were taken up later.

Schellenberg had been amazed at the flow of information which arrived daily in the SD offices in Berlin. He learned that though Himmler insisted on being kept informed of progress, he was kept in the dark on various matters, for by then Heydrich preferred a certain independence of direction. By 1938 he had begun to regard himself as a separate force. He had little or no contact with other SS departments, and even his liaisons with the *Gestapo* were reduced. In short, Heydrich was carving out his own empire through his SD, much as did some other Nazi leaders. In this first really major task, the taking over of a neighbouring state, Heydrich saw his SD as the one organisation capable of ensuring a peaceful union between Austria and Germany. He pursued the operation with great zeal, to the exclusion of other matters, even though Hitler and others were following their own line.

All of these Nazi efforts put very great pressure on Chancellor Schussnigg.

Franz von Papen discovered to his astonishment and fear that he himself figured on a Nazi hit list. He was shaken enough to deposit written notes and documents in a safe place before hurrying back to Berlin to see Hitler, who had in the meantime sacked him. Von Papen was one of the old school of diplomats who made the mistake of trying to suck up to Hitler, perhaps in the hope of curbing his excesses. Unabashed by the recent and menacing disclosures, he came up with a bright idea, suggesting Hitler meet the Austrian Chancellor. Hitler agreed, and Schussnigg arrived in Berchtesgarden on 12 February.

It was a frosty morning, and the Austrian was greeted affably by von Papen, who assured him the *Führer* was 'in excellent mood'. But Hitler had no intention of doing other than browbeating the visitor into submission. He intimidated him from the start by having three of his generals attend the talks, a fact von Papen alluded to, hoping the Chancellor would not be offended. The three soldiers 'just happened to be in the building'. They were Keitel, and the two men responsible for the German troop and air build-up against the Austrian border, Generals Reichenau and Sperrle. Yet, Schussnigg found himself alone at one point with Hitler in a spacious second-floor study, a large picture window affording grand views across the snow-capped Alps into Austria itself. The visitor's polite comments on the views and weather were cut short by Hitler who said, 'We do not gather here to speak of the fine views or weather'. He then launched into a bullying tirade, accusing Austria of one long act of treason through its history, of the present government's unfriendliness, and so on. The argument and dissension that followed even touched on the true birthplace of Beethoven. Hitler gave his guest no leeway, he was 'determined to solve the problem one way or another', and he had a 'historic mission'. He added, 'Listen! You don't really think you can move a single stone in Austria without my hearing about it next day, do you?'

Hitler ranted on, assuring Schussnigg no help could be expected from other powers; Mussolini was his friend; France had missed its chance when Germany re-occupied the Rhineland, now it was too late. England? They would not lift a finger, the English did not care about Austria.

When they finally broke for lunch, Hitler became affable again, quipping to his worried guest that Germany was building bigger and better skyscrapers than the USA! But when Schussnigg left for home he did so with Hitler's final ultimatum ringing in his ears: either he accept the *Führer's* three provisions, or face immediate invasion by the *Wehrmacht.* The three clauses were:

- The appointment of the Austrian Nazi Dr Seyss-Inquart as Minister of the Interior and Security.
- An amnesty and release of all Nazis in custody in Austria.

136

- The Austrian Nazi Party to be incorporated into the Austrians' own Patriotic Front Party.

In effect, Hitler was demanding the Austrians turn over their administration to the Nazis – and within three days. Von Papen had been amazed at this act of bullying, but like von Ribbentrop urged Schussnigg to agree. At one point the talks with the Austrian had turned into tragi-comedy, Hitler losing control of himself and rushing to the doors to yell for Keitel – an obvious act of further intimidation taken to absurdity. In fact, just as suddenly, Hitler, the ham actor, became all smiles and told Schussnigg, 'For the first time in my life I have changed my mind. But I warn you, this is your last chance!'

The Austrian Chancellor retreated like a beaten child, having told Hitler that only the Austrian President could decide and sign any agreement.

During these days, Heydrich's men stepped up the pressure in Austria, principally in Vienna, organising demonstrations by Nazis, beefed up by SD agents, demanding union with Germany. The population had in turn been bemused then alarmed; Heydrich made certain they saw the sense of such a union, having pamphlets distributed extolling the virtues of such an arrangement and the benefits to be gained. It was in fact a case of the stick and carrot. There were many Austrians perfectly willing to accept such a union, for they thought of themselves as 'Germanic', bombarded by Nazi propaganda proclaiming that their natural place lay with their German brothers and sisters. A lot of this was mere poppycock, as Heydrich well knew. He was to some extent familiar with Austrian history, feeling that like the Swiss the Austrians were inclined to be self-indulgent and far more like the Hungarians, with whom they had enjoyed a past union. Hitler, utterly cynical, displayed no great love for his native land, which he saw as having failed him in his youth. It was the Jews in Vienna who had prevented him from entering academia, only Germany had provided him with hope and the chance to prove his talents. He owed Austria nothing, it was a mere stepping stone on his road East.

Hardly had Schussnigg left Germany when Hitler ordered Keitel to arrange sham manoeuvres by the *Wehrmacht* forces against the Austrian border. The Austrian President was known as a rather feeble, peasant type whose best achievement had been the fathering of a large family. Yet he refused at first to cave in to Hitler's demands, agreeing only to free imprisoned Nazis, including the men accused of murdering the former chancellor Dollfuss. German troop movements caused a change of heart, and Schussnigg was able to inform Hitler that his government would be able to sign the agreement by 18 February. The Austrian Nazis were released on 16 February and Seyss-Inquart became Minister of the Interior, and he hurried to Berlin to receive his orders. He had been careful to distance himself from the rowdies parading the streets of Austria, and was looked on with some trust and tolerance by Schussnigg and President Miklas; he

137

had served in the same Austrian Tyrolean rifle regiment as the Chancellor and was a regular church-going Catholic.

In his postponed speech to the Nazi Parliament on 20 February, Hitler made pointed reference to 'over ten million Germans' living in the two states bordering Germany; he was referring to not only Austria but Czechoslovakia. Hitler said he would not tolerate the refusal of rights due to these Germans, and his speech was the signal for yet another round of even bigger demonstrations organised by the SD. Behind the scenes, Seyss-Inquart worked hard to further undermine Austrian independence. Chancellor Schussnigg's response to Hitler's speech was to make one of his own, four days later, obviously having recovered his nerve and now defiant. He declared: 'Red – white – red! Until we're dead!'

Schussnigg roared his challenge, referring to the Austrian national colours. Hitler was surprised and infuriated, von Papen trying to assure him the Austrian was only trying to ensure his domestic position. But the speech was met by an SD-organised mob demonstrating in the town square of Graz. At this point von Papen left for a skiing vacation, while chaos grew in Austria as depositors began withdrawing money from banks and the famous conductor Toscanini wired that he would not appear at the Salzburg Festival. In desperation, Schussnigg called on all workers to turn out in counter-demonstrations; there was nothing Hitler or Heydrich could do to stop this. But the *Führer* summoned one hundred Austrian-Nazi Army officers, ensuring they would do all in their power to stop their troops fighting.

Then Schussnigg played one last card. He called a referendum for Sunday 13 March. Hitler reacted by ordering his generals to prepare to invade Austria the day before, but was dismayed to find they were unprepared. He therefore summoned the promising military genius General Manstein to work on it all night. Meanwhile, Seyss-Inquart tried to persuade Schussnigg to cancel the referendum. Schussnigg complied, '. . . to save spilling German blood', and knowing that many of his police chiefs had been won over by the Nazis. It was not enough for those in Berlin. Goering joined others in making bullying telephone calls to Schussnigg demanding his resignation – which came on 11 March.

That night Walter Schellenberg was ordered to fly to Vienna with Himmler, a detachment of the SS *Leibstandarte* and a few men of the 'Austrian Legion' formed in Germany. The parties left Berlin in two large transport aircraft, overloaded and subject to disagreeable weather conditions; radio contact with Vienna was lost. Schellenberg withdrew to the rear of his plane because noise from the engines was making his conversation with Himmler difficult. The *Reichsführer* wanted to go over the problems resulting from the establishment of the Ostmark – as the Nazis had dubbed their new province. As Himmler began speaking he leaned against the door of the plane, which Schellenberg suddenly saw was not latched. Lunging forward, he seized hold of Himmler and pulled him aside,

Himmler and Heydrich arrive in Vienna in 1938

much to the *Reichsführer*'s astonishment. But Himmler was grateful when Schellenberg pointed out the danger.

Heydrich did not travel to Vienna by aircraft, but instead took two squads of chosen men by car across the frontier, overtaking long convoys of German troops before entering the Austrian capital. Heading straight for the police headquarters, he was greeted most effusively by the Austrian-Nazi chief who appraised him of the situation in the city and throughout the country. Heydrich was anxious to lay hands on the Austrian secret police files, and after greeting Himmler he went with Schellenberg to see Colonel Runge, who seemed quite co-operative, though saying little. The two SD men began examining the files, Heydrich's chief aim to find out all he could about known foreign agents in the country. He was very disappointed; Colonel Runge's department – the *Geheime Kommando* – had been very inefficient, and all he found was some useful data on decoding.

In fact, Heydrich had been beaten to the prizes by Canaris, as Runge's assistant, Colonel Erwin von Lahousen Vivremont, was candid enough to divulge. To the SD men's surprise and anger, they learned from the rather smug von Lahousen Vivremont that Admiral Canaris had arrived two hours before, accompanied by his assistants who had removed several dossiers which seemed to interest them greatly. Four files in particular took their attention: they were labelled Hitler, Goering, Heydrich and Canaris. Clearly, Heydrich had underestimated his rival. He was intrigued, wondering what the Austrian Secret Service had dug up on them. In fact, the file on Hitler contained full details of his earlier life, facts that are well known today.

His disappointment laid aside for the moment, Heydrich ordered an immediate round-up of all suspects, including prominent anti-Nazis. They were to be locked up in local jails until more long-term arrangements could be made. Most of the prisoners ended up in Mauthausen concentration camp, north of the River Danube, and set up very quickly on Austrian soil. The arrests were supervised by the Austrian police chief, Ernst Kaltenbrunner. In another direction, an SS officer called Karl Adolf Eichmann set up an 'Office for Jewish Emigration', which when staffed had by August 1938 begun the task of throwing out all Jews from Austria – a quarter of a million people. Karl Adolf Eichmann was himself Austrian, and of rather Jewish appearance. His SS squads began looting Jewish premises and extorting cash and valuables in exchange for safe passage out

Hitler motors into Vienna with Seyss-Inquart

of *Reich* territory. This was gangster robbery on a grand scale, perfectly agreeable to Heydrich and Himmler, who believed such 'vermin' should be deprived of everything before being kicked out. Even Baron Louis de Rothschild was obliged to turn over his great steel mills, the complex becoming part of the Hermann Goering Werke. Eventually, once the war was well under way, no Jews would be allowed to escape, though there were ambiguities and disagreements among the top Nazi chieftains as to their fate. In due course, it is said that Mauthausen claimed the greatest number of victims, 35,318 people killed (not all Jews) in six-and-a-half years; the SS camp commandant naturally kept exact records.

Heydrich now contributed an article to *Das Schwarze Korps*, the SS newspaper which, under its editor Gunther D'Alquen, published items surprisingly critical of some aspects of Nazi life and policy:

> The *Führer's* will can henceforth be performed in Austria after the happy conclusion of the fierce struggle against the political, intellectual and criminal elements opposed to the unification of the German people.

The Austrian police, Heydrich noted, would henceforth be 'happily subordinated to the Federal Chancellery', in other words, to Himmler's and Heydrich's SS, SD and *Gestapo.*

Whatever the efforts of Hitler, the rape of Austria succeeded largely through SD subversion. It was certainly the first time an independent nation had been taken over in such a fashion. Heydrich had good cause for great satisfaction over the way terrorism had resulted in the disintegration of a neighbouring nation without a shot being fired.

Next on Hitler's agenda, once he had returned in triumph to his native land and digested all this entailed, came 'Case Green', the swallowing of Czechoslovakia.

By 1 April 1938, the German Army had grown to twenty-eight divisions; by autumn, including reserves, it numbered fifty-five divisions. For his military build-up, Hitler had sacked the *Reich* Treasury of 6.2 milliard marks (6.2 thousand million). In the year 1938–9 this rose to 16 milliard.

Hitler, a man ever driven by hatreds, had always disliked Czechoslovakia, an unreasoning bile dating from his youthful days in Vienna when he perceived the neighbouring state as challenging the Hapsburg monarchy. The land to the east had been cobbled together as one of the 'settlements' of 1919, following the 'Great War'. The old names denoting lands containing a polyglot people, Ruthenia, Moravia, Slovakia had gone, with Hungary, Poland and Russia squabbling over slices of territory lost in the settlement or by annexations. The three million Germans living in the portion of Czechoslovakia called the Sudetenland were Hitler's pretext for intervention. In fact, the new state contained deep divisions since it consisted of several peoples brought together forcibly in the postwar 're-arrangements' largely brokered by the US President Wilson. In fact, three different segments lived in disharmony, and despite all the efforts of the Czech government, these divisions remained, especially between Czechs and Slovaks.

Hitler's problem was how to swallow this country without choking on its powerful army and defence system, which rivalled the French Maginot Line in modern fortifications. The Czechs, lumped in with most others to the East as *Untermenschen* (sub-humans), had their great Skoda arms works and a high degree of engineering skill; Skodas would add greatly to the German war-making capacity. Hitler had walked a diplomatic tightrope over the Austrian affair, placating the Western powers and his friend Mussolini. He now knew that further and possibly far greater difficulties would have to be overcome if 'Case Green' was to be implemented. Powerful though the *Wehrmacht* had become, Hitler knew his forces were not yet strong enough to take on several armies at once. He would, with astonishing nerve, play several games together, rather like a master chess player. France, Hitler reckoned, was no longer a power to be reckoned with in world politics; England was too weak, both politically and militarily, though it would certainly lift an enfeebled hand in protest through Prime Minister Chamberlain. However, Hitler had not reckoned on more active intervention from the Italian dictator, Benito Mussolini.

The move-by-move game that resulted in the dismemberment and final absorption of Czechoslovakia into the Greater German *Reich* as a 'Protectorate' has been told and re-told. The period that became known in Britain as the first 'Munich Crisis' involved visits by Prime Minister Neville Chamberlain to try and placate Hitler and arrange some settlement – almost anything to prevent war. Chamberlain came from a family line used to acting as mayor in the city of Birmingham; he had not long succeeded Stanley Baldwin and was no doubt thankful the Abdication Crisis was not on his plate when the latest threat from '*Herr* Hitler' erupted. The situation seemed so serious in Britain that the digging of air raid shelters in public parks was begun, as was the issuing of gas masks and a scheme for the evacuating of children from big city areas.

Suitably incited by SD and *Gestapo* agents, the Sudeten Germans had demonstrated and rioted against their Czech 'masters', marching through the streets bawling '*Ein Reich, ein Volk, ein Führer!*' Leader of this movement was Konrad Henlein, who initially had been anti-Nazi but was anxious to secure power within the Czech legislature; he and his followers were not interested in union with Germany. But between May and September a complete about-face took place. When Henlein met Hitler he was presented with forcible arguments that his own cause was best served by joining Hitler's. Henlein now donned a uniform cap bearing an outsize swastika, but if he had any notion of being appointed *Gauleiter* of a Nazified Czechoslovakia he was much mistaken. The power went to Heydrich and his man Karl Hermann Frank, a German-Czech whose life would end on the gallows.

Some of Hitler's private utterances tell the story of the days when the fate of the Czech nation was decided:

It is not my intention to smash Czechoslovakia by military action in the immediate future without provocation . . . (20 May 1938)

It is my unalterable decision to smash Czechoslovakia by military action in the near future. (30 May)

You will understand, my comrades, that a Great Power cannot for a second time suffer such an infamous encroachment on its rights . . . I am in no way willing that here in the heart of Germany a second Palestine should be permitted to arise. The poor Arabs are defenceless and deserted. The Germans in Czechoslovakia are neither defenceless nor deserted and people should take notice of that fact. (12 September)

No doubts should arise as to my absolute determination not to tolerate any longer that a small, second-rate country should treat the mighty thousand-year-old German *Reich* as something inferior . . . Three hundred Sudeten Germans have been killed . . . I am determined to settle it; I do not care if there is a world war or not . . . I am prepared to risk a world war, rather than allow this to drag on. (15 September)

Oh, Mr Prime Minister, I am so sorry, I had looked forward to showing you this beautiful view of the Rhine . . . but now it is hidden by mist. (22 September)

This Czech state began with a lie, and the father of this lie is named Benes . . . There is no such thing as a Czechoslovak nation, but only Czechs and Slovaks, and the Slovaks do not wish to have anything to do with the Czechs! (28 September)

The daily number of refugees has risen from ten thousand to two hundred and fourteen thousand today! In the last resort, *Herr* Benes has seven million Czechs, but here stands a people of over seventy-five million! (28 September)

This fellow Chamberlain has spoiled my entry into Prague!

The last quotation is how Hitler complained to his SS entourage after the British Prime Minister, with the help of Daladier of France and Mussolini, had persuaded him to settle for occupation of the Sudetenland. The Czechs were not consulted and felt utterly betrayed.

Hitler's profound hatred of President Benes and his determination to take over Czechoslovakia finally bore fruit in October, when the German Army and *Luftwaffe* marched in to complete stage one of the creation of the Czech 'Protectorate' that would last until 1945. For months Hitler had provided headlines in his relentless campaign to get his way. Now, only partially successful, he let it be known that he had 'no more territorial claims' in Europe. Prime Minister Chamberlain returned to Britain in great relief, waving the piece of paper that was to prove worthless, an 'agreement' signed by the German Chancellor, *Herr* Hitler, to guarantee 'peace for our time'. Despite his great aversion to the fiery dictator, Winston Churchill was honest enough to comment on Hitler's 'amazing willpower'. That willpower would overcome those who were weaker and lacked the determination to stand firm.

Following a series of underhand manoeuvres, the Nazi government concocted a telegram ostensibly emanating from the cleric leader Mnsr Tiso of Slovakia, pleading for Hitler's protection; the German Army marched across the borders and entered Prague in a snowstorm. The Czech population watched mostly in silent, impotent grief as their state ceased to exist, becoming overnight the Protectorate of Bohemia-Moravia. Slovakia was granted independent (but puppet) status. The Western allies did nothing bar protest, Chamberlain in particular suffering the rudest awakening as he realised how Hitler had duped him again.

Behind the shock headlines of yet another triumph of Nazi bullyboy tactics lay the reality of Heydrich's Secret Service machinations that had set the Sudetenland aflame and undermined the opposition. No matter how much Hitler blazed away with threats and lies, without the subversions of the SD events might have taken a different turn. 'Case Green' had presented Heydrich with another chance to prove the worth of his service. But it was not another 'Austria'; there were different factors to contend with, especially the Czech Secret Service, which was alive to the threat of Germans living within its borders. Heydrich's SD spies had begun their work in 1937, posing as tourists, photographing everything, including of course the frontier defences in the west and in other regions. It was impossible for the Czechs to stop these activities, though some were caught, as were Czechs spying in Germany. In this kind of work Heydrich employed a team of camera specialists who, with aid from civilian experts in the industry, developed a new type of mini-camera that fitted very conveniently into a top pocket. Its lens was actually disguised as a jacket button; all the operator had to do was operate the shutter by leaving a hand in one pocket, a normal cable release did the rest. The results were excellent, though the 'tourists' needed some practice before setting off on their 'holidays'.

In this way the SD built up a very comprehensive picture of the target country even before Hitler began his public campaign to capture it. Heydrich knew for certain that his rival Canaris was up to the same game, as there were occasions when the agents of both services actually met in the same vacation spots and certainly recognised what the others were up to.

Other spies were tasked to photograph buildings of importance in the major cities, principally in Prague, especially police stations, headquarters, post offices and utilities. Airfields naturally received priority, posing special problems as they were guarded by alert sentries. One of the best disguises used by the SD was to employ 'families'; that is to say, SD agents were encouraged to take womenfolk, children, even relatives, along with them on vacations funded by the Nazi Secret Service. Obviously, innocent-looking families picnicking on the grass alongside airfields caused less suspicion. Proud fathers holding their little boys by the hand as they excitedly watched planes taking off and landing seemed quite innocuous. In this connection, Himmler insisted on checking all expense claims and on some occasions baulked at meeting the bill. But when Heydrich showed him a few sample files he was suitably impressed and remarked how the *Abwehr* had been trounced at its own game.

This was of course military espionage, work which in the event proved superfluous. Heydrich's greater efforts were, as indicated, directed towards inciting the Sudeten German population and the Slovaks to demonstrate against the Czech authorities. Alfred Naujocks proved his worth again by despatching 'intervention groups' to act as political saboteurs, influencing opinion by word of mouth and well-designed literature. The office work involved was run by Walter Schellenberg and the chief of SS recruiting, Gottlob Berger, who found suitable men, some from among the Sudeten Germans who spoke Czech and were called to Berlin for consultation. They were screened, given tuition and put into teams to cross back into Czechoslovakia. It was not the kind of work either Schellenberg or Berger was cut out for; unlike Naujocks, who revelled in the chance to escape from office work. He went into Czechoslovakia with a team to assess the situation and to activate more intervention groups, on Hitler's direct order, for the *Führer* did not trust Mnsr Tiso and his followers. Naujocks organised a train of terrorist acts designed to stir up the Czechs and increase tension. Bombs were placed in public places, not powerful enough to cause casualties, but enough to bring alarm and cause a small amount of damage, giving an impression of Slovaks pressing for independence from their Czech masters. Naujocks also surveyed the so-called 'Hlinka' Guard, a fascist group much like the Nazis but reckoned by Hitler to be of little value.

While these subversive operations went on, other crises blew up, especially when Hungary was pressed by Poland to settle common frontiers, proposing that Romania divide the province of Ruthenia with her. For its part, the Hungarian government not only claimed Ruthenia, but all of Slovakia. These disputes were a result of the 1919 'settlements'.

Such manoeuvres had no effect on Naujocks's operation. His teams were seemingly integrated into the communities, but actually living with firm and reliable contacts wholly committed to the Nazi cause. Naujocks made frequent trips back to Berlin, reporting to Heydrich, travelling by road through the Sudetenland and meeting no problems, though on one occasion he was forced to bribe an overzealous policeman who was intent on searching his luggage, which contained report notes and a camera. If it came to it, Naujocks was prepared to shoot him with his little Walther PPK.

Somehow, the absurd sabre rattling of the central powers never resulted in war, even though Hungary began massing troops on the Slovakian border, a threat which if carried through would have upset Hitler's plans considerably. Romania and Poland hastened to reinforce their forces in the affected zones.

Heydrich himself made no visits into Czechoslovakia in this period. Only after the greater takeover in 1939 did he and his entourage go to Prague to rummage through the files in police headquarters. The Czech spy chief, Lt-Colonel Moravec, had by then fled, taking with him the most important documents and burning the rest. His escape route was via France to England, where his hosts provided him with a very modest home in South London until it was bombed during the Blitz. President Benes had earlier confided in him that with such powerful adversaries as England, France and Poland, Hitler would not dare to try anything. If he did it would bring his downfall. Despite his close ties with Stalin, the Soviet dictator did not find it expedient to try and intervene on the Czech side. Moravec tried to co-operate with French Intelligence, finding they would not reveal very much; the Czech did, however, receive a new developer for secret writing from a French scientist and criminologist. But:

> My overall impression was not favourable, and often I had reason to feel distrust . . . we ascertained that important information (passed by us) was 'lost in transit' to the higher French policy makers and even to the Command of the French Army.

The Czech Army Commander-in-Chief, General Syrovy, was well warned in advance by Moravec of the coming German invasion, a warning already given to the Foreign Minister. For his pains Moravec was reprimanded and warned to stop spreading false information – or face prosecution. In fact, he had precise information on the coming invasion from his agent A-54, who Moravec was later convinced was a captain in the *Abwehr*. At first it seemed the man was no more than a mercenary, but his erect military bearing and, in time, comradely feelings spoke of more. Agent A-54 predicted the exact time of the German invasion, dawn on 15 March 1939, plus the precise movement of the four Army corps involved. He even produced an original Nazi document ordering the *Gestapo* to seize all Czech intelligence officers and to interrogate them 'with great severity' in order to learn the identity of Czech agents in the *Reich*.

The agent, obviously German, warned Moravec to get out while he could, and not to choose France as a haven; 'No matter where you go I will find you, and continue the collaboration', the man added, rather optimistically. Lt-Colonel Moravec only gained permission at the very last moment to begin destroying files of the Czech General Staff, as well as his own. Leaving his wife and children in ignorance of his true destination, he flew out of the country by arrangement with the British. He took eleven of his key intelligence staff with him, plus some £32,000 in *Reichsmarks* and

Dutch guilders, reckoning this amount, plus funds already abroad, would be sufficient to begin operations anew from elsewhere. Admiral Canaris arrived with his team in Prague a few hours later, hurrying into the Second Bureau of the Czech Intelligence building, demanding files from the only officer left on the premises.

'Everything has been destroyed', the man told him.

'That is what we expected,' an *Abwehr* major replied. 'We would have done the same.'

That much Moravec learned later. On that bleak morning in March 1939 he looked out of the aircraft window at the mountains below, dropped his head and cried.

The Czech spy's presence in London did not go unnoticed, for his picture appeared in a British newspaper as 'part of a mysterious group' which had arrived in the capital. The same photograph then appeared in a German-controlled paper in Prague, being seen by Moravec's wife, who learned of his safety and whereabouts. Next, Moravec received a note asking him to attend the Grosvenor Hotel, and with it came the torn half of a visiting card signed 'Rudolf', the cover name used by successive Soviet spies in Prague. As he commented later, Soviet methods smacked of fifth-rate spy fiction novels. Meeting the Russian, he was asked to continue the co-operation against the Germans. He gave the same response already made to a French officer – he would comply, but the British had priority as they had been the most helpful.

Heydrich, and perhaps even Canaris (it is impossible to be certain), would have been aghast if they had known how every German 'invasion date', from the Czech takeover, the attack on Poland, the assault in the West in May 1940, and the invasion of the Balkans and USSR, was passed to Moravec by A-54 who maintained his contact after the Czechs began operating from Holland and other locations, such as Belgrade.

Admiral Canaris's rush to try and seize the Czech files may have had more than one motive; he had been most active in various directions and ways not conducive to Hitler's policies. He had been sounding out and prodding certain high-ranking German staff officers to carry out an uprising against the *Führer* before it was too late. Plans were more than tentative, and Generals Beck, Halder and Witzleben were up to their necks in the talks. The latter was in command of the Berlin garrison and charged in the event of a *Putsch* to take over the capital. Much depended on attitudes in London, and it seemed to the conspirators that help from that quarter could not be relied upon. The true facts of this matter are not known, and whether Britain missed a real chance to get rid of Hitler before September 1939 is open to conjecture. It is especially relevant in view of events to come in October–November of that year. Prime Minister Chamberlain's agreement over the Czech affair in September the previous year seems to have scotched hopes held by Canaris and his friends.

In any event, and despite his excellent warning system, Canaris did not realise that his machinations had become known to Himmler and Heydrich. The feelers put out in London did not remain secret because of the German generals' lack of security, as the chief conspirators were under constant surveillance by SD and *Gestapo*. However, Canaris himself escaped arrest because no final proof was forthcoming. He put nothing in writing, except in his diary, and it never proved possible to tap his telephone. Certain of his treachery, by the weaknesses among the military staff he conspired with, Himmler nevertheless decided to bide his time.

As for the von Fritsch affair, his trial was resumed and he was acquitted, then killed fighting with his regiment in Poland in late September 1939.

11
'LET NAUJOCKS DO IT!'

Hitler could be astonishingly frank with his intimates, without regard for recorded history. Following his success in forcing war on Poland he said:

> I needed an alibi, especially with the German people, to show them that I had done everything to maintain peace. That explains my generous offer about the settlement of Danzig and the Corridor.

It was an offer he never intended to allow anyone to take up. But then, Hitler's word was law, as the Nazi lawyer Hans Frank made clear when he wrote in the *Völkischer Beobachter* on 20 May 1936: 'Our Constitution is the will of the *Führer*.'

This had been the case ever since Hitler came to power: he had scrapped the German Constitution introduced by the democratic *Weimar* government, replacing it by decrees issued under the Enabling Act, a device that permitted Hitler to do exactly as he pleased. The Act was renewed every so often, giving Hitler (as Alan Bullock pointed out) greater power than Stalin, Mussolini, or even Napoleon, with no restrictions on mere trivial details of legality. Indeed, if Hitler made the laws, then whatever he did within them was legal. It was gangster rule by an all-powerful clique possessing unbridled power. All this meant that the troops of the *Gestapo* and SS, etc. did not act lawlessly, since their actions were in essence governed by orders that were lawful. Every man was ultimately answerable to Hitler, who had no restrictions placed on him at all.

When the 'race police' set out to corral and later destroy the Jews and others, they were not acting under mere whim or prejudice of Heydrich and Himmler. They were in their minds performing under legal orders. Yet, conscience did prick Hitler, that much is obvious. It was why he put up 'alibis' and excuses and pretexts for his barbarous acts, because he had some small regard for what 'his people' thought of him. He did not wish to lose face and kudos by appearing a barefaced liar or aggressor, even if he was. Likewise, the hunters still rummaging in various places for some document or scrap of paper signed by Adolf Hitler assigning the Jews to extinction will never meet with success. Hitler knew perfectly well, despite his twisted hatred, that he could be condemned by history for such an act. But the sheer scale of the crime precluded any notions of another 'alibi'; it was something that would have to be done without written orders and instructions from him or his associates. That did not mean a complete lack of documentation, for it was needed by the men actually assigned the grisly task, and in this Heydrich's 'Secret Service' became involved. Involved, that is, following one of Hitler's hysterical outbursts of hate: 'I will destroy them! Do you hear? See to it!' These were allegedly the actual words spoken to Himmler, who interpreted the utterance to mean the actual, physical extinction of the Jewish race in Europe.

Himmler, already completely immersed in his prejudices and 'studies' of racial questions, agreed wholeheartedly that the pestilence had to be removed. He passed on the necessary order to Heydrich, who had no qualms in setting up the necessary organisation, clumsy though at first it was. But Heydrich, the Secret Service chief, was not the chief executioner of course, though as the war got under way the SD had its 'executive' arm of uniformed men as part of the SIPO set-up. These men carried out raids on Jewish premises and quarters to round up those destined for the camps and eventual extinction. The concentration camps already existed, the staffs were in place, SS men who adhered to orders, no matter how inhumane; all that was needed (eventually, given the scale of the task) was an efficient method of mass execution, and in this German industry proved quite co-operative.

Angry Czechs hurl abuse as German troops enter Prague

There is no intention here of repeating the familiar history of the Holocaust, as it is called. But it is worth noting that there was far from harmony among the Nazi leaders on the Jewish question. On the one hand, the policy of enforced exodus had begun in the thirties, and this course seemed perfectly reasonable to some Nazis. Then, as the war spread and more and more labour was needed for the war effort, other Nazis saw no sense in doing away with such a useful human resource. Other Nazis, as shown, had only one blind thought, to expunge the Jews completely from all spheres of German life and territory. These contradicting views were never resolved, the evidence for them left for history – but no written order for the enforced demise of a race.

But the pogrom to top all pogroms came later. It would prove no more than a comparatively mild diversion for Heydrich, who in 1939 was still preoccupied with espionage. Politics would come later.

Incidentally, it may have been Walter Schellenberg who first coined the word *Einsatzgruppen,* later used as a term for the mobile 'action squads' numbering a few hundred men and women ordered to liquidate undesirables in the East. In the earlier days the term '*Einsatzgruppen*' signified the 'intervention groups' who penetrated into Czechoslovakia, as a note from Schellenberg to Heinz Jost dated 13 September 1938 makes clear. This paper also contains the following phrase, which is not without interest: 'This has been ordered by C, in the manner indicated above.'

'C' was the simple way Heydrich designated himself, and of course well known as the identity used by the head of the SIS in London, though it has been said that the SD chief could not have known that then. However, being an avid reader of spy fiction, Heydrich may have picked it up somewhere.

It cannot have come as any great surprise to the Western democracies when Hitler, after a short pause following the occupation of the rest of Czechoslovakia, began a similar round of threats and bluster against Poland. Hardly a democracy, and certainly involved in questionable politics against some of their neighbours, the Poles now awoke more fully to the greater threat. Hitler had taken over two independent nations without a war, but this could not happen with Poland because of the far sterner attitude now being adopted in Paris and London. While the British were willing to consider Hitler's claim to the largely German-populated city of Danzig, anything beyond that would entail grave risks for Germany.

Goering's Swedish friend Birger Dahlerus was called in to try and sound out the British attitude. He carried 'six points' to London put forward by the *Führer:*

1 Germany wants an alliance with Britain.
2 England to help Germany obtain Danzig and the 'Polish Corridor'.
3 Germany would guarantee Polish frontiers.
4 Germany must have its old colonies returned.

5 Guarantees needed for the German minorities in Poland.
6 Germany to pledge defence of the British Empire.

Neither Goering nor Hitler would permit these ideas to be committed to paper, which seemed strange to the Swede, who asked what they wanted regarding the Polish 'Corridor' to Danzig. In response, Goering sent for an atlas, tore out the appropriate page and marked it in lines with a red pencil. He then handed the sheet over to Dahlerus with a grin. That was Nazi-style diplomacy.

Some of the points raised were clearly nonsense, and in any case Hitler had already decided that this time he would settle the issue by force. The diplomacy was a mere smokescreen designed to force Poland and the Allies into a corner. In other words, Hitler was preparing another alibi for German and foreign consumption.

Neville Chamberlain had voiced his dismay the year before:

> How horrible, fantastic, incredible it is that we should be digging trenches and trying on gas-masks here, because of a quarrel in a far-away country between people of whom we know nothing.

After making this public complaint, he had gone off to help sign away Czech independence. His utterance would add fuel to his critics later, though history would judge him less harshly. Unfortunate in a sense though his choice of phrase had been, it did express a grim reality, for most Britons did know little or nothing of these 'far-away' countries and had little desire to risk another blood bath on the lines of the 'Great War'. Across the Atlantic, the Americans at large felt even more isolationist, desiring only to stay clear of European squabbles.

Though Hitler was trying to use the British to pressure the Poles to accept his demands, he had a two-way attitude on the matter. On the one hand it would have pleased him to see London fall in line once again, but on the other he did not want peace, as von Ribbentrop made plain to their Italian ally. Mussolini had basked in the limelight of his believed intervention over the Czech crisis, only to see his friendly dictator and ally apparently ready to throw it all away a year later. Mussolini felt sidelined as the more dangerous partner once again threatened to set Europe ablaze. The negotiations dragged on, the British refusing to play Hitler's game, for even the more moderate Chamberlain had learned by now the true nature of his adversary. As even the hapless Dahlerus, who had tried in all sincerity (and naïvety) to step onto the world stage to try and preserve peace, became increasingly disenchanted in his attempts to understand Hitler as the dictator railed and blasted away about 'Germany's irresistibility' and Polish atrocities against German minorities in the border areas. 'If there should be war I shall build U-boats, build U-boats, U-boats, U-boats, U-boats . . .' His voice became more and more indistinct, until finally Dahlerus could not follow him at all. Then, Hitler pulled himself together again and began bawling a similar threat, as if addressing a large audience: 'I shall build aeroplanes, build aeroplanes, aeroplanes, aeroplanes – and I shall annihilate my enemies!'

To the open-mouthed Swede, Hitler seemed more like some phantom from a story book than a real person. When the Swede glanced at Goering the rotund marshal had not turned a hair. But there were some moments when even Goering was forced to turn away and hide his face as his leader raved in seeming uncontrolled fashion. When calmer, Hitler asked Dahlerus why the people in London could not be more accommodating; in reply the Swede told him candidly that the English had no confidence in Hitler personally. This brought another outburst. 'Idiots! Have I ever told a lie in my life?' Hitler yelled, beating his breast with his clenched fist.

His barefaced effrontery knew no bounds as in secret he set in train his arrangements for the new alibi and start of World War Two. Heydrich and Canaris were to stage various 'incidents' on the German–Polish border. They were made to appear as if the Poles were committing new crimes, and would give Hitler ample reason to launch his forces into Poland. Apprised of Hitler's tactics, Heydrich sent for the trusty Naujocks; he had an important job for him. Unfortunately, they were compelled to liaise with the *Abwehr* in the matter.

Canaris, meanwhile, had taken part in a conference with *Wehrmacht* chiefs in Berchtesgarden in which Hitler harangued them for several hours on the situation *vis-à-vis* Poland and the world in general, a marathon session mercifully interrupted by lunch. Everything was settled. Von Ribbentrop, despite his failure to woo the British, had managed to restore Hitler's belief in him by pulling off a coup in Moscow, by signing a German-Soviet Non-Aggression Pact, which contained a secret clause permitting the two powers to carve up Poland. At the big conference attended by Canaris, three summaries were made of Hitler's lecture, which were to be presented at the Nuremberg Trials in 1946 as proof of his guilt in waging aggressive war. However, another version was taken down by Canaris, who hovered in the background, and used later to brief his *Abwehr* staff on the *Führer's* latest undertaking. As usual, the admiral made notes in his diary. Everything he worked for seemed in the process of collapse, yet he felt obliged to do his duty. This included complying with a mysterious order received from Keitel.

The *Abwehr* was ordered to provide Polish uniforms, identity papers and weapons for Operation 'Undertaking'. Keitel's order was delivered verbally on 17 August 1939; he seemed rather uncomfortable, but it was a Hitler order. The goods must be delivered to the SS as quickly as possible. Baffled, Canaris consulted with Pickenbrock and Lahousen, the latter having been promoted from his former employment in Vienna. These aides carried out their chief's instructions, and when Heydrich's SD man called he found everything ready for collection. He signed for the gear and took it away by truck to an SD depot. That was the end of the matter as far as Canaris was concerned, though his curiosity continued.

Naujocks was briefed by Heydrich on Operation 'Himmler'. His boss had told him of the extreme seriousness of the job in hand; they were to stage an incident, but if Naujocks allowed himself to be captured it would prove disastrous for him and Germany. Heydrich showed him a place called Gleiwitz on the border with Poland, asking if he felt confident enough to do the job. Naujocks assured him he would do his best, whereupon Heydrich said, 'You will do better than that, Alfred, I'm counting on you! Failure could ruin the efforts of thousands and bring disgrace on us.'

Heydrich saw one of his agents who had just returned from Poland. Otto Ulitz had been recruited six years before and had set up the so-called 'German Popular League for Polish Upper Silesia', responsible for various sub-groups which made alarmist agitations for union with the *Reich* in precisely the same way as had the 'intervention groups' in Austria and the Sudetenland. There had been constant demonstrations in the German-populated areas of Poland, and a stream of accusations had been made against the Poles alleging harassment, injustices and atrocities, most of which were untrue. These were reported to Berlin, where they were re-issued as dressed-up, virulent and anti-Polish propaganda, tales which the German people on the whole swallowed. It was Ulitz who briefed Naujocks on the zone of operations, also providing two technicians, a radio expert called Karl Berger, and Heinrich Neumann, who spoke Polish fluently. Two more SD men would complete the team.

The Naujocks group motored to Gleiwitz, booking into a hotel as 'mining engineers', and using false names when they signed in the hotel register. The staff believed they were in the region to do a survey and collect mineral rock specimens, with the local agent – Otto Ulitz – assisting them.

The successful launch of Hitler's invasion of Poland depended on the Gleiwitz incident, everything rested on the Naujocks team. Not until Heydrich signalled success to Himmler could the *Wehrmacht* begin its attack, which was scheduled to begin at dawn on 26 August. At Gleiwitz there existed a small radio station, and its prime staff of two Germans had been enrolled in the conspiracy and sworn to secrecy. Satisfied that all was in place, Naujocks returned to Berlin where Heydrich handed him a slip of paper bearing a message to be broadcast by 'Polish terrorists' from the radio station at Gleiwitz. The other essential ingredients for the operation were a few bodies which would be delivered before the action by the *Gestapo* chief Müller. Naujocks returned to Gleiwitz, where a message awaited him: it was from Müller, who asked him to rendezvous in Oppeln, fifty miles away. Naujocks complied, meeting him in a temporary *Gestapo* stelle and learning that one corpse would be delivered personally by him to Gleiwitz at 7.30 p.m. on 25 August. The body would appear to be a Polish soldier, in reality a Jew from a concentration camp. The 'Pole' would be killed in a gun battle with German police.

Müller then brought in Herbert Mehlhorn and Otto Rasch, who had been organising other 'incidents' along the border. Müller told them he had a dozen or so common criminals who were to be dressed in Polish outfits, killed and used as evidence of Polish 'guilt' in these incidents. The victims would be given fatal injections by a doctor before being shot in various places to simulate battle wounds. Naujocks would be given one body to deposit outside the Gleiwitz radio station; for this aspect of the operation they would use the code name 'Canned Goods'. Other 'goods' of the same nature were to be dropped off at Hochlinden and Pitschen.

On the evening of 21 August Hitler was in a state of increased nerves, as his juggling act with the other powers reached new heights of tension. He wished to confirm beyond doubt Soviet commitment to the partition of Poland, and had asked Stalin to receive his envoy to this end. Stalin kept the emissary waiting for hours, but agreement eventually came, and on learning this Hitler became ecstatic, crying out, 'We've won! Now we can spit in anybody's face!' Hitler's anxiety was unjustified, as Stalin was anxious to grab some spoils, especially from Poland. Hitler then called another conference, attended by one hundred generals and their aides, to inform them the attack on Poland would begin at dawn on 26 August.

At this juncture one of the SD agents heavily involved in the Nazi provocations got cold feet. Herbert Mehlhorn called Schellenberg, meeting him later to express his great apprehension over Hitler's decision to make war. Above all, he was nervous about the dark role he had been assigned by Heydrich, who Mehlhorn was convinced wanted him out of the way. According to his own later testimony, Schellenberg expressed amazement over the madness of the diabolical scheme hatched to take place as an excuse for aggression, apparently horrified by the use of concentration camp prisoners for such purpose. These feelings may have been genuine, it is hard to tell; certainly, Schellenberg could never himself have partaken in such shady work. 'Let Naujocks do it!' he told Mehlhorn. 'He's a thug!'

As the last days of peace slipped away the tension grew across Europe; German columns moved east to take up their jump-off stations. In neighbouring countries partial mobilization took place, President Roosevelt and the Pope called for peace talks, while Allied politicians talked and talked over what was to be done.

On 24 August the SS Commando groups were on standby. The night before, German Customs and Border Police, almost certainly SS men, raided a Polish outpost near Kattowice, shooting and creating mayhem. The next day, further incidents were staged along the frontier. Eight deaths and several injuries were reported on the German side after another skirmish at Bielitz. Hitler fumed, as part of his act, though his nerves were at breaking point. News from London numbed him, the Chamberlain government was now offering the Poles guarantees. Hitler called Keitel: could the German columns be halted? When the British ambassador, Sir Neville Henderson, called on Hitler it was to inform him his government had now concluded a treaty of alliance with Poland, France already having such an agreement and special ties with the country, chiefly through religion. Hitler was now left in no doubt that an attack on Poland would almost certainly mean war with the two main Western powers, even though von Ribbentrop assured him otherwise. The Allies, the Foreign Minister said, were decadent and bluffing, they would not fight for Poland. On the strength of such assurances Hitler called General Vormann: Plan White would commence the next day.

On receiving this news, Heydrich called his co-ordinator at Oppeln, Lieutenant-Colonel Hellwig, alerting him to three hours' notice. Hellwig informed Müller, who in turn ordered his men to get the concentration camp prisoners split into two groups; half would be dressed in German *Grenzschutz* (Border Police) uniforms, the rest as Poles. Three trucks stood ready to take the unfortunate victims to the action zones.

Meanwhile, Hitler tried to clear up final diplomatic hurdles, interviewing the French ambassador to assure him Germany did not want war. Then Hitler sent a letter to Mussolini explaining the inevitability of action in the face of Polish provocations, which brought a cold douche response from the Italian leader. Italy, Mussolini wrote, was not ready for war, and while he approved the pact with Stalin, he warned against misunderstandings with Japan – a curious diversion. He also irritated Hitler by asking for huge deliveries of raw materials, reminding him of their 'Pact of Steel', which specifically ruled out conflict – until at least 1942.

As Alfred Naujocks confessed in his lengthy sworn affidavits given to American interrogators following his desertion on 19 October 1944,

The radio station at Gleiwitz

Heydrich had told him that actual evidence was needed to show to the German and foreign Press. But, late in August 1939, the comings and goings of various diplomats in Berlin and Berchtesgarden, all trying to placate Hitler, had produced a delay to his plans. As a result, Naujocks spent fourteen days in all in Gleiwitz, waiting for the signal to go ahead. Much of that time was spent with his men in the Oberschlesischer Hotel, until at last the code word arrived from Heydrich to commence action. Proceeding that evening to the vicinity of the radio station, Naujocks waited until Müller drove up in a black Opel, one body being removed and laid on the ground. The victim was still alive, but had obviously been injected with something and had blood over his face. He was still wearing civilian clothes.

Naujocks then took his squad into the radio station, finding the two men on duty ready and compliant. The Polish speaker then yelled a short tirade into the microphone calling for war to begin between Poland and Germany. The squad then ran outside, firing off their pistols as they went. Years later, Naujocks would try to cash in on his claim as the 'man who started the war'.

Hitler had signed his first war directive that day, having covered himself with an alibi, Berlin Radio announcing his sixteen-point plan for negotiations to try and solve the German–Polish problem; to many his proposals seemed quite reasonable. But Hitler and his controlled media pretended that the Poles were refusing to negotiate. His timetable now ticked away like clockwork, the SD and *Gestapo* playing their parts in launching the war. At dawn German troops attacked, and at 10 a.m. Hitler addressed his mock 'parliament' in his final move to bamboozle them and the world. After describing all his tireless efforts to reach a settlement he said:

> For the first time Polish regulars fired into our territory, since 5.45 a.m. we have been returning the fire, and from now on bombs will be met with bombs!

His utterance was greeted by a storm of applause from the Nazi deputies, but in the streets of the capital crowds were noticeably absent. If Hitler had hoped for a throng similar to the grand and enthusiastic turnout on 4 August 1914 then he was greatly disappointed. Friday 1 September 1939 commenced quietly among the German population, who seemed strangely muted as the fateful news of a new war dawned across the nation. An American correspondent noted that there seemed to be few takers among the passers-by being offered papers by newsboys.

It took a further two days for Britain to act, Sir Neville Henderson arriving rather early on Sunday morning to hand over an ultimatum to von Ribbentrop, who was absent from his office in the Wilhelmstrasse. An aide called the interpreter, Dr Schmidt, who rushed from his office elsewhere, using the side door of the Foreign Ministry building to greet Sir Neville and receive his explosive document, which gave Hitler until 11 a.m. to issue withdrawal orders to his troops invading Poland or face war with Britain.

Heydrich arrives in Poland with an 'action group', September 1939

After the Britisher left, Schmidt hurried to Hitler's Chancellery, to find a number of officials hanging about anxiously in the corridor outside Hitler's study. Schmidt found Hitler seated at his desk, von Ribbentrop gazing out of the window. As Schmidt translated the British note, both men remained mute, Hitler's expression one of surprise and then gloom. At length, he looked somewhat accusingly at von Ribbentrop, saying simply, 'Well, what now?'

The man who had convinced his *Führer* the Allies were helpless looked distinctly uncomfortable, saying only that he supposed the French would follow suit. This they did, but not until some hours after the British ultimatum deadline had expired and both nations were at war with Germany.

Outside the room again, Schmidt saw Goering, who heard the news given the other officials. His reaction was, 'If we lose this war, God have mercy on us!'

After the British ultimatum had expired, von Ribbentrop saw Sir Neville Henderson in his office, to hand over a harsh and concocted German response containing all the familiar propaganda and lies. Henderson read through the catalogue of falsity, remarking that history would judge where the blame lay. Von Ribbentrop coldly retorted, 'History has already proved the facts'.

Sir Neville left sadly for his embassy, where his staff were already packing for home. The *Gestapo* and SD phone taps would soon be removed from the Allied embassies. Birger Dahlerus, ever hopeful and naïve to the last, continued his well-meant but futile efforts to avert catastrophe, appealing to Goering to fly to London in a 'past-midnight' attempt to stop hostilities between Britain and Germany. According to Dahlerus, agreement was obtained from Hitler, but nothing came of it since the British government told the Swede by telephone there was nothing more to discuss.

Hitler had warned his new Army Commander-in-Chief, von Brauchitsch, before the Polish campaign began, that the military must ignore security matters, which would be handled exclusively by the SIPO units. Within two days, Heydrich had set off for Polish territory with a hand-picked SS commando to organise the work of rounding up suspects. The campaign against the Jews would be a far bigger and lengthier process. Owing to the fierce fighting, considerable damage was being caused to Polish towns and cities, so that little was recovered in the way of documents by Heydrich. The Polish Intelligence system had worked well in Germany for years, as proved by the unmasking of just one of its star agents, Major Sosnowski. But it came to Heydrich's notice that there were those among the Polish spy staff who would be willing to co-operate in an anti-Soviet role; these officers Heydrich hoped to meet in Warsaw, though no actual arrangements had been made. However much the Poles detested the Germans, their hatred for the Soviets was even greater. Obviously, this was of great interest to Heydrich in his attempts to penetrate the USSR, which had so far proved largely abortive. As ever, he was anxious to beat Canaris to any intelligence loot in the Polish archives, though without help this did not seem likely. Above all, he wanted to get his hands on Polish data on the Soviets, on their agents in the West, and of course any Poles still at large in the *Reich.*

In 1941 the Nazis made great propaganda of their discovery of thousands of Polish corpses in the eastern part of the country overrun by the *Wehrmacht* after the attack against the Soviets in June. These were the remains of Polish officers and intelligentsia murdered by the Soviet secret police. Early in the Polish campaign in September 1939, Admiral Canaris attended conferences in Hitler's special command train, where the HQ unit was commanded by Erwin Rommel. Canaris told Keitel during one of these meetings that he was aware of 'extensive executions' planned by Hitler of the Polish aristocracy and ecclesiastics. The *Führer* had already told Brauchitsch that each Army district would be appointed its own civilian governor who would oversee such actions, which would be none of the Army's business. This murderous campaign would be termed Operation 'Spring Cleaning'. Keitel, responding to a warning from Canaris of the effects on foreign opinion, said the extreme measures had already been decided on by Hitler and Goering. Details of how this murder programme was to be carried out were arranged between SD and *Gestapo*. Before the end of September, the German Army and *Luftwaffe* had concluded its campaign in Poland; Stalin, surprised by the speed of the German victory, had hastened to rush his own troops into attacking in the East, and before long a programme very similar to Hitler's was under way beyond the demarcation line between the two armies. The Soviets 'secured' their areas of occupation by arresting many Poles in military and political life, and indeed others, for little or no known reason, who were either shot or deported to the East to face months of interrogations designed to force 'confessions' of anti-Soviet activity. Ironically, and even long after the Germans attacked them, the Soviets were slow to release Poles to fight the enemy, and then did not have the uniforms and equipment for such units. Numbers of these men, near physical and mental wrecks, were eventually released to the British via the Middle East, turned into soldiers and in many cases shipped back to England.

Warsaw, defended in the final days of the battle, had been bombed by the *Luftwaffe*. The Allies added these raids to a list of German aerial blitz atrocities. When Heydrich and his men arrived among the ruins they sought out the police headquarters and found some officers still present, but nothing turned up of value in the way of documents. However, one policeman told the Germans he knew the whereabouts of certain staff who would be willing to work with them against the Soviets. Thus began German–Polish co-operation, which, though proving fruitful, was uneasy from the start; Heydrich never trusted the Poles and suspected they knew far more than they disclosed. He never knew the extent of the Poles' contacts with the Allies, principally the British, both before his arrival and later. He certainly never suspected they had already smuggled a German Enigma code machine to the West.

It is perhaps tragic that better contacts with the Poles were not established by the British Secret Service, as the people under German and Soviet occupation could have provided a constant source of excellent information.

12

SD vs MI6

The British Secret Service in the thirties was commanded by Admiral Hugh Sinclair, officially CSS-Chief of Secret Service, and known in that body as 'C'. The actual running of MI6 was left to C's two executives: Colonel Valentine Vivian had served as a high-ranking officer in the Indian Police, while Colonel Claude Dansey was an ex-Territorial Army officer who entered the spy game after World War One. It would have surprised the British public to know that their own leadership was prey to rivalries and deceptions like the totalitarian regime of Adolf Hitler. The two chief executives of MI6 are recorded as having great distaste for each other – and rivals; in fact, it has also been recorded that the British Secret Service of that era was so locked in feud as to be paralysed.

While Colonel Claude Dansey has gone down in every record as someone of bad reputation, Colonel Valentine Vivian is noted as a rather gentle type. If so, then he was doomed when faced with the kind of Machiavellian character Dansey seems to have been. Amazingly, when Admiral Sinclair decided enough was enough, he dismissed Dansey from the Broadway (London SW) headquarters, permitting him only to call weekly to collect mail. What the *Abwehr* would have made of this situation is anyone's guess; knowing what we do of Dansey he would have exploited any attempt to use him to the full. Unabashed and a dedicated spymaster, Dansey obtained C's permission to set up an anti-German operation from the continent, at first starting up in Italy, but soon moving to Switzerland. In fact, the 'Z' organisation he began was a rival 'MI6', and he had enough contacts to establish British businessmen in legitimate commercial premises in Germany and the surrounding countries as fronts for espionage. They were provided with codes, cyphers and procedures quite separate from the official SIS run by Vivian from London. Indeed, very few SIS had any idea that the dismissed executive had set up on his own, as it were. Though this has a familiar ring to it, that of the agent thrown out of his own firm in order to lure the enemy into a trap, there seems little reason to doubt that the Secret Intelligence Service of Britain was fractured. Whether in the long run this proved wasteful and pointless is hard to say, but it seems so. One must assume that Dansey was still funded by London.

The Z organisation set to work, gaining success and losing agents. Canaris learned that some percentage of spies caught in the *Reich* belonged to some new network. Dansey used anyone he felt useful, not only pure businessmen, but foreigners and old hands innured and fascinated by the game. All the capital cities around the *Reich* held Z outposts, the most important being Copenhagen and the Hague in Holland. Two big networks were controlled from these locations, one dedicated to pure espionage, the other sabotage. But, in parallel with SIS, Dansey opted for the Hague as his chief base of operations, and, like his rivals, co-operated with Dutch Intelligence. In Holland he appointed an ex-Army captain as his chief player.

Sigismund Payton Best is said to have spent all his adult life spying, travelling to Holland in World War One and staying on later as a 'sleeper'. As cover he used the old ploy of an 'import-export' business, even taking on two Dutch partners and marrying a woman of that country who was the daughter of a retired admiral. He continued to be known as 'Captain Best', living and dressing like a gentleman, generally putting on a swell front. He became a well-known figure in the Hague and also well regarded for the excellent dinner parties and musical soirées laid on in his home. In short, he appeared to have settled down very nicely in Dutch life as a businessman-socialite – while his real occupation, carried on behind the façade of the 'Continental Trading Company', was spying on Germany. His spy rings operated quite independently of each other in the best security traditions. Best was regarded highly by his boss Dansey, who, whatever the seedier sides of his character, always remained loyal to his employees.

It is not without humour to record that not far from the Best spy HQ could be found (if one were in the know), the 'other' British spy service. Housed in one of the elegant streets near a canal this other espionage centre was under the command of Major Hugh Reginald Dalton, who employed about eleven top men under his roof, which like Best's HQ had its own radio room link to London. Dalton relied heavily on one man in his outfit, a Dutch ex-detective called Vrinten, who used a variety of aliases in his work and had his own front, a detective and credit bureau. Vrinten had very good connections, including old friends in the Dutch police and intelligence. Dalton placed his real trust in another Dutch-born assistant, mistakenly as it turned out. John 'Jack' Hooper had become a naturalised Briton and would prove one of the worst weaknesses in the British set-up.

The SIS in Holland and particularly the post in the Hague functioned well, with results coming in and some promising leads opening up among anti-Nazi candidates in Germany. Then disaster struck, which ultimately ruined the British spy networks in Holland and Germany.

On 4 September 1936 Major Dalton shot himself, and when an SIS team arrived hotfoot from London to investigate they discovered the station chief had put his hand in the till. London had, as part of government policy, sent the SIS in the Hague a large sum of money to fund investigation and subversion of illegal Jewish attempts to smuggle refugees to Palestine, this itself inciting even more friction with the Arabs. It was a not unfamiliar story, though the spy chief should have known better: he had acquired an expensive girl friend and had been using the special fund to lavish her with whatever kept her favours.

The 'Passport Control Officer' sent to replace Dalton seemed eminently suited to the task of propping up the shaky SIS HQ in the Hague. He was already married to a Dutchwoman and spoke her language fluently. But by early 1937 he had proved himself unsuitable, in turn being replaced by Major Richard Henry Stevens, who was another old India hand and fluent in German, French and Russian. But he was new to secret operations on the continent, more used to dealing with difficult tribal chieftains on the north-west frontier of India. His chief in London told him nothing of the parallel British spy net operating from Holland.

Best took his post just as things started to hot up. Hitler was inaugurating his campaign of agitation in Austria, and more and more British spies were starting work on the continent, in Czechoslovakia, Poland, France, in the USSR and of course in Germany itself. The Germans executed spies caught even in peacetime, unlike Britain, and of six charged in 1936, four had been working for the British. But the top *Abwehr* investigators, Commander Protze and Captain von Feldmann, failed to discover any more about this fresh employer – until that summer, when one Gustav Hoffmann was caught taking photographs in a prohibited zone near Magdeburg. He confessed to receiving orders from a Dutchman who worked for the British in Holland. A few months later, Richard Lange was also arrested by the *Abwehr* and proved to be working for the same source. This arrest proved to be the big lead Canaris had been waiting for.

The British had been working true to form, like the *Abwehr*, paying most agents small sums to spy for them and never using the £60,000 allocated for action against the Jewish Zionists. Richard Lange had grown sick of British parsimony, and following his complaints the Dutchman Vrinten had made the big mistake of introducing him to his boss Major Dalton, who of all people should have known better. Obviously the British station boss was defective in various ways. By the time Lange was in German custody he knew much of the British Secret Service set-up in Holland, and specifically at the Hague. But Captain von Feldmann travelled to that city rather late; Dalton was dead.

While Claude Dansey's staff knew him as 'Uncle Claude', Canaris called his star agent Richard Protze 'Uncle Richard'. Protze was by then in his sixties, but Canaris sent him to tackle the big job in Holland. The ex-navy man had actually 'resigned' from Section IIIF of the *Abwehr* to enter Holland, ostensibly on a private visit with 'Aunt Lena', as she was known in that service. She used the alias *Fraulein* Schneider. Despite the leads gained, it was six months before Protze began to make any real headway.

First, Protze found he was being tailed, quite brazenly, by a young man with a bicycle. This went on for several days, and obviously one of the 'enemy' spy organisations in the Hague knew of his arrival, but whether it

'Uncle' Claude Dansey set up his own spies

was the British, French, Polish or Soviet he had no idea. Finally, Protze arranged a little confrontation. Turning on the youth, he threatened to call the police, and right then a 'Dutch policeman' just happened on the scene – in reality a disguised German agent.

This proved a fantastic coup for the *Abwehr*, for the Dutchman was van Koutrick, one of the men employed by the British. From then on he worked for the Germans, who paid him double and found out all they needed to know. Richard Protze learned that there was a traitor working among the German diplomat staff in the Hague. Despite his experience and ability, Protze now made a stupid error, informing the German ambassador, who was naturally shocked. He in turn, incredibly, assembled all his staff to convey the terrible news – one of them was a traitor. *Herr* zu Pulitz was well warned and soon spirited out of the country by his employers, the British. This incident was one of several recorded later in the diary of Dr Goebbels to lambast the German diplomats.

Now the *Abwehr* began photographing everyone who came and went at the British SIS HQ of Major Stevens, identifying them all with the help of van Koutrik. Captain von Feldmann was called in to assist in the operation, as with great daring the German agents hired a barge, cruising up and down the canal near the SIS building before anchoring nearby to observe and film at leisure. It was the start of a string of further German triumphs through the *Abwehr* which proved how their enemy the British had underestimated them.

It was the Danes, however, who now became agitated over the number of spies operating in their country. They started a clampdown, capturing two agents they assumed to be working for the Germans, startled to find their employers were the British. Once more the *Abwehr* triumphed, for although the two spies were taken to court and tried in secret, the Germans had help in the Danish administration and obtained copies of the two men's confessions. Canaris now learned the great extent of British spying operations throughout Scandinavia.

Meanwhile in Holland, van Koutrick was still employed by the British, but telling the Germans all they needed to know, having been won over completely by the *Abwehr*. He was in fact an impressionable youth, enjoying the game and earning good money, completely oblivious to the harm that resulted. He would live to express his regrets in older age. Every time an agent left the SIS Hague station on a job it became known to the *Abwehr*, so it was not long before Major Stevens and his staff realised their schemes were going wrong. However, there was worse to come.

The late Major Dalton had been rumbled by his aide Jack Hooper and forced to cut him in on his racket. But Hooper was weak and confessed his part to the investigators from London, who instead of getting rid of him 'for good', as Claude Dansey suggested (Hooper was now a tremendous risk), simply gave him the sack, on the orders of Colonel Vivian. Protze heard all about it from his man in the SIS, van Koutrick, so he started to hunt for Hooper, who had remained in Holland. It was the reliable sleuthing of van Koutrick who ran their quarry to earth in Rotterdam. He fixed up a meeting with Protze.

Hooper, devious and realising what was afoot, told Protze plenty, but retained a few gems in order to extract more cash from the Germans later. Out of a job, he intended to spin out his usefulness as long as possible. But now Richard Protze brought in a new man, one who would repeatedly prove his worth to his *Abwehr* bosses.

Captain Hermann Giskes was an ex-World War One Army captain, turned wine salesman when the conflict ended. In 1937 he rejoined the German Army, went into the *Abwehr* and now took over the Hooper case. The Dutch-Englishman's usefulness continued into 1939, but by April Giskes knew the turncoat was stringing him along, elaborating on old data or inventing new. The German gave him short shrift, whereupon Hooper pulled out his last nugget, telling Giskes about the most important British spy in the *Reich* – a 'Dr K'. The man was actually a German ex-naval officer and engineer the British had 'rescued' from unemployment in 1919 – he had spied for them ever since. Dr K was so successful he had moved freely in German business circles and had been elected into the Federation of German Industries. Captain Giskes was so amazed and hooked by what he heard that he at once offered Hooper ten thousand Dutch guilders (in sterling), half in advance, for the master spy's capture.

Dr K was traced and put under surveillance. His mail was opened and his telephone tapped – but nothing incriminating came to light. The light dawned when Protze mentioned Dr K's visits to a villa at Scheveningen in Holland to his man van Koutrick, who at once told him it was the home of August de Fremery, a Belgian, who worked for the British in the Hague under the name Captain Hendricks. Dr K, actually Otto Krueger, was arrested on 7 July 1939 in Hamburg and confessed all. His long career was over.

Before long every British-run spy in Germany was either dead or awaiting execution. The No. 1 British network lay in ruins.

When war came in September, Claude Dansey was forced to order Captain Best to move in with the SIS HQ in the Hague, while he himself moved from Brussels to London. For Dansey, things also continued to go wrong, for his men in the Hague were obliged to try and work with the 'official' SIS and use their radio communication set-up. Van Koutrick discovered all of this and passed it on to the *Abwehr*, who now learned to their great interest the existence of the Z network and about its boss Dansey. It had taken 'Uncle Claude' six long years of patient labour to build up his organisation, but within a comparatively short time it was collapsed by the Germans. It was the worst disaster in British Secret Service history, directly due to the two traitors van Koutrick and Hooper, but basically due to weakness in the British organisation itself.

These climaxes, worthy of any spy thriller, occurred during the so-called 'Phoney War', quite outside public knowledge. British naïvety would now lead the SIS into its final disaster of the period.

In a further twist, Jack Hooper, having given his new employer, the *Abwehr*, the last he had to offer, and been handsomely paid, decided to play a change of heart and returned to the British fold. He had of course been dismissed, but now evidently felt he had in turn information to offer his old bosses, who would hopefully pardon him and give him a fresh start. The ineptitude of Major Stevens shows again. He swallowed Hooper's tale of having 'played a little ball' with the *Abwehr*, forgave him and decided to plot the kidnapping of Captain Giskes, using of course Hooper as bait. Hooper had not quite cut off his link with the German, and let him know he now had something so big they must meet. Giskes arranged to visit Holland again. However, once again the fly in the ointment ruined the British scheme; van Koutrick blew it to the Germans so that Richard Protze, fearing the worst, sent an urgent message warning Giskes not to attend the rendezvous. It should be realised that the meeting place was of course in neutral Holland, and carrying out a kidnapping would have affronted the authorities of most such countries. But the British were unlikely to get into difficulties over such an incident, as they had the best of connections, despite a large fascist faction and allies of the Germans in Holland.

In this tense drama, Protze's urgent warning arrived too late to stop Giskes travelling by train to Holland, but he was traced at the last moment on the border at Enschede and abandoned his intended meeting with Hooper.

This failed British plot to catch a star German agent would be followed by a counter-plot by the enemy – one that succeeded and smashed home further nails into the coffin of British Intelligence on the continent.

Reinhard Heydrich's great chance to cross swords with MI6 came quite early in the war. It is interesting to conject just what might have developed in the Venlo affair, had Hitler not intervened.

Pre-war surveillance of British diplomatic and military staffs in Germany had enabled the German security services to discover which men were engaged in subversive activities, that is, espionage of one kind or another. Similar surveillance, though on a far lesser scale, was carried out in the larger neutral countries, particularly in Spain, Portugal, Sweden and Holland. From his agents, Heydrich learned of British methods, how SIS agents worked under diplomatic cover to develop and maintain trade and military contacts. He became certain that in Germany itself British spies were gathering information from Germans befriended in the course of duty and off-duty hours. It was, however, in Holland that Heydrich achieved his first great success against the British in the world of spying.

By the autumn of 1939 the SD had succeeded in buying several Dutch informers in the police force, among them detectives, one or more already engaged to some degree in working with, or being well aware of, British Secret Service activities in their country. It was this kind of activity which Hitler forwarded as one excuse for invading Holland the next year. Heydrich discovered a British spy net operating against the *Reich* from over the border. His Dutch contacts were able to point out certain buildings in prominent locations used by the SIS as HQs and radio stations for contact with London. Heydrich had everyone entering these premises photo-graphed, and with the help of his informers pinpointed which were agents. For the moment, since Holland was still neutral, he could do no more than that. For their part, the British had no idea their cover had been blown, and that they had been identified as spies.

The British Secret Service, according to some opinions, declined in quality, widespread though its work still was. Largely recruited through the 'old boy' and university system, it had been taken over by Steward Menzies after the death of the old 'C', his deputy, the coldly efficient, one hundred per cent spymaster, Claude Dansey. Dansey had coveted the top job. He was ambitious, fanatical, and had, as shown, set up his own spy net before the war. If Steward Menzies ever suspected Dansey's 'other', second-line

Stewart Menzies, head of Britain's SIS

outfit, he did nothing, judging by available evidence. Dansey was by far the biggest driving force in MI6, and by 1945 had earned himself the most unflattering terms, vitriolic comments from well-known names who had occasion to work with him or brush past him in some way. Most probably such men were not of the same ruthless and utterly dedicated breed as Dansey; even so, there is no doubt he was a very cunning and dangerous man.

It was not two of Dansey's spies but regular SIS officers who became trapped in an SD web in Holland. In this amazing and even amusing tale Walter Schellenberg came to the fore, thrust into the field by Heydrich. He was completely suited in one sense to the double-dealing which preceded the kidnapping of the two British spies from neutral territory, but out of his depth in the hot action which ensued.

According to his own account later, Schellenberg had been touring the Ruhr, scenting out and unmasking one or two spies. Sent for by his chief in Berlin, he was surprised and excited to learn he would now get the chance to enter the real spy world as a genuine counter-espionage agent. To do this he needed to adopt an alias, but first, Heydrich briefed him on certain other matters. This was new to Schellenberg, for Heydrich never divulged matters of no concern to others in his organisation.

Schellenberg learned of an ex-Czech agent, actually a German and an ex-Hamburg policeman suborned by the Czechs, who had somehow reached London to play a double game, passing his hosts and French Intelligence true but innocuous pieces of information. The man used various aliases, Moertz, Michelsen or Fischer, and had belonged to Otto Strasser's Black Front movement and had escaped to Switzerland following the Roehm affair. He proved very useful to the Czechs, who passed him on to the British. When Heydrich heard Moertz had gone to Prague, he used a Czech to try and locate him, a racing car champion and ex-officer thrown out of the Czech Army for fraud. Having been snapped up by the SD, Heydrich was delighted when the man managed to find Moertz, who was snatched back into the *Reich* by SD agents – in fear of his life as a traitor. But he had a wife and loved the good life, and once interviewed by Heydrich he soon jumped at a way to save his skin, being registered in the SD files as agent F479.

In the summer of 1939, Moertz, kept under watch, was despatched back into Holland under orders to renew his spy contacts, particularly among the Czechs, who had themselves set up an organisation in that country, liaising closely with the British. Moertz, inevitably, came into contact with two British agents, Major Stevens and Captain Payne Best, who sent one of their Czechs to meet the German and generally sound him out. Major Bartik travelled from London, met Moertz and distrusted him from the start, believing he was a double agent, and broke off contact at once. The British agents disagreed with his assessment, but failed to convince Major Bartik.

Heydrich had other irons in the same fire. His promising agent Dr Helmut Knochen had also succeeded in making contact with the two British agents, sparking their interest and belief by posing as an anti-Nazi in touch with a group of officer dissidents in the *Wehrmacht*. The two Britons, meantime, had taken Moertz back to London where they again failed to convince Major Bartik of his usefulness. Moertz was allowed back to Holland, from where he at once returned to Germany to report. Heydrich ordered him to continue his work of deceiving the British, by confirming the tale told by Knochen, 'beefing it up' by telling them he was in touch with a certain Captain Schaemmel of the German Army transport service. Schaemmel, so Heydrich briefed Moertz, was a member of the same group anxious to get rid of Hitler; they wanted contact with the British government for support. The upshot of all this was a promise by Moertz to try and arrange a meeting between the German officer and the two British agents.

During his own briefing, Schellenberg asked if Captain Schaemmel worked for the SD. He was amazed by Heydrich's reply: he, Schellenberg, was 'Schaemmel' – he would be the one to meet the British spies.

Heydrich went on to explain that he suspected there really was a conspiracy among certain German generals, and by leading on the British the SD could well end up entrapping both sides. In any case, there was nothing to lose in the game. It was mid-October. Heydrich passed all the papers over to Schellenberg, who went off in excitement to study them in his own office. He was now twenty-nine years old, had served five years in the Nazi Secret Service, and at last stood at the top, ready and willing to step into the big league of spying. Schellenberg sat down to peruse the file, learning at once that 'Captain Schaemmel' was real and serving in Poland. There was one detail, the man wore a monocle; Schellenberg decided that if he was to masquerade as this officer then he too must adopt such an appendage. His natural vanity touched, he began imagining himself into the part.

The SD had set up a special headquarters base in the Ruhr, actually in Düsseldorf. It was a large villa with several bedrooms, complete with various equipment such as cameras, radios and recorders, a laboratory and a direct line to Berlin. Schellenberg discovered all this when he arrived in company with SS Colonel Christensen at the SD villa, just as a teleprinter was being installed. That evening, a message arrived from Heydrich: 'Captain Schaemmel' was to meet the two British agents at Zutphen in Holland next day. A black Buick would pick him up at the Issel bridge. He had *carte blanche* to conduct 'negotiations' with Stevens and Best, but was to proceed with caution.

Next morning, Schellenberg and his companion, the SS colonel, made careful checks of their outfits and passports before setting off by car in the rain for Holland. There was no problem with formalities on the German side of the frontier, but once past the barrier the Dutch customs officers checked their car over thoroughly before allowing them to proceed. When they reached the River Issel they found the Buick already in place on the bridge. Trembling slightly with nervous excitement, Schellenberg left his car and strolled across to the Buick. Introducing himself to the only man in the car as Captain Schaemmel, he learned the driver was Captain Best.

Major Richard Stevens and Captain Payne Best

Schellenberg got into the Buick and they drove away, Christensen following in their own vehicle. Best conversed easily in excellent German. Schellenberg, warming to his part, joined in to chat on a variety of topics, especially music, learning that Best played the violin 'reasonably well'. If only Heydrich were present, the German thought, knowing of his chief's passion for that instrument.

No mention was made of the purpose of the meeting, and on reaching Arnhem they met Major Stevens and a Dutch lieutenant called Coppens. These two climbed into the rear seat. The talks then got under way as they drove off through the flat countryside. Schellenberg tried hard to keep his wits about him, alert to every possibility, especially of the British playing a double game. He wondered if Moertz had betrayed them and if he would be taken back to England as a prisoner. His worst problem proved to be keeping the troublesome monocle in place; he had been startled to find Captain Best also wore one.

Schellenberg told his hosts he knew the name of the German general leading the conspiracy against Hitler, but he was not yet at liberty to divulge his identity. The dissidents were ready to kill their *Führer* and sign a peace deal with the Allies. In reply, the two Britons told him their government was very interested and anxious to prevent the war spreading further. The two were in direct contact with the Foreign Office in London and would soon be able to give a binding commitment to the German dissidents.

The meeting seemed to be a great success to both sides, each believing in the bona fides of the other, only the two Germans enjoying the charade for what it was. When they separated it was in agreement to meet again at the Hague on 30 October. The two SD agents then drove back to Düsseldorf, where Schellenberg telephoned Heydrich in Berlin. Delighted, Heydrich told Schellenberg to go ahead and pursue the negotiations in such a way that the British would be convinced in what they wanted to believe, a definite conspiracy against Hitler and a real chance of an end to the war. This belief would, Heydrich explained, help to lull the Allies into a sense of false security and unreadiness for the blow the *Führer* planned against them.

As it happened, Prime Minister Chamberlain had made a speech on 12 October, certain phrases of which indicated to Heydrich that the British were indeed assuring support to any group who toppled Hitler. In this connection, 'Captain Schaemmel's' approaches seemed to be exactly what the British government wanted to hear; they were ready and willing (especially Chamberlain) to clutch at any straw which offered hope of ending the war which could prove so costly to Britain and its Empire. In fact, whatever the British wanted to believe, and whatever Heydrich and the *Gestapo* suspected, there was a real conspiracy against Hitler among certain German generals. But, as Canaris thought, they had missed their best chance, and further designs in this direction in 1939 came to nothing. Plainly, the leading professionals among the *Wehrmacht* were incapable of organising such a coup efficiently. In their jobs they proceeded with the assurance which came from many years of training and experience, but in the field of subversion and conspiracy they were complete amateurs. Moreover, some, if not all, felt constrained by not only their 'gentlemanly' code of military ethics, but their oath of allegiance to Hitler.

Through the rest of October, Walter Schellenberg mulled over his own ideas for dangling tempting bait before the British. When he went horse-riding in Berlin he was accompanied by a friend, Professor Max von Crinis, a psychiatrist at the Charite Hospital. An Austrian, von Crinis was clever and very friendly. He was a reserve medical colonel in the Army and SS. Schellenberg had some inspiration: trusting his friend completely, he confided the matter in hand with the British agents. Amazed and flattered to be so trusted, von Crinis was also amused, then astounded when his friend proposed that the Austrian join the charade as a leading participant. Suppose he adopted the part of a right-hand man to the general leading the conspiracy? Von Crinis seemed ideal for such a role, as he had both breeding and military bearing and could easily pass himself off as a conservative Prussian staff officer. Laughing and excited by this prospect, von Crinis agreed; it sounded like a singular adventure, and the fact of the *Führer's* approval of the game impressed him tremendously.

As a result of these new arrangements, when Schellenberg and Christensen next set off to meet the British they were accompanied by Max von Crinis. All went well until they reached the agreed rendezvous, the crossroads at Arnhem – the two Britons did not show up. Following almost a whole hour of anxious waiting, they were approached by two Dutch policemen, who after some preliminary questioning invited the three to drive to the nearest police station. Surprised and irritated, the Germans felt the game was up – the British and their Dutch collaborators must have rumbled them.

In the police station the policemen proceeded to search the Germans' toilet kit. Just in time, Schellenberg noticed Colonel Christensen's phial of aspirins, which still bore an *SS Sanität* label. Unnoticed, he swiftly moved his own toilet case forward, snatched the aspirins from beneath it and put them in his pocket. The Dutchmen never noticed.

Then, as if on cue, the Dutch Lieutenant Coppens hurried into the room. After a brief word with the policemen, he began apologising to the Germans, who were at once taken outside to find the two British agents waiting in their own car. They offered profound apologies, telling the Germans they had been to the wrong crossroads. Schellenberg guessed it had all been a ploy, the enemy was being careful.

At the Hague the Britons led their contacts into a building Schellenberg assumed to be the British spy HQ. Seated round a table, they began the negotiations, which from the Germans' side included the standard demands, the return of former colonies, etc., Schellenberg emphasising that this was a necessary 'safety valve' for the surplus German population. The

'compression' of Western and Eastern frontiers would continue to consti-
tute an element of danger in Central Europe. It was in fact the old Hitler
cry and ploy for *Lebensraum* – 'living space' for the large German population that had already spilled over into Eastern states. In exchange,
Germany promised a return to the gold standard and a withdrawal of
German forces from Austria, Czechoslovakia and Poland. It was all fiction,
part of the game played by Schellenberg to impress the two enemy agents.

The discussion went on for over three hours, until at last Major Stevens
excused himself 'to call London', returning soon to inform the Germans he
had received approval, but needed further instructions from Lord Halifax.
Schellenberg, while pleased with himself, felt exhausted and suffered (he
told himself) from the effects of too many strong English cigarettes. He
pleaded a migraine and retired to the bathroom, where Captain Best
discovered him having a refreshing wash and trying to adjust his monocle.
Best enquired if he always wore one. Schellenberg laughed, parrying this
by returning the question. It passed off in easy bonhomie.

The Germans were next driven to the home of a Dutchman, being shown
to three bedrooms which served as guest accommodation. Then the Britons
took them on to another substantial house where Captain Best introduced
a woman as his wife. She was, it transpired, the daughter of a retired Dutch
Admiral. Then Heydrich's agent Moertz (F479) arrived, and the whole
party sat down to a sumptuous meal which included succulent oysters.
Schellenberg was thoroughly enjoying himself, noting how well his friend
von Crinis was playing his part to perfection. The guests gained a clear
picture of how the British regarded the war, which, if it continued, they
would fight to the end, even from Canada if necessary – should England
be invaded.

After spending a night at their lodgings, the visitors were taken the next
morning to yet another British base, in the premises of the Dutch
Commerce Bank. It was then that the Germans were even more astounded
to be handed a transceiver and code book with which to contact the British
agents in the Hague. By this method they could fix another rendezvous. That day, Captain Best saw them off at the frontier, shaking
hands with them and watching them drive back into the *Reich* in high
fettle. Schellenberg returned in triumph to Berlin to make his report to
Heydrich.

His chief's congratulations were muted. Heydrich had begun to smell a
trap, it all seemed too good to be true. How could the world's oldest and
greatest spy service fall for such a ploy? Schellenberg was ordered back to
Düsseldorf to await further instructions; Heydrich decided to consult
Himmler, and if need be the *Führer*. Schellenberg felt deflated, as he had
by now dreamed up a grander, even bolder scheme. He proposed asking
the British agents to take him to London to meet more important people.
But Heydrich would not hear of it, such an idea was far too dangerous; he
also believed it possible that Schellenberg might become lulled by life in

London into changing sides. In any case, once the British had him in their hands in England anything was possible. For his part, Schellenberg had so relished the game and his leading role that his mind raced ahead, exploring many new possibilities.

A few days later, the SD in Düsseldorf established contact with the British in the Hague by radio, and over the following days Major Stevens called back to try and arrange another meeting. Schellenberg was obliged to stall, having received no further instructions from Berlin. Growing impatient, he decided to go ahead on his own initiative, agreeing to meet the two British agents at a café over the frontier by the River Meuse.

One of Major Stevens's important allies in Holland was another Czech Intelligence officer; Colonel Alois Frank had received a good deal of help from the British. When he next met Stevens in a café in Leyden he was surprised by his ally's disclosures on the negotiations in progress with German dissidents. Major Stevens seemed to have complete faith in the people he had met. Frank listened in silence as Stevens told all, emphasising that a complete cessation of hostilities was at stake. It was a major move, the Czech could see that Stevens was agog with excitement and hope – he was in the thick of great events. Frank advised caution, suggesting the

Cafe Backhus, Venlo, site of the kidnapping

rendezvous be changed to a place further from the German border. Stevens seemed put out, assuring the Czech that security would be well handled by Lieutenant Coppens. As one historian has commented, Major Stevens allowed himself to be hoodwinked 'like a child falling into the hands of brigands'.

The two British agents met Schellenberg and his men at the Café Backhus near Venlo on 7 November. The Britons were disappointed to learn that 'the opposition general has been unable to get away from his duties in Berlin'. Major Stevens pressed the Germans to bring the general along the next day, Schellenberg agreeing to do his best. On arrival back in Düsseldorf, he called Heydrich urgently to explain the situation and request orders. These were not forthcoming, Heydrich telling him that the *Führer* had now turned sour on the scheme. There would be no visits to London by Schellenberg or a bogus general; neither did Hitler care to further any talk of a *Putsch* by his General Staff. The *Führer* was scheduled to attend the annual 9 November anniversary meeting at the Munich Burgerbraukeller, and if need be Heydrich would pass further orders following his return to Berlin.

Schellenberg had to be satisfied with that. He would have to improvise, yet had no notion that the whole situation was about to be snatched from his jurisdiction by a totally unexpected event.

By the morning of 9 November, Schellenberg had not only decided to continue the game in Holland, he had also found another player. This man was willing to play the part of 'the general', the alleged leader of the conspiracy to kill Hitler. The new entrant was an industrialist, and like von Crinis also held an honorary SS rank. Leaving this man behind, Schellenberg again went with Christensen to meet the British agents, and once at the café in Venlo assured Stevens and Best that all was well, the general was about to make himself available.

But, back again in Düsseldorf a surprise awaited him, and not one Schellenberg enjoyed. Heydrich, alerted that Schellenberg was getting too involved, had despatched Alfred Naujocks to take charge of security and more. Briefed for the first time on what was afoot, Naujocks was astonished and even more so when his boss told him to generally oversee the business and make sure Schellenberg did nothing rash – such as departing for London with the two enemy agents. On reaching Düsseldorf again, Schellenberg was taken by surprise when Naujocks appeared with a posse of SS toughs. He was also flattered to think Heydrich valued him and wished to ensure his safety. That evening, however, he preferred to dine with his original team, and included the new recruit who was to play 'the general', going over his plans and rehearsing their respective roles.

That night, Schellenberg slept soundly, until jerked rudely awake by the insistent jangling of the telephone. The caller was none other than Himmler himself, who told him there had been an explosion in the Munich beer cellar the previous evening. By extraordinary good fortune, the *Führer* had

Georg Elser, 'bomb plotter'?

completed his speech and just left the building and was safe – others among his comrades had not been so lucky.

The origins of this event, perhaps the first real attempt to assassinate Hitler, had come about in the summer of that year, when an apparently innocuous German carpenter and clockmaker named Georg Elser had been arrested by the *Gestapo* as a communist and thrown into a concentration camp. Then, late in October, he was sent for by the camp commandant to be interviewed by two men in civilian clothes (*Gestapo* agents), who took him into a private room to offer concessions and freedom in a new life in Switzerland if he co-operated. Elser was mystified, but agreed, and at once his way of life in the camp was improved. Then the same two men returned, taking him by car to the beer cellar in Munich where he was shown the podium where Hitler spoke each 9 November. Elser was ordered to construct a time bomb, fixed to a pillar near the podium and set to explode at a precise moment. They assured Elser the *Führer* would escape the blast and remain safe, and that it was not a real assassination attempt. He need know no more.

By the evening of 8 November, Elser was taken to the beer hall by the two *Gestapo* men, carrying the time bomb he had made with the materials provided. The beer hall staff were dismissed, and the *Gestapo* men helped Elser to fix the bomb into a cavity cut into a pillar. It contained enough explosive to cause considerable damage.

Curiously, Hitler left early after making a shorter speech than usual on the evening of 9 November. He hurried away from the building and was on his train when the bomb exploded, killing and injuring a number of Nazi comrades and causing much damage.

Hitler speaks in the
Munich beer cellar,
9 November 1939

Meanwhile, Georg Elser had been escorted to the border by the *Gestapo*, who gave him money, a passport – and significantly – a picture postcard of the Munich beer cellar. Elser pocketed the items and was about to cross over into Switzerland when the Germans arrested him and took him away. That night, Hitler raged, asserting the British Secret Service had tried to kill him, but that Providence had spared him for the work to be done. *The two British agents in Holland were to be seized at once!*

Germany and indeed the whole world heard the amazing news that Hitler had survived an assassination attempt. But at once conjecture arose – who had planted the bomb? Why had Hitler so uncharacteristically left the beer hall early? It all smelled rather fishy.

Then came the dramatic news of Elser's arrest, a known Bolshevik who

177

The beer cellar was severely damaged

tried to murder the *Führer*, and following interrogation his version of how he came to make the attempt became known. It differed markedly from the account given above, which was told to one of the British agents in a prison camp. According to the tale printed in German newspapers, Elser confessed that as a communist it was his duty to try and kill Hitler. He had made a bomb entirely on his own initiative, and the security police had traced the sources of the materials he used. There was no one else involved. Elser, so the papers alleged, had been caught trying to flee into Switzerland.

If all that were true, then Georg Elser would have been tried and executed in short order. Instead, he was given a comparatively easy life in a prison camp, only being executed on Himmler's orders in the very last days of the war. It seemed he knew too much. The 'bomb plot' of 9 November 1939 had been a contrived attempt by Hitler and the *Gestapo* 'to improve the *Führer*'s popularity and depict him as the God-protected saviour of Germany', as one historian saw it. Although no evidence to prove either version is available, there seems no reason to doubt the story which emerged via the SIS agents who survived the war.

However, the explosion in Munich put paid to Schellenberg's masquerade. Himmler ordered the kidnapping of the two SIS agents from Holland. Naujocks and his squad would prove indispensable, as there was no way Schellenberg could carry out such an operation, and this he knew as he went at once to waken his protector. But Naujocks, amazed, expressed scepticism that the job could be done. Nevertheless, orders were orders, and next morning Schellenberg left with his own team for Venlo, Naujocks and the SS squad following in two cars forty-five minutes later. They had worked out a plan: Schellenberg would wait for the two Britons, but get clear once the action started. Fearful of shooting and to prevent any chance of misidentification, he had paraded himself before the SS toughs before leaving, to ensure they would not confuse him with Captain Best, who would also be wearing a monocle. The chance of a gun battle had to be taken, and the rumpus that would surely follow such flagrant violation of Dutch neutrality.

All went well. On reaching the German side of the frontier Naujocks briefed the elderly Customs officer to stay clear. He then took his two cars just past the barrier, half concealing them behind a building, and well short of Café Backhus. Schellenberg had not taken his 'general' or von Crinis with him; there was no longer any point. He entered the café and sat down with Colonel Christensen to wait for the Britons' arrival. And wait they did, with no sign of the enemy – but an unusual number of Dutchmen, including some policemen with dogs. The situation began to look very tricky, and the Germans' anxiety grew. Then, an hour late, Schellenberg spotted the familiar black American car appear outside. He stood up and went to the door of the café with his companion.

This was the signal for the Naujocks squads to act. The SS men leapt from their vehicles, dashing forward and brandishing pistols. As Naujocks led his men to wrench open the doors of the Britons' car, the Dutch Lieutenant Coppens appeared, drew his own gun and opened fire. The SS fired back and Coppens slumped to the ground. Stevens and Best were dragged out of the car, stupefied by the suddenness of it all. Schellenberg's impressions were blurred, it seemed like a few action-packed seconds. It was terrifying for him as he ran off towards the SS cars – only to be grabbed by one of the Naujocks squad who pointed a pistol at him. Schellenberg thought his last moment had come, as the SS man seemed in the wild confusion to have mistaken him for Captain Best, just as he feared. But, suddenly, the man's pistol barrel was knocked aside by his superior. With yells and curses the two British agents were dragged across to the SS vehicles and thrown inside. Schellenberg managed to pull himself together and regain his own car, driving off in great haste and leaving Naujocks to follow as best he could before the Dutch reacted more violently.

By the time the Naujocks squads drove off there were Dutch people hurling insults at them. When they reached the German Customs officer he appeared shaken and begged Naujocks to leave some men to protect him from Dutch reprisals. Two of the SS men stayed with him.

The SS teams returned in triumph with their prisoners to Düsseldorf, and within hours the Dutch government had launched strong protests to Berlin over the incident. Naujocks, perhaps without thinking, had taken the wounded Dutch lieutenant with him. He was hurried to a German hospital, but died that night. Major Stevens and Captain Best were taken to Berlin and at first interviewed separately by Müller, then Heydrich, who used an interpreter since both prisoners refused to speak German. At first, Heydrich confined his comments to advising the pair he was well aware of their activities in Holland, they had been followed and photographed. Smiling, he told them to forget about any military conspiracy to kill Hitler, it was mere wishful thinking on their part. He also told them that though they had been taken from neutral territory, they were still spies acting against the interests of the *Reich*. However, because of the unusual circumstances they would not be tried and executed, he had the *Führer*'s word on that.

Later, Heydrich questioned them on the British Secret Service in general, surprising them by his apparent knowledge of its operations on the continent. He assured them that all their agents were known and either about to be arrested or kept under close surveillance – 'at our convenience'. Heydrich wanted to squeeze everything of use out of them, but without any rough stuff; these were not any old 'Bolshevik' or *Untermensch* spies, but obvious English gentlemen of His Majesty's Secret Service. He therefore invited them to dine with him, and so well did the atmosphere progress during the general conversations that both Britons became most talkative. They had got over the shock of being violently kidnapped, perhaps surprised and relieved by their treatment once in Germany. They certainly found the Nazi spy chief most friendly, quite cultured in fact. In truth, Heydrich had nothing against them, and struck up a real rapport with Captain Best through their common love of music and violin playing.

After the war, when writing his memoirs, Payne Best submitted that though they had talked, the Germans seemed to know it all anyway. This was not of course strictly true, though both *Abwehr* and SD did have much information on British agents on the continent.

There was no talk of trying to pin the Munich bomb plot on Stevens and Best, and Heydrich barely mentioned the incident. When he did, the shock on the faces of his prisoners was obvious, the very idea of such dirty tricks would never have occurred to such members of the old school. Things changed later of course, as disclosed recently, when after years of savage conflict the British SOE organisation was prepared to look at ways to get rid of Hitler. In fact, quite detailed schemes were prepared for his killing, but military opinion was, rightly, that the Nazi *Führer* was of greater value alive to the Allies. His blunders made him almost an asset, incongruous though this sounds.

Heydrich eventually parted from his prisoners, who were taken to a comparatively mild life in a concentration camp where, as mentioned, they eventually met Georg Elser. Both Britons survived, unlike their captor.

13

THE SD AND THE
DUKE OF WINDSOR

The long-delayed German attack in the West began at dawn on 10 May 1940, the military operations helped by a great deal of information obtained by Hitler's *Abwehr* and SD spies. Both these services had already contributed much to the invasion of Denmark and Norway the previous month. Heydrich had long targeted German sympathisers in Denmark, especially families of German descent in Jutland. There were recruits in plenty, selection was easy and the tasks given the chosen ones far from difficult. Owing to its small population of four million, Denmark's armed forces were very small and presented no problem to the *Wehrmacht*, which was provided with all the information it required long before the occupation took place. Every frontier fortification and military installation was noted, photographed and mapped. Apart from this kind of intelligence there were those in the Danish military who were not averse to a German takeover, and the same men very quickly formed a 'Danish Free Corps' to fight for the enemy once their country was occupied.

In Norway things were rather different; the people and armed forces took their defence more seriously and the SD agents had more problems. There were, however, various ways of subversion, and the softly-softly approach sometimes worked wonders. This approach was carried out by various youth groups and other Nazi organisations, which sent in 'good will' missions which invariably contained at least one spy. The Norwegians were not fools; however, they never managed to catch the majority of German spies. Only occasionally was an agent stopped from leaving the country with a camera full of film.

The French, Belgian and Dutch populations provided many collaborators, both before and after the German invasion, and once the battle was over a resident SD agent was set up by Heydrich in every city and large town. These agents were often natives, able and willing to provide answers to intelligence questions. They were paid for their work and in some cases provided with suitable rewards beyond that, such as positions of power in the occupying administration.

In Paris, there were policiticans to be bought who already had fascist leanings, right-wingers of the extreme kind who had often spoken out in favour of a lasting understanding with Hitler. Such men were not difficult to subvert, and often provided valuable information on their anti-fascist colleagues, especially communists and Jews. There were also a few individuals of the same kind who had been to Germany and had been given the VIP treatment and promised lucrative contracts 'when the right time comes'.

Another method which *never* failed was sexual entrapment. The right kind of women were no problem for the SD to find, and at least one high-class brothel in Paris was owned by the SD through a French front man. It proved a hotbed in more than one sense, a constant stream of tittle-tattle being relayed to Heydrich's agent in control, who sifted out the most useful for Berlin, the reports being sent via the weekly diplomatic bag. The brothel became very popular with not only a number of French politicians, but also businessmen and military. One captain happened to be a cavalryman, and regularly told his favourite female in the hothouse how his unit was progressing in its conversion to armour. He was extremely peeved to lose his beloved horses and talked freely. The brothel manageress reserved her best rooms and women for the most promising clients, the rooms of course being bugged.

This operation, it must be emphasised, was in progress in peace-time, prior to September 1939. It required a full-time staff in Berlin to handle the great flow of information from this one source in Paris. Naturally, the French had their counter-spies run by the Deuxième Bureau, and the 'SD' brothel did not escape inspection, usually by a police spy in plain clothes. But the 'madame' already knew him as an informer and soon wheedled out of him the real reason for his visit. The result was that she promised to give him special attention and keep watch on her rooms for indiscretions. Heydrich had no problems.

However, some German agents were put under surveillance by the French, a few being arrested and deported. The same thing happened in reverse, the upshot of such affairs being that the matters were hushed up, and sometimes exchanges took place in quite amicable circumstances.

Heydrich gained a very comprehensive picture of the generally chaotic and corrupt state of French politics – the rivalries, intrigues and plots went on continuously. The military was not much better, having petty, childish differences at many levels, which reduced the effectiveness of field forma-tions. As for the common French soldiery, it was widely known that in the main they cared only for wine and women and seemed to have little interest in what Hitler and *le Boche* were up to. So long as the *Poilu* was given his daily wine ration he remained content. All of this merely confirmed Heydrich's view that France as a nation provided no obstacle.

Although the Dutch had the largest fascist party in Europe under Mussert and provided a few agents for the enemy, the SD preferred to use Germans posing as businessmen or tourists. These went through the motions, which

183

in the case of the former were often genuine. No problems were encountered in completely mapping Holland from the espionage point of view. The same applied in Belgium and Luxembourg, the former having its right-wing Rexists, of whom Leon Degrelle became best known, raised up by the Germans as a hero of their anti-Bolshevik 'crusade' during the war in Russia. Men like Degrelle really believed in such a cause, but fought as soldiers and were not usable by Heydrich.

Following the astonishing successes in the West during 1940, the *Abwehr* was ordered to improve its military knowledge of England. It had of course carried out a certain amount of work before the war, but its files were deficient in many respects. Specifically, with the enormous loss of equipment suffered by the British Expeditionary Force in France, how were the people in England re-organising their defences in the face of invasion? This question was of vital interest to the *Wehrmacht* chiefs charged with drawing up detailed plans for the cross-Channel assault.

The *Abwehr*'s attempts to land spies in Britain in 1940 proved a fiasco. No matter how successful Canaris had been on the continent, the barrier of water separating the Germans from their target proved too much for the admiral spy chief to surmount. British security was sewn up tight in short order following the successful evacuations from Dunkirk and other points on the continental coast. The south and east coasts of England were virtually inpenetrable by subversives. The whole nation was in a state of enhanced alert, with tension at such a pitch that 'enemy parachutists' and spies were reported everywhere. This is not to imply it was utterly impossible to land agents on the British coast by submarine or seaplane. It was impossible to guard every yard of shoreline, and there were many inlets and more remote areas where such operations were possible. The real problems for Canaris began once the agents were ashore, and here the *Abwehr* proved amateurish.

The history of such attempts is familiar, and every episode will not be recounted here. This brief mention of the *Abwehr*'s efforts to infiltrate spies across the sea serves to highlight the problems which would have faced Heydrich's SD, had they made any similar forays, and they did not.

There were non-Germans taken on by the *Abwehr*, provided with hurried grounding in spy work, and sent across by sea to Britain around September 1940. One man managed to row ashore in a dinghy on the pebbly Kent shore, one of the most carefully watched sectors of England at the time. Naturally, he was soon under lock and key. Another agent landed on the Scottish coast, finding his way to the nearest hamlet and railway, where at the wayside halt station he enquired about trains to London. In such a spot strangers stood out conspicuously – whatever their place of origin. To arrive as if out of nowhere carrying a suitcase was suspicious enough, and by the time the stranger boarded the London-bound train he had been noted by the local police. As the spy sat comfortably on his upholstered seat on the London, Midland and Scottish train speeding south he took out his packet of *Wurst* to eat his breakfast, unaware that long before he reached the capital's terminus detectives had also boarded the train. When the amateur *Abwehr* spy alighted at King's Cross station in London he was already under arrest.

This success had been quietly accomplished, with no great hue and cry and interminable inspections through the train or at stopping stations by hordes of '*Gestapo*' and uniformed police.

Unfortunately for Canaris, his 'agents' sent to detail and report on British anti-invasion preparations were quickly rounded up, and in some cases executed after secret trials. Tiny paragraphs in the Press announced their demise by hanging or shooting, the former fate awarded to any agents belonging to the military. The British were quite cold-blooded about it, even if one spy sentenced to death was ill or injured and permitted to sit in a chair to meet his Maker. Those who preferred to co-operate and save their skins became the tools of the Double-X Committee, who through MI5 controlled turned agents to fool Canaris throughout the war with bogus information radioed to the *Abwehr*. These cunning operations involved the use of 'sub-agents' and 'notional spies' employed by those caught, a network of almost total fiction. The occasional snippet of truth was inserted to provide enough meat to convince the German spymasters all was going well. Money and equipment was dropped to the waiting British by the *Luftwaffe*, all this a precursor to a similar and even larger operation run by the *Abwehr* and SD in Holland later.

Neither Heydrich nor Canaris had discovered the most important enemy secret, despite the great amount of work carried out by the SD chief's two agents before the war. The 'radio towers' observed by the Germans across the Channel from the cliffs at Cap Gris Nez were presumed to be just that. The *Luftwaffe* Signals Intelligence chief, General Martini, eventually concluded the structures must be concerned with the excellent fighter control system operating in the Battle of Britain. They were not recognised as vital radar towers, and in any case proved almost impossible to put out of action. The ferreting out of such important information by German spies earlier would have proved of much military significance.

At a conference following Hitler's order to plan Operation 'Sea Lion', at which both Heydrich and Admiral Canaris were present, the SD chief heard various proposals for bringing the existing intelligence data up to date. All these proposals seemed unworkable to him, or at least, unlikely to succeed for various reasons. Yet, as he discovered later, several of the proposals were in fact carried out by the *Abwehr*, assumedly with the blessing of Canaris. Heydrich also learned in due course that the rival organisation was operating spies from England – with reported good results. This surprised him, but he was never able to check on the truth. Since he was not pressed on the matter, Heydrich made no attempt to follow suit and try to organise spying in wartime Britain, his impression being that the *Wehrmacht* chiefs were satisfied with the results passed on by the *Abwehr*. In any case, the SD had a very great deal of work to tackle following the successive occupations of the lands conquered by the German Army.

There were ways in which the Germans (both SD and *Abwehr*) might well have succeeded with wartime spying activities in Britain, if only they had planned beforehand. There were rabid Irish and Welsh nationalists ever anxious to harm England, who could have been sufficiently cultivated before the war. The results gained could easily have been passed back to Germany via (for example) the Spanish diplomats in London.

The 'Eddie Chapman' story is well known. A petty crook and safebreaker, he was in jail in the Channel Isles when the Germans arrived. He soon curried favour and was taken on by the *Abwehr*. Chapman was successfully parachuted into England, only to give himself up to the authorities, so that MI5 had no trouble in 'turning' him to act as a successful double agent. One ploy used by the British to fool Chapman's *Abwehr* controllers was to carry out a little piece of 'sabotage' at the de Havilland plane factory in Hertfordshire. The resulting story of a fire was fed to the Press and in due course collected by the *Abwehr*, who swallowed it as proof their *Englander* was doing the job for which they had trained and paid him. Precisely the same piece of foolery was used by the Germans later in Holland to successfully hoodwink the more gullible Special Operations Executive in London.

Not without interest is another method the Germans may have found feasible in certain narrow parameters, put forward by a modern writer of World War Two fiction. In his tale the *Abwehr*, employing considerably more brain power than it actually displayed, managed to infiltrate its man into England by having him included in one of the rare PoW exchanges. One or two of these took place during the war, the affairs overseen by a neutral power, such as the Swedes or Swiss through the Red Cross. The adventure is worth briefly telling because of its originality and one must say ingenuity – not shown by the enemy.

A British Tommy, we may call him Atkins, was something of a rascal, and when the lead started to fly during the Battle of France, he ran away. This is not an unusual event in first battles, when officers were trained to expect anything up to a quarter of their men to desert; most returned later once the shock of combat wore off. In Private Atkins's case, his defection was noted in company records, and these would by luck survive to reach his unit's depot, the Royal Norfolks in Norwich. However, Atkins and many of his regiment were caught up in very heavy fighting and killed, though a sizeable group was taken prisoner and massacred by SS troops soon afterwards. Naturally, German Intelligence officers went through the dead Britons' papers, and those of Tommy Atkins found their way to the *Abwehr*. It was some time before one of its cleverer minds came up with the scheme to use a pending PoW exchange to slip a man into Britain. The man chosen knew England, as he had been an exchange student in Cambridge before the war, and by good chance established an affair with an Irish girl working in the area.

The brave *Abwehr* spy was placed in the special camp reserved for would-be repatriates, British soldiers deemed too unfit for further war service. A similar group of Germans was assembled in Britain. The men were inspected and certified unfit by the neutral inspection team, each man presenting his documents, which in the case of Tommy Atkins (Richard Bregmann) consisted of his British Army Pay and Service Book (AB64) in the name of Private Atkins, of the Royal Norfolk Regiment. 'Atkins' had been furnished with an X-ray plate proving he suffered from incipient tuberculosis; he had also been suitably starved and shut up by his *Abwehr* trainers, so he appeared quite sickly to the neutral inspectors, who passed him without query.

All went well, and the ship, displaying large red crosses on its hull, docked at a south coast port. The sick PoWs disembarked and following various formalities and the provision of a meal were either dispatched to military hospitals or allowed home leave. In the case of 'Private Atkins', the address he gave was that of his former Irish mistress in Cambridgeshire. It was to her remote cottage that he travelled, finding her at home and willing to take him in. But within days, the German had successfully received supplies of explosives dropped by Dornier in the nearest available field. Suitably outfitted in second-hand civilian gear bought cheap in the nearest town, he embarked on a programme of sabotaging airfields and repair depots.

By a very feasible twist, the saboteur's activities were brought to a sudden and quite unexpected halt when he was arrested by military police as a deserter from the Norfolks and sentenced to a suitable period in detention. The idea is ludicrous, a German spy-saboteur incarcerated in a British Army 'glasshouse', but stranger things have happened. That is not the end of the story, but it will suffice to indicate one method of inserting agents into wartime Britain; maybe the *Abwehr* could never have got away with it, but the scheme had the merit of being far more cunning than simply dumping half-trained dupes onto our seashore.

Before leaving the realms of spy fiction, the same author indicates yet another ploy, this more along the lines of the first mentioned, which both SD and *Abwehr* might have considered.

The British Union of Fascists had many members, and one of Sir Oswald Mosley's London meetings was said to have drawn twenty thousand uniformed adherents who came to hear their '*Führer*' speak. It is true the organisation was infiltrated by MI5 and the Special Branch, as was the Communist Party, and that most Mosleyites were detained under Regulation 18b when war came, including the leader. But not all were imprisoned, and some 'camp followers' escaped jail. In this other tale, a fascist is enrolled by the Germans to spy on RAF airfields, his role quite undetected (at first), though the hero and central character of these stories catches up with the traitor in the end. But that is again fiction, the hero must win through; in real life, in those circumstances, important information gathered by a British citizen could easily have been passed (as indicated) to the enemy via neutral embassies, for transmission to the *Reich.*

The fiction author in question also touches on one aspect rarely mentioned in histories (see *Target England* (Airlife 1997)), using it to assist his story involving another Nazi sabotage plot. This was the fact of *Luftwaffe* recce pilots using captured RAF aircraft made serviceable to overfly Britain. This was accomplished by choosing any of the very many days when Allied warplanes were streaming homewards after raiding the continent. Some of these were damaged, many flying at various heights. It was easy to simulate one of these. Once over the British mainland, the enemy pilots roamed around, photographing RAF airfields and anything else, unsuspected by the defences below. When they roared eastwards again the coast watchers saw nothing unusual, just another Allied plane on a mission.

Two successful Nazi saboteurs are snatched off North Weald RAF base by a *Luftwaffe* crew flying a captured Vickers Wellington bomber, the twin-engined plane on the ground for only a moment or two. This is almost what happened in Lincolnshire when a Dornier 217 touched down on an RAF base and took off again. It was not the only incident of that nature, but quite unique since the crew were in the employ of MI6 and delivering a package of secrets (*Fatal Decisions* (Airlife 1999)).

Returning once more to the more regular tracks of history, in late 1940, while the *Abwehr* sought to infiltrate Britain, all the Nazi security agency headquarters in Berlin began to receive reports of communist cells operating in occupied territories, and of the first ugly incidents of German personnel being assassinated, in France. According to Germans then and later, the killings disgusted the majority of French people, who were only really interested in carrying on with their lives in increasingly difficult circumstances.

Then came the broadcasts over the BBC which incited the conquered peoples on the continent to acts of sabotage, pinpricks to annoy and harass the occupiers. As a result the security measures already taken by the Germans had to be stepped up and more agents sent in. This placed a strain on SD resources. Heydrich was forced to recruit more men, and although these were forthcoming, they had to be trained, and this took time.

Meanwhile, the Battle of Britain had come and gone, with enemy aircraft still raiding Britain in reduced numbers. Heydrich, already a qualified pilot, and having mastered the Messerschmitt 109 fighter as a challenge, now decided he must fly a few combat missions. The very notion of a Nazi spy chief in Berlin going off to a *Luftwaffe* base on the Belgian coast to fly against the RAF seems a little fantastic, but that is precisely what happened. At least, having learned all he needed to know about the various procedures, including call signs, *Gruppenführer* Heydrich had a chosen 'Emil' suitably decorated with SS lightning flash insignia and went off with a squadron of regular *Luftwaffe* fighter pilots. These flights took Heydrich over the North Sea and were not fighter-bomber raids on the British coast or RAF bases such as Manston; they were more in the nature of routine offensive patrols. Following three such flights, Heydrich was peremptorily ordered to cease, for Hitler had come to hear of it and forbade Heydrich from ever taking off in a fighter aircraft again. Heydrich was disappointed, but became so embroiled in additional work that he felt content with what had been accomplished. His uniform already bore the *Luftwaffe* pilot badge, and to this he now added a fighter pilot's war flights clasp. His collection typified the kind of assortment the Germans loved to adorn their uniforms with, rather like Boy Scout merit awards.

The slowly deteriorating situation with regard to security in the conquered lands led to not only an increase in SD surveillance, but the posting of *Abwehr* agents and members of the *Geheime Feldpolizei*, the Secret Field Police of the *Wehrmacht*. When in uniform the latter could be readily identified by the metal letters 'GFP' on their shoulder straps. But, in the roles assigned them against the various Resistance groups, these personnel wore plain clothes and, naturally, needed to have fluent knowledge of the appropriate language in order to mix with and infiltrate the Resisters. In this work one Hugo Bleicher of the GFP became most successful.

Heydrich had not neglected his new wireless intercept team, and following the occupation of France he had them set up a base on the coast just outside Calais. It was a mobile detector van with accommodation nearby and enough men to man the radio on a 24-hour basis. His object was to catch secret transmissions from England to French and British agents, but once the BBC began broadcasting such messages quite openly by way of code phrases the effort was abandoned and the van with its personnel utilised on a more mobile basis.

The plan to invade England had not been abandoned, only postponed. At least, that was the impression Hitler wished to give, not only to the British but to his people and *Wehrmacht* – apart from those at the very top level, that is, who knew the *Führer's* mind was now concentrating on the East. Heydrich's own proposed part in an occupation of Britain had been worked out in broad outline under the general order issued by Hitler's Army Commander-in-Chief, Field Marshal von Brauchitsch. He was presumably one of the old school of conservative military hierarchy, one of the 'non-Nazi' gentlemen Prime Minister Chamberlain and his government believed they could do business with back in October 1939. Here is one of the Field Marshal's edicts concerning the fate of the British people, though it must be said that whether he actually dreamed up such orders or merely put his signature to the *Führer's* wishes is unknown. It can be borne in mind, however, that it was von Brauchitsch who in similar fashion passed on Hitler's cruel orders for the suppression of the Poles.

> ... the able-bodied male population between the ages of seventeen and forty-five will, unless the local situation calls for an exceptional ruling, be interned and despatched to the continent.

This was part of the orders issued through the German Quartermaster General's office to the Ninth and Sixteenth Armies assembled on the Channel coast waiting to invade Britain. The orders signed by Hitler's Army chief went into considerable detail, obviously unique since nothing like it had been planned before. The plans included the military and economic governing of England, and were designed to plunder and terrorise the British nation. To execute these plans Hitler set up a special Military Economic Staff England, which provided for the confiscation of *everything* barring household goods. Britain was to be stripped bare and those allowed to remain on the island permitted only the most meagre living. Naturally, hostage taking and executions would be the rule. The security aspect, under the proud gaze of a British-born but long Germanised *Gauleiter*, would be taken care of by Himmler and Heydrich, who appointed SS Colonel Dr Six to administer the right kind of medicine to the '*Englanders*'. Six was, according to William Shirer, 'another peculiar intellectual gangster'. He was an alleged specialist in economic and scientific matters in a Berlin university. He never got the chance to prove his worth as 'Security *Führer, Grossbritannien*'; his chance came later, in Russia, where he became head of an *Einsatzgruppe*. Dr Six received a twenty-year jail sentence at the Nuremberg trials for his crimes of overseeing mass murder in the East, but was released after four years under an Allied occupation regime incredibly benevolent by comparison with that planned for Britain in 1940.

Indeed, it was the Nazi most loved by Allied cartoonists who proved yet again to be as ruthless and vindictive as any. *Reichsmarschall* Hermann Goering was a man who applied every ounce of his energy and enthusiasm towards whatever project came to hand, whether it was the persecution of the Jews and Reds, his beloved model train layout – or the subjugation of England. Of course, having lost face following his boast that his *Luftwaffe* would subdue England, he now directed Heydrich to simultaneously commence harsh measures against the British with the military invasion. The man once described by a *Luftwaffe* aircrewman as rather like a fat, jovial, made-up schoolboy, saw the stubborn and decadent *Englanders* as overdue for a lesson in the Nazi manner. A blacklist was drawn up of individuals and organisations to be arrested and smashed, from Winston Churchill to the Boy Scout movement. On the very day Hitler decided to postpone the invasion, Heydrich appointed Dr Six as Security Chief in Britain, to combat all anti-Nazi organisations, institutions and opposition groups in England. He was to set up his base in London and seize all relevant documents. Six was authorised to form small *Einsatzgruppen* in the island as the situation demanded. Heydrich had already, on paper at least, ·assigned six such groups to Great Britain. Their headquarters were to be located in Bristol, Birmingham, Liverpool, Manchester, Edinburgh or Glasgow (depending on whether the Forth bridge remained intact) and London.

Interestingly, the 'Special Search List GB' had been hurriedly drawn up by Walter Schellenberg in May 1940, evidently during the triumphal onrush of the *Wehrmacht* across France. He had by then risen to chief of *Amt* (bureau) IVe, the Counter-Espionage Branch of the *Reich* State Security Office (RSHA) in Heydrich's Berlin HQ. Schellenberg's list contained 2,300 names, probably extracted from a *Who's Who*, old SD lists of British correspondents, editors of papers hostile to the Nazi regime. In certain directions the list seems foolish and pointless: H.G. Wells, Virginia Woolf, J.B. Priestley, Stephen Spender, C.P. Snow and Noel Coward featured among the writers, etc. to be arrested. Others were economists and intellectuals, such as Bertrand Russell, but foreign emigrés were also seen as important targets for Nazi retribution. Among them were President Benes, who had fled to Britain, and others such as Jan Masaryk, the world-famous pianist Paderewski and Hitler's ex-piano entertainer, Hans 'Putzi' Hanfstaengel. Even the famous psychoanalyst, Sigmund Freud figured on Schellenberg's list, the compiler apparently unaware the old man had died the year before.

Naturally, and since the Nazi hierarchy had failed to burn all their secret documents before the collapse in 1945, the SD files, and especially Schellenberg's 'Special' list, provided amusement in Britain after its contents became known. There were names like Lady Bonham-Carter, described by Schellenberg rather quaintly as an 'Encirclement lady politician'. Beside each name on the list was marked the appropriate department of the RSHA which would deal with them. Churchill would be handed over to Schellenberg's own Counter-Intelligence bureau for example, but most would be taken by *Amt* IV – the *Gestapo*. Schellenberg also compiled an *Informationsheft*, or supplement, a kind of Black Book detailing British organisations to be eliminated. All Masonic Lodges would be smashed, plus all Jewish groups, private schools and the Church of England, which was seen as a 'powerful tool of British Imperial Politics'. The Boy Scout movement was listed as 'an excellent source of information for the British Intelligence Service', and its leader Lord Baden-Powell was to be arrested.

This was the standard of 'intelligence' mustered by Walter Schellenberg, who was of schoolboyish character and of no real use whatsoever. Since men like Himmler looked on him as the brains of the SD Counter-Intelligence, there can be little doubt that his foolish recommendations would most likely have been accepted; what Heydrich thought of the list is another matter. Prime Minister Churchill was in no doubt that terror

The Duke of Windsor inspects an SS honour guard during a mid-thirties visit – and poses with wife Wallis Simpson beside the Führer

would be meted out against the British population, but, curiously enough, when the enemy did take over British territory – the Channel Isles – no such harsh measures took place. At least, not on the scale envisaged by the document quoted. Following the probably mistaken bombing of the ports, the *Wehrmacht* behaved correctly. There was no sudden influx of SD and SS to carry out deportations and executions, and an island administration was allowed to continue its work under the eye of the German Commandant.

Schellenberg was again sent out into the field following the French collapse, in June 1940, when Hitler thought he saw a chance to suborn the Duke of Windsor. Ever since meeting the Windsors in the thirties, Hitler had been under the impression they were under his spell, or at least very sympathetic to him and the Nazi cause. The *Führer* had put on his very best behaviour when receiving such 'Royals'. One photograph depicts him holding Wallis Simpson's hand and bowing deeply. As was usually the case, Hitler had taken foreign visitors' politeness in listening to his lectures as agreement with all he said. The friendliness and understanding shown by the Windsors encouraged him to view them as allies, quite apart from their family and the British government in London. The Duke had, Hitler and his followers believed, been driven further towards friendship with Germany by the shabby treatment he had received in England. Should events take a certain course, the Duke might be persuaded to act favourably to Hitler's cause, even regaining the English throne with Nazi help. When Britain seemed close to defeat such ideas loomed larger, though it is difficult to know how seriously Hitler could have envisaged Edward once again King of England. By late summer 1940, it had all come to nothing, and Edward could hardly have been persuaded to climb onto the throne again in a land deprived of much of its male population.

But in June, as France fell apart and the *Wehrmacht* seemed all-triumphant, Walter Schellenberg was sent for by von Ribbentrop and told with enthusiasm of the *Führer*'s idea. We now know the nature of the Duke's 'escape' to the South of France and thence to Spain and Portugal. Disclosures point to a serious dereliction of duty, though the suggestion that Edward was traitorous seems far-fetched.

The German ambassador in Madrid, Eberhard von Stohrer, cabled Berlin, reporting that the Spanish Foreign Minister had sought advice on how best to treat the Duke and Duchess. It was to the Germans the Spaniard had turned, as he wondered if his friends were interested in detaining the Duke, assuming Edward was *en route* to England. But the British preferred him abroad, and began a protracted battle to have Edward take up a post as Governor of the Bahamas. Von Ribbentrop responded at once, advising that it would be appropriate for the Windsors to be detained for a couple of weeks, though cautioning that the idea they remain a while as 'guests' should not of course appear to come from Berlin. Accordingly, the Spanish minister received the Windsors, reporting all his conversations to the

Germans. It seemed Wallis Simpson absolutely refused to go home until she was admitted into the Royal family and the Duke was given a position of importance. Otherwise, Edward intended settling down in the castle the Spanish had offered him. The Duke, so von Stohrer reported to Berlin, had expressed himself as 'against Churchill and against the war'. This was grist to the Nazi mill, exactly the kind of utterance that confirmed Hitler's view of the Windsors, who travelled on to Lisbon in July. The fact that he was supposed to be a serving officer in the British Army seems to have escaped the Duke entirely. Ever since the German breakthrough in May he had behaved as an individual quite independent of military orders, and had returned to the kind of lifestyle he loved best. In Lisbon, the German minister soon learned that Edward had been offered a job in the Bahamas; such facts were easy to come by owing to the lack of security displayed by the pair. The German diplomat also reported to Berlin how the Windsors were delaying things in the hope that something better would turn up.

The Duke, von Ribbentrop learned, was a convinced supporter of a peace settlement with Germany, and believed severe bombing would persuade his country to sue for peace. 'He is convinced that if he had remained on the throne war could have been avoided.'

If such an utterance had become known to the British people while they were suffering the Blitz, much if not all the sympathy shown to him earlier would have vanished. If that was in fact his belief, that the British would soon cave in under air attack, then Edward proved how little he knew his people and how unfit he had been to sit on the throne in 1936. But it was great news for von Ribbentrop, who hurried to get Hitler's sanction to have the Duke and Duchess somehow prevented from sailing from Lisbon. They should be taken back to Spain, preferably by the Spanish, and the Duke perhaps interned as 'an English officer'. The British Prime Minister, Winston Churchill, was becoming increasingly exasperated with the Duke. Meanwhile, von Ribbentrop wanted him informed of Germany's great desire for peace with England. 'We would be prepared to assure him and his wife a subsistence which would permit him to lead the life suitable for a king.' To add urgency to the notion, von Ribbentrop told Hitler he had information the British Secret Service planned to 'do away' with the Duke as soon as he reached the Bahamas. Accordingly, with Hitler's approval, the Spanish became involved in a plot to detain the Duke until Nazi plans for him could mature. A good friend and ally of General Franco would invite the Windsors back to Spain for some hunting, where, at an appropriate moment, the Duke would be told of the British plan to get rid of him.

Miguel Primo de Rivera was an old friend of the Duke and called on the Windsors on 16 July. He returned to Spain to report his findings to his Foreign Minister, who told von Stohrer, who in turn informed Berlin. Churchill, so Hitler learned, had told the Duke to leave for his post in the Bahamas at once – or face court martial. That such details should become known to Hitler proved the total lack of security surrounding the Windsors, who not only talked freely, but were attended by Portuguese staff, some of whom were in German pay. Though not really a traitor, Edward chattered to friends in quite indiscreet fashion, voicing criticisms of his country and its leaders, which seemed to compromise his loyalty to Britain. In the circumstances, the Spaniards agreed to act for their German friends and warn the Duke not to go to the Bahamas for fear of assassination by his own side.

De Rivera's next visit to the Windsors on 22 July resulted in yet more blatant indiscretions reaching Hitler. The Duke was reported to have remarked that he was now more distant from the English King and government, that his brother George was foolish, his wife the Queen shrewd and intriguing successfully against Edward – but even more against his wife Wallis. He was considering making a public statement, distancing himself from British policy and finally breaking with his brother. The Windsors seemed anxious to return to Spain. In these talks, de Rivera seems to have had no idea he was acting as a tool for the Germans, and overplayed his hand when he stated they (the Germans) would almost certainly want the Duke to play some role in the war, and perhaps even re-ascend the throne. The Duke was apparently 'astonished' by this latter assertion, knowing full well it was impossible.

The Spaniards made their arrangements: the Windsors were to be secretly escorted back into Spain, where they would be at the Germans' mercy. The SD (i.e. Schellenberg) was ordered to bring the pair back to Germany. He therefore flew to Madrid in the last few days of July, to be briefed by von Stohrer. Although the plot had been hatched by von Ribbentrop, none of the proceedings escaped Heydrich's attention, who had no great respect for the Foreign Minister but was obliged to allow his man to leave on the job because it was a *Führer* order. Heydrich briefed Schellenberg to be doubly vigilant as he knew the British Secret Service was very active in Spain and Portugal. Beyond that there was little he could do, for von Ribbentrop employed his own agents and had prevailed on the Spanish to provide secret policemen for the job.

Schellenberg listened as von Stohrer put forward various suggestions for the *modus operandi* of the plan, including the need not to induce any feeling of flight or coercion in the Duke, and above all to convince him the Spaniards really were trying to help him escape from the British assassins. To further this, von Stohrer suggested a suitable scare manoeuvre – to be charged to the British Secret Service. Prey to such foolishness, Schellenberg complied, going to the Windsors' villa to lurk in the shadowy grounds after dark and have his agents hurl pebbles at the windows, before starting rumours among the servants that the culprits were British agents trying to intimidate the guests. Other ideas, such as the firing of pistols in the grounds, were not pursued.

Increasingly irked, Churchill sent the Duke's old friend Sir Walter Monckton to work on the Windsors and speed their departure.

Schellenberg reported the envoy's arrival in Lisbon on 30 July, the same day von Stohrer urgently cabled Berlin that one of his own agents had discovered the Windsors intended to sail for the Bahamas on 1 August. Further, the Duke had, according to a Portuguese banker friend, expressed a desire to meet Hitler. Von Stohrer felt it was now urgent to expedite matters, as time seemed to be running out. Next, von Ribbentrop learned that despite being impressed by Spanish warnings, the Duke intended to leave for the Bahamas, but was trying to conceal the date. Stung by the urgency, von Ribbentrop sent a long cable detailing German attitudes which he hoped von Stohrer would prevail on the banker to place before the Duke and finally persuade him to act as required. Receiving the cable just before midnight, von Stohrer was obliged to rouse the Portuguese in the night. The banker played his part the next day, duly passing on to the Duke all the German views. The response seemed very favourable. Yet, to the consternation of the Germans, the Windsors sailed from Lisbon that very day on the American liner *Excalibur.*

So ended German attempts to suborn their friend the Duke of Windsor, who went on at his insistence to see his friends in New York, enjoying the kind of fantastically extravagant lifestyle to which he and his wife were accustomed. Whether the Duke was still, nominally, an Army officer is open to question. He was, one assumes, the Governor intent of the Bahamas. Not that it made any difference, he no longer wore uniform – that had been abandoned across the Atlantic.

Schellenberg reported dismally to his superiors in Berlin that everything possible had been done to stop the Windsors' departure, short of physical force. Franco's brother, who was ambassador in Lisbon, had appealed to the couple; the car carrying their luggage was sabotaged; he had spread rumours of a bomb aboard the ship, which forced the Portuguese police to delay the sailing while a thorough search was made. Schellenberg blamed Sir Walter Monckton, the Spaniards, and the Duke's 'mentality'.

It is alleged that the Duchess maintained contact with known friends and agents of Hitler, and that her husband used a 'confidante' in Lisbon to let him know the moment action became necessary for him to use his influence to try and secure peace between Britain and Germany. There is no doubt the Duke saw the Germans as 'blood brothers' through the royal lineage. However, when various unsavoury whispers came following the discovery of German documents at the end of the war, the Duke finally (in 1957) issued a statement through his solicitor refuting the von Ribbentrop version of events in 1940, asserting his complete loyalty to Britain. Certainly, both Hitler and von Ribbentrop swallowed their own high hopes. They probably stood little or no chance of winning 'Royal' patronage for their cause via the Windsors.

The forming of the Special Operations Executive (SOE) in London to further Churchill's dream of 'setting Europe ablaze' led to the equipping of

Resistant networks on the continent, chiefly in France. Though very little occurred during the first months of the German occupation, the vast majority among the conquered populations wished only to make the best of things. They wanted to keep their heads down and trust the enemy would leave them alone. For their part, the Germans did their best to maintain correct relations with the people, while behind the scenes steps were taken to transfer the necessary economic production to the needs of the *Reich*. The communists had been quite strong in France, and their cells were maintained after the occupation, awaiting orders from Moscow. Only following the start of Operation 'Barbarossa' in June 1941 did these communists begin active sabotage and murder against the Germans.

The German SIPO forces worked to catch their prey among the Resistance chiefly by infiltration, though once the supply of radios began to flow from England the detector vans were increasingly busy. Their crews became adept in tracing illegal signalling. Heydrich had a wireless expert advise him on such matters, which was how the system of a master receiver and controller came into use later. It saved a great deal of time and effort if detector teams were allotted certain areas where they waited, sometimes for days on end, before being ordered to a particular district from where unauthorised transmissions had been detected. Sometimes, these signals emanated from the middle of armed groups, and gun battles resulted, losses occurring on both sides. Special squads of SD agents needed to be on standby, armed with all kinds of weapons, when such operations were in progress. Some of these men were French, even Russian, and in many cases the French police co-operated, as did the German military. When prisoners were taken the results were usually harsh; neither the SD, *Gestapo* nor the French *Milice* auxiliary police treated prisoners gently during interrogations. On some occasions, Germans or their helpers captured by the Resistance were later found executed.

The *Milice* became the most hated, for both their treachery and cruelty. The war between patriots and those hunting them was no gentlemanly affair. Both sides displayed ruthlessness. Women who consorted with the enemy, and more than a few did, were not always required to wait until the Liberation in 1944 before receiving retribution by way of shaven heads and beatings. One *Luftwaffe* bomber crewman took on a French girl friend, her father having no objection, and the two became lovers. One evening when the airman called the Frenchman told him his daughter was missing, and within minutes a short but decisive note was slipped through the letterbox which made it clear the Resistance had taken action. The girl was never seen again.

The greatest danger to any indulging in anti-German activities was lack of security, as 'keeping mum' did not come very easily to the French. The successes gained by the SD and other German agencies against resisters and their helpers all too often came through this means, and of course traitors. Yet, not until almost the end of the occupation did greater numbers spring up among the population claiming to be members of the Resistance. The veterans were indeed very few by comparison, extremely brave and utterly dedicated to France.

The Resistance movement as a whole, as Claude Dansey in London well realised, was a hindrance to the work of MI6. Its activities, especially when sabotage occurred, stirred up a hornet's nest as the German counter-forces turned out in force. Agents who had settled into comparative safety and obscurity to gather pure intelligence material for the Secret Intelligence Service in London found themselves turfed out of hiding by thorough German searches and round-ups when hostages were seized and all too often shot. Such conditions were not conducive to pure spying, small wonder Dansey and MI6 in general looked askance at the 'amateurs' and, as a rule, ordered agents to steer clear of them.

Heydrich received regular reports from all SD commanders in these occupied territories, but rarely visited them. Exceptions were in the East, where special problems arose in Czechoslovakia and Poland concerning subversion, the usual measures being taken. It was in the latter country that the SD joined Military Intelligence in trying to penetrate the Soviet Zone.

During a conference in Cracow, Heydrich proposed the best way to progress in work beyond the Demarcation Line against the Soviets was through the Poles. The Army Intelligence representative was General Gehlen, an 'Eastern expert', and on the Soviets in particular. His files and services would become available to the Americans in the Cold War. As indicated, neither SD nor *Abwehr* had succeeded to any worthwhile degree in penetrating Soviet military and economic secrets. Not until the weeks immediately preceding Operation 'Barbarossa' was a greater, combined co-operation attempted in order to provide the *Wehrmacht* and SIPO with a better picture. Gehlen too had made contact with virulently anti-Soviet Poles, among them ordinary Army officers, but also intelligence personnel found in 1939.

It was therefore agreed to set up a joint staff, including Polish officers, who could do much of the directing of their spies in the Eastern zone, though everything would be monitored by German staff. Yet, despite this degree of co-operation with the military, Heydrich still maintained distance between them, rarely visiting the new intelligence centre. He believed, as did General Gehlen, that the Soviets already had their own agents at work in the German-occupied zone of Poland. To counter them it was necessary to maintain strict vigilance on all sides, using counter-agents of the SD, *Gestapo*, *Abwehr* and GFP. This was a unique period when the SD and Army co-operated for the good of both. Successes were, however, slow in coming, and when they did it was through the use of Polish *agent provocateurs*, who were employed in the same way as French people in the West. As in the concentration camps and elsewhere, the Nazis were not beyond using Jews in essential work, one Jew on the

198

German payroll becoming very good in ferreting out Soviet spies. In fact, the man was often paid in foodstuffs. He was of course provided with a special pass of identification.

Despite occasional fraternisation between German and Soviet troops on the border, both sides remained wary of the other. It happened that the Germans were lucky to have several Russian deserters enter their zone after September 1939. These were mainly private soldiers, but well able to provide much information on Soviet forces and dispositions before being allowed limited freedom under restriction. They did, however, pose a risk as the Germans could never be sure they were genuine deserters. Eventually they were all sent back to Germany as prisoners, with one exception. A higher Soviet NCO proved extremely valuable then and later when used to interrogate Russian prisoners in the war that came.

After advance warning was circulated to all German units concerning the huge operation to start on 22 June 1941, security was stepped up. Military police were everywhere and a zone ten miles deep behind the jump-off positions was closed to all civilian and non-essential personnel. General Gehlen increased the number of Polish subversives, losing many. Some were caught, others, almost certainly communists, deserted with valuable information for the Soviets. It had been risky using them, but the Germans felt they had no alternative. A very brave few regained the German sector, usually those with best knowledge of the local terrain. Much was gained from these men concerning Soviet dispositions.

The kidnapping of two British secret agents by the SD in November 1939 was preceded the previous month by a crucial leak of information from within the *Reich* itself.

The British embassy in Berne was informed that Hitler planned to strike in the West on 12 November. The information was correct, it had emanated from the heart of the *Wehrmacht* headquarters in Berlin. British scepticism seemed justified when that date passed and no offensive came; in fact, Hitler had been forced to postpone his plans for various reasons. Even though the Belgian and Dutch diplomats were also warned, there was little they could do, even if they believed the news. The Belgians especially were being extra-careful not to 'offend' the *Führer* by mobilising troops to defend their frontier.

Then both Danish and Norwegian governments received warning of Hitler's plan to invade their countries, in late March 1940. The event was to take place on 9 April, with the Danes 'taken by surprise'.

Next, detailed plans were received by the British and French of a revised German offensive to begin in the West on 10 May.

All these secrets were passed by a German living in Switzerland and posing as an innocent publisher. Rudolf Rössler was a liberal Protestant brought up in Bavaria. Friends he had made during service in World War One gained promotion in Hitler's new *Wehrmacht*, though not in sympathy with Germany's new leader. As an anti-Nazi himself, Rössler took the

Anti-Nazi master spy Rudolf Rössler

advice of a Swiss communist and emigrated to Berne, from where he maintained his contacts among the German military staff in Berlin. In May 1939 two of these, both now generals, took a vacation in Switzerland, calling on Rössler to deliver a radio transceiver, codes and callsigns – and providing details of Hitler's plans for a war of conquest. Rössler learned that eight anti-Nazi Germans were placed in the Army staff in Berlin, two more in the *Luftwaffe* headquarters.

and his Swiss contact-mentor, General Masson

Rössler received his further information from these German military direct by radio, but never passed it to the Allied embassies. Instead, he gave it to Swiss Intelligence, and since the commander of that neutral country's army was also anti-Hitler, he made certain the data reached the right quarters. General Masson, chief of Swiss Intelligence, was soon put in the picture and made such arrangements.

However, the Allies seemed indifferent to this amazing source, so Rössler turned to his communist friend for advice; it was not long before Moscow took up the source. Rössler became 'Lucy', head of the ring which thereafter sent all it learned from inside Hitler's *Reich* to the Soviets. Included among Rössler's aides was a Briton, Alexander Foote, who had fought with the Red-dominated International Brigade in the Spanish Civil War. Before June 1941, 'Lucy' had passed Stalin details of Operation 'Barbarossa', the attack on the Soviet Union.

In August 1941 the German invasion was plunging deeper and deeper into Western Russia; when German troops captured Smolensk they found a safe containing documents which proved the enemy knew all about Hitler's plans in advance. Such information could only have come from the German military itself.

SS *Brigadeführer* Walter Schellenberg was given the task of discovering the source of the leak. Deducing the information had to be transmitted by radio from Germany, he urgently began setting up SD monitoring units to try and track down the traitorous transmitter. It was no simple task, as the airwaves were thick with the mush of many perfectly legitimate signals. By then his boss Heydrich was becoming more involved in politics and the holding down of the populations in the occupied territories. In any case, the former law student was now chief of Counter Espionage in the SD.

Yet, despite all these efforts, the SD failed to locate the source of the information being radioed to enemy spies. Time and time again the Red Army, despite suffering enormous losses, seemed able to slip out of the intended German pincers. One thing Schellenberg did learn, the information was being sifted through Switzerland, probably with the help of Swiss Intelligence. To be sure, Schellenberg proposed to Hitler that a trap be laid: a plan would be hatched in Berlin whereby it appeared Hitler was planning to invade Switzerland. Troops actually began assembling around Munich, and the wily SD officer travelled to Berne, where he met General Masson. Masson soon gave the game away by enquiring about the divisions massing in Bavaria. Obviously, the Swiss had been warned. Schellenberg brazenly asked Masson to give him the names of the traitors in the German military, but the Swiss refused. This was not only galling to Schellenberg but a dangerous affront to Hitler, for it had also become clear these secrets were being radioed to Moscow from Switzerland.

The officer-conspirators in the *Wehrmacht* had been ultra-careful. Schellenberg failed in his task, but succeeded with the other Nazi security forces in smashing the much wider 'Red Orchestra', some of whose military members may have been among those supplying 'Lucy' with secret information.

Rudolf Rössler was never tracked down by the Germans, living out the remainder of his life in Switzerland and dying in 1958. His spy ring is alleged to have been the most successful of World War Two although some, or even much of his information, may have been supplied by MI6 via Ultra intercepts.

14
OPERATION 'NORTH POLE'

A British infantry officer of the Highland Division entering Holland from the south-west in late 1944 recorded these observations of the people in his diary:

> The Dutch certainly have a very high standard of living, at our expense. In two wars have we saved their freedom, and not least in spending money on armaments while they have invested in *kloosters* [a kind of luxury barn], schools and houses. As a nation they are fat, rich and lazy. I only hope they will face up to their responsibilities after the war, and take up their full share of garrisoning Germany and Japan, instead of leaving it all to us.

Billeted with a Dutch family, he learned from the host that it had been mainly treachery and the Fifth Column which had defeated them in 1940. The Germans had generously offered 20,000 'domestics' before the war. The Dutch accepted, realising too late that many were spies. Holland became full of German technicians, and the Dutchman had employed seven but sacked them all in 1937. This had led to trouble with his own government, who were afraid of offending their big neighbour. The Dutch Army was 'rotten to the core', inefficient, badly paid, poorly trained and corrupt, with men commissioned on the basis of secondary school education.

However much truth there was in all this, the Dutch people suffered increasingly under occupation, and by 1945 were starving. But in the beginning there had been very little for Heydrich's men to do. The population remained largely passive, there were few incidents. The wearing of patriotic orange buttonholes here and there hardly signified subversive activity, and the occupiers were to some extent keen to treat the Dutch as blood brothers, to demonstrate the more benevolent side of National Socialism.

Intelligence matters remained fairly quiescent. The Dutch Royal Family and part of the government had fled to Britain, leaving no resistance core or intelligence set-up behind them to keep the exiles posted on conditions under the enemy's heel. In fact, the Dutch intelligence officers who remained in Holland were known to the Germans, who extracted promises from them to retire into peaceful living, promises which were in the main adhered to. But in London, officers anxious to continue the war from Britain set up a new intelligence section. To do this they needed British help, which was forthcoming, though the Dutchmen were to find strings attached. The British, initially through MI6, remained in control. The Dutch had not the means to begin anything very much in operations across the sea. But the British Secret Service had suffered a severe set-back through the loss of its continental bases and key personnel, such as Messrs Stevens and Best. As stated elsewhere, MI6 was not at its best in this period, though one historian has recorded that the service carried out brilliant work from 1940 to 1945. Whether its record in Holland can be termed that is still open to debate. Its successes have never been trumpeted, but that has always been the way with the 'Silent Service'. At least, it was until more recent times. The failures in Holland that cost so many brave Dutch lives seem, according to published evidence, to have been the responsibility of SOE.

Orders that MI6 should cooperate and assist both SOE and the embryo Allied intelligence agencies were accepted by Stewart Menzies and Claude Dansey with reluctance, and in the latter's case at least, so cunningly that MI6, while remaining aloof from them in the field, contrived to either control or oversee their activities. The very fact that initially, at least, both SOE and Allied intelligence departments were forced to rely on MI6 communications put them at risk; Claude Dansey knew everything of the newcomers' activities, but the reverse did not happen. Further, Dansey is alleged to have been responsible for the destruction of vital SOE networks in France, using a known double-agent who worked for the SD. The question then arises, was Dansey also guilty in sabotaging SOE operations in Holland? The Dutch authorities laid the blame on the British for the loss of their people, all SOE agents, suggesting the British played a cunning double game against the enemy. If so, then that almost certainly was masterminded by Dansey. However, the idea that the British (through MI6) tried to fool the Germans in believing Holland was the D-day target seems

Himmler and his police chiefs: left to right – Daluege, Nebe, Heydrich and Müller

very unlikely. The cause of SOE's disasters in its operations in Holland seems to be simply their own incompetence.

It was of course the practice of MI6 to use agents native to the countries targeted. For Holland, the service called on a young Dutch naval lieutenant who had proved himself during the Dunkirk evacuation. Obviously, MI6 wasted little time in rebuilding its Dutch network, returning Lieutenant van Hamel to his own country by parachute in August. The handsome young Dutchman proved brave and utterly reliable, and within a few weeks had set up a spy ring which astonishingly included a member of the *Luftwaffe* he had met before the war. The German apologised for his country's invasion, and began passing information. Van Hamel operated under the noses of the Germans, reporting to London by radio; but by October the strain was beginning to tell and he asked his masters the British to fulfil their promise to lift him back to England. This at first they refused to do, but van Hamel persisted until MI6 set a rendezvous at a lake some distance away. There he would be picked up by seaplane.

Hamel cycled with two friends and helpers, taking his suitcase radio with him, and on reaching the area scouted the lake to await rescue. Spotted by

The Dutch spy for MI6, Lt van Hamel, shot 1941

a local constable and challenged, the trio explained they were bird watchers, which did not satisfy the policeman, who kept them under observation. It was some three days before a floatplane of the free Dutch Air Force arrived one night to pick up the agent, but by then the three were in custody. It was a painful lesson the British now learned, that no help should be sought from the police of the occupied lands, whose first duty in many cases seemed to be co-operation with the enemy. The Dutch constable had reported to his superior, the local police chief, a Dutch Nazi who wasted no time in calling in the German SIPO and military. As the Dutch plane came in to alight on the lake it was suddenly illuminated by a searchlight and met by flak. The aircraft was damaged and the crew barely managed to escape back to England.

With the three spies in German hands a search began for the suitcase Hamel had been seen carrying – it was finally found by a Dutch constable and handed over to the Germans. The German SIPO chief, Joseph Schreieder, had been informed of the episode, shocked that a British spy ring had been freely operating under his nose for weeks. He authorised his interrogators to use severe methods with the ringleader, van Hamel, but they learned nothing. The young lieutenant repeated over and over again that he was only a patriot doing his duty for Queen and country. The *Abwehr* officers called into the case were impressed by his bearing and fortitude, perhaps scornful of the crude methods resorted to by the SS and *Gestapo*. Like the British, they may have known that beatings and torture are not the best ways to elicit truth. But Schreieder was under pressure and embarrassed that the Dutchman was brought to trial without his secrets being revealed. Furthermore, this point was driven home to him by the officers of the court, but van Hamel was obviously guilty and sentenced to death. Again, his courage impressed the *Abwehr* officers, who

Dutch Fokker floatplane used to rescue Hamel

Josef Schreieder, chief of SIPO in Holland

are alleged to have walked out in disgust when the verdict was announced.

It had not been a happy episode for the SD, which had failed to detect the spy before important information was transmitted to England. Indeed, but for the Dutch police, Hamel and his accomplices might never have been caught. Nor had the *Abwehr* shone, but the *Abwehr*'s own ace sleuth Major Herman Giskes now did the most to retrieve the Germans' reputation.

Despite lengthy experience, MI6 had sent van Hamel into Holland with flawed papers, the date of birth on his ID card being shown as 29 February 1915. Any worthwhile co-operation with the new SOE's Dutch Section was marred by the latter's incompetence. Later, Dutch agents surviving to return to England were disgusted to find their compatriots involved in comfortable lifestyles in London while divided among themselves and achieving virtually nothing. They were petty bureaucrats more intent on establishing little empires. The agents' complaints were vociferous enough for them to be 'disciplined' by despatch to Scotland. The general amateurishness and lack of security among SOE's Dutch Section continued and would pay the enemy large dividends. It augured well for Messrs Schreieder and Giskes.

Now thoroughly alerted, and helped by Dutchmen willing to sell their services for money, the German SIPO and *Abwehr* were well prepared to receive further agents when MI6 and SOE continued operations. The 'firm' of Schreieder–Giskes proved a very unusual co-operation between SD and *Abwehr*, to great mutual advantage. Schreieder was by comparison a starter, and Giskes had already proved himself a professional detective in the counter-espionage game. As their co-operation grew, so did complications in the Allied camp across the sea. The Dutch wanted to run their own show, quite independent from their British hosts. This was impossible, the British could not allow a foreign spy agency to operate from their territory un-monitored, quite apart from the fact that facilities and equipment came from the hosts. Apart from some money, the Dutch had arrived in Britain with nothing, and the performance of the Dutch intelligence team set up in London proved to Dansey and MI6 seriously flawed, with three of four departments often acting against each other's interests. For one thing, MI6 had maintained from the start that Holland, owing to its terrain and dense population, was unsuitable for acts of sabotage and terrorism, which SOE began promoting by the despatch of arms and explosives.

But MI6 itself now encountered problems, for the enemy, thoroughly on the alert, had instituted many watchers and patrols along the Dutch inlets and coastline of the North Sea, among them troops of the *Waffen*-SS. Agents trying to land by motor-boat were captured. The agents were brave, but as in France, often not careful enough in matters of security; errors proved fatal. Yet, SOE was now getting into its stride, intent on establishing Dutch networks to undermine the German occupation. The Dutch agents fully believed in the British, convinced their masters directing them in London could not be flawed. For, whatever failings had been shown among the Dutch staff, the overall direction came from the British bosses of SOE. One agent called Lauwens, also believing the British invincible, was picked up by the Germans, who were now well up to the game and beginning to enjoy themselves. Major Giskes, following long, patient sessions with Lauwens, finally persuaded him to contact London. The Germans had at last decided, as had their opponents long ago in London, to enter the 'radio game', which for the Germans became known as Operation 'North Pole', or the *Englandspiel* – the England Game.

As with the British, the object of this game was to convince the opponent that their agent was alive and well, ready to carry out fresh orders. But unlike their British opposites, the *Abwehr* and SD chiefs in Holland would now encourage the despatch of arms and explosives by air. The RAF machines would occasionally be intercepted by *Luftwaffe* night-fighters waiting for them. Not too often, however, as that would give the game away. In fact, in due course the RAF questioned the all too frequent losses among the special-duty crews despatched to Dutch airspace.

The first Dutch agent, Lieutenant van Hamel, was finally shot by the Germans in June 1941. By then, agent Lauwens had begun calling London, the radio transmitter conveniently set up by the Germans in their own quarters. A crowd of *Abwehr* and SD officers gathered about him in considerable excitement and anticipation as they waited for an acknowledgement from London. When it came, they knew they were at last in direct contact with the enemy spy and sabotage organisation in Britain. The firm of Schreieder–Giskes was now in business – the Germans were exultant. As for Lauwens, despite his predicament, he had (by pre-arrangement should those very circumstances befall him) deliberately omitted his vital security check. This of course had gone unnoticed by the closely watching Germans. When the Dutchman let go his morse key and awaited the reply he prayed that those in London were now alerted to his fate – or at least would flash a query to try and establish whether their man was operating under duress.

However, the only signal received from London made it clear they had failed to heed his warning. But Lauwens decided they must have noticed, and were bluffing it out. He believed London knew the truth.

The game of deception now went into higher gear as Lauwens was induced by his new masters to call London again and again, requesting more agents, arms and explosives. SOE obliged by sending flight after flight, agents and containers dropped to the waiting Germans below. This happened month after month, until the receivers of all this booty were obliged to commandeer a whole warehouse to stockpile it all. Sten guns by the hundreds, plastic explosives and detonators, clothing, boots, cases, food supplies were sent, everything to sustain the growing army of subversion believed by SOE to be building and operating in Holland. The Germans grew more cocky and jubilant, and in Berlin, Himmler and Heydrich were agog as the great game of deception against the British continued unabated. So this was the true mettle of the once greatest spy organisation in the world? How could the people in London be so stupid?

The Nazi leaders were aware of the operation, which seemed to go on and on, with their enemy seemingly quite unaware of the truth. The number of agents which fell into German hands soon passed double figures, and Dr Goebbels was moved to visit Holland just to set eyes on a real, live enemy spy, albeit a Dutchman working for London. The possibilities inherent in the operation seemed endless, and various ideas to exploit this continuing contact with the British were put forward by Heydrich. Among them was the impersonating of agents by Dutch and German infiltrators taken back to England. Naturally, the *Führer* was kept informed and rubbed his hands with glee as each new report was passed to him on the latest triumph of German counter-intelligence and British stupidity. Hitler was also of course receiving the *Abwehr* reports from its 'spies' in England, most of them fiction dreamed up by the British. Obviously, both sides were involved in a bizarre situation, each playing the game to success, yet unaware of being deceived in other directions.

The grand play the Germans dubbed Operation 'North Pole' lasted about two years, an incredible length of time for such an episode. It cost SOE many lives before those in command in London finally began to wake up to the many pointers and warnings passed to them, some from agents who had escaped back to England. At least fifty agents paid with their lives for this gross incompetence. During the two-year period those in charge of operations, including General Gubbins at the top, seemed again and again to turn a blind eye to the truth – if it did not fit in with their preconceived notions of reality in Holland. For example, at one time when the flow of agents captured by the Germans had just begun, they were as a temporary measure accommodated in a former monks' training school dormitory. This was comparatively luxurious, its rooms retaining beds, sheets, hot and cold water, and other fittings that made life quite tolerable (except of course for the interrogations and Dutch SS guards outside the locked 'cells'). The people in London refused to believe the enemy could be so lenient, but for the *Abwehr* and SD it had been purely for their own convenience, not the prisoners' comfort; indeed, the spies had first been placed in rooms at the Orange Hotel.

When SOE finally wound up the operation in Holland, Major Giskes, knowing it was the end, sent a laconic, sarcastic signal in plain English to London, which confirmed the Britons' worst fears once and for all.

Despite this great success, attempts by Giskes–Schreieder to inveigle MI6 came to nought. Once Dansey had absorbed the early lessons very few of his agents were caught later in Holland. In truth, the Germans never really grasped the fact that they were grappling with two different agencies, only one of them the fabled British Secret Service.

One small and interesting spin-off for the Germans came through the capture of so many Sten machine-carbines. Not very accurate, with a tendency to jam, the weapon had been rushed out by the Sterling arms company at Dagenham in Essex during Britain's darkest days, at a time when the British Army had no personal light automatics of its own. Only a few hundred Thompson sub-machine guns had arrived from America, and the urgency of the situation precluded the design and production of a British weapon. The Sten gun in none of its forms compared for quality and usage with, for example, the German MP 38 or 40, or the Thompson for that matter, which the Germans easily discovered. Nevertheless, it was light and cheap to make, so the enemy made a copy, though this version was only produced in small numbers. A few captured Stens were issued to *Volkssturm* units late in the war, the British gun conveniently using the same 9 mm calibre ammunition.

15

THE DEATH OF HEYDRICH

B y mid-May 1942, Reinhard Heydrich's great energy had begun to
flag; he had worked hard to solve problems of occupation in West
and East. His initial success in pacifying the Czech workers had won
praise and gratitude from Hitler. 'The *Führer* confers with me alone', he
remarked to Schellenberg who after a period of shabby treatment was
suddenly back in favour, for good reason.

In fact, Heydrich's position had become less secure. For a start, and at
long last, his relations with Himmler had become tense. This Heydrich put
down to his success in Czechoslovakia, for he believed the *Reichsführer* had
become jealous. Worse, the man Heydrich had allied with, the poisonous
head of the Party Chancellery, Bormann, had now turned against him and
was intriguing with Himmler. It was inconvenient, to say the least, to
suspect plots were being hatched behind his back in Berlin, while he
was fully engaged in trying to keep the lid on a deteriorating situation
in Czechoslovakia. The workers there had once more begun to falter in
production, and Heydrich saw his policies failing. Not that it mattered
in the long run, for the Czechs were to be dealt with by a long-term
programme of 'Germanisation' and extermination. Those deemed to
qualify via the correct racial characteristics would be sent to the *Reich* to be
absorbed thereafter as Germans. All others would be 'deported', a Nazi
euphemism for wiped out. All the measures publicly announced for self-
rule and concessions were a sham; the Czech nation would cease to exist.

Under the guise of an anti-TB drive in that country, mobile clinics and
specialists would in fact secure details of all those Czechs suitable for
'Germanisation'. This would be via the just-started *Kennkarten*, or Identity
Card, system.

To counter the Himmler-Bormann alliance, Heydrich proposed
to Schellenberg he be sent as his chief's representative and liaison man to
Hitler's headquarters. Once there he would watch events and inaugurate a
counter-plot. It was a move that would never be implemented.

In wartime Germany the work of the Nazi Intelligence Service was
increased by the flow of foreign workers. Though these had been screened
before being allowed to enter the *Reich,* they needed watching. Obviously,
as the war progressed and ever-increasing numbers of forced labourers and
more specialist foreigners became part of Germany's population, it proved

Heydrich excelled in sports, seen here in fencing rig

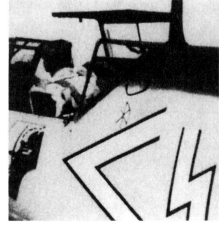

Heydrich flew combat flights with the Luftwaffe, *seen here with his specially marked Me 109.*

mpossible to keep them all under surveillance. As a result both the *Gestapo* and SD resorted to the proved method of using 'V-men', the same kind of trusted sub-agents who it was hoped could be relied upon to report anything suspicious to their controllers. Only a few arrests resulted, chiefly because most of the foreign workers had families back in their occupied homelands and knew that reprisals would be taken against them if any misdemeanours occurred in the *Reich.*

One aspect did, however, cause problems, and this was the consorting of foreign labourers (mostly Frenchmen) with German females. The reputation of Frenchmen as great and skilful lovers was known, and in some cases German women became involved – to their cost. Imprisonment was automatic for any *Reich* female having sexual relations with a foreign worker. However, it was hard to prevent and did happen, sometimes never becoming known to the authorities.

On another level, crimes were committed by foreign workers, though on a very small scale. Culprits received short shrift, and if Germans were found to be involved, then they too were severely punished. Although the civil police usually dealt with such matters, the *Gestapo* and/or the SD were sometimes called in, such as when there could be wider implications on the military or political levels. But these instances were rare.

In one case a Belgian worker employed in Württemberg became a prime suspect when damage was caused to rolling stock carrying munitions. The man was watched by the German CID, but when nothing came to light they gave up. They therefore warned the *Gestapo* and SD, who took up the case, the two agencies co-ordinating their efforts. Things then took a more serious turn when a fire broke out in the same railway sidings, an explosion being only narrowly averted. If it had happened among the stacked munitions it could have been catastrophic for the whole neighbourhood.

The Nazi security police staff in Paris

Heydrich's man in Paris (right)
Karl Oberg, seen here with the
Belgian W/SS hero Leon
Degrelle

The Belgian was allowed to stay in his job, which involved driving munitions to the sidings. Obviously, he had the opportunity to carry out sabotage, but when he was allotted a mate (provided by the *Gestapo*), caution seemed to overcome the man, who probably guessed by then that he was now under close watch. After several weeks had passed, with no more sabotage, the *Gestapo*'s man was withdrawn – and another fire resulted at once. The Belgian was arrested for questioning but revealed nothing. However, he provided one clue when he mentioned his brother was with a unit fighting on the Russian front and had suffered terribly. Furthermore, not wishing to face their parents in Belgium he had spent leave with his brother in Germany. The authorities concluded the disgruntled foreign volunteer soldier was the root cause of the sabotage, and enquiries revealed the man had only recently completed a long sick leave in Germany. He was brought back from Russia, and after confessing everything, was shot.

It became the role of both SD and *Gestapo* to monitor home opinion, to generally watch over the people's mood and arrest any who spread unwholesome rumours or defeatist talk. But it was specifically the SD's duty to produce reports which were circulated on a very restricted basis among top Nazi leaders, including Hitler and especially Goebbels, whose prime task it was to mould public opinion. This SD work continued right up to the final weeks of the war.

SD and SIPO making a raid

There was another aspect in German wartime life which certainly gave the authorities problems and especially angered Goebbels. This too involved the SD internal service. It was the subversive broadcasting by the BBC's German services, known as 'black propaganda' (i.e. untruths compared to the 'white' truth). In fact, a certain amount of this very cunningly contrived material was the simple truth which had been concealed from the German people. Despite penalties and the manufacture of domestic wireless receivers (*Volksempfangen*) designed to receive only the *Reichssender* stations, some Germans managed to listen to London, though few would be brave enough to disseminate what they heard.

The news and talks on the BBC's German programmes for the *Reich* were distinct from the 'special' programmes broadcast from Caversham by its 'other' departments under the skilled hands of the 'German' expert Sefton Delmer. His schemes were often extremely funny, though with serious intent. Separate programmes were broadcast for the different *Wehrmacht* services, and it is obvious that despite all Hitler's findings regarding the great harm caused to Germany by British propaganda in the earlier war, and all Dr Goebbels's efforts in the current conflict, the Germans lagged far behind in terms of broadcasting propaganda to the British. The samples put over stations Hamburg and Bremen featuring 'Lord Haw-Haw' had passed their 'sell-by' interest date after 1940, while the dance music by 'Charlie and his Orchestra', incorporating propaganda lyrics, can be seen

215

as crude and infantile by comparison, even though the music itself was perfectly agreeable, comprising as it did British and American popular tunes. One of the most absurd and counter-productive of such early efforts in this direction was quite offensive, since it allowed the classic 'Onward Christian Soldiers' to be sung by an almost comic vocalist sporting the most blatant German-accented English. The crude propaganda lyrics seemed even to have turned off the performer's producers. But, as indicated, the changes were not too effective either.

All this was a far cry from the snippets culled from German newspapers, which, served up verbatim, twisted or added to, were fed back to listeners in the *Reich* or in the services. German U-boat crews anxious for their kin in towns and cities under air bombardment found news of such events via the BBC, coupled of course with black propaganda. *Luftwaffe* aircrews could hear startling reports on their particular units and equipment delivered not only by British experts using exact knowledge gained from PoWs, but from ex-*Luftwaffe* airmen, a few of whom had been successfully 'turned' by the British. The British Station *Soldatensender Calais* combined such programmes with top-quality dance music and swing to capture German service audiences, who, while refuting or laughing at some more obvious propaganda, certainly recognised the truth which was included.

There was very little that Goebbels could do about this. Jamming failed, as the broadcasts were especially powerful.

However, the most worrying aspect to German morale and good order was the dropping of fake ration cards by the RAF. Dire penalties for using such cards did not always prevent usage, the chief thinking behind the British effort to disrupt the enemy's food rationing system. It worked brilliantly, for the cards seemed to be exact facsimiles of the originals in use in the *Reich*. Even the paper and card used had been as near matched as to appear perfect. The British organisers used a specially chosen private printing firm whose brilliance certainly equalled that of the artist used by Heydrich in the Tutachevsky affair of the mid-thirties. When the exasperated German authorities changed the design or format of the ration cards, as they were forced to do, at, of course, extra trouble and cost, the British followed suit. The new 'authentic' cards would fall over Germany, courtesy of the RAF, within a comparatively short time.

One family caught and arrested by the SD with such cards protested they had just been issued them by the local Party ration office. Sure enough, when the SD agents checked they found this to be true. Baffled, the Party officials checked with the supplier, and after a thorough and painful investigation, discovered that somehow a large consignment of fake cards had become mixed up with genuine ones. The mystery was never solved, despite a long and stringent search.

In another case, the wife of a Party officer was caught using a fake card, which still had mud over it, having arrived during an air raid. The officer pleaded for his wife, but she was awarded six months' imprisonment and he resigned and joined the *Wehrmacht.*

It had not been too difficult for the British to get their hands on samples of the real ration cards, and indeed any other papers such as identity cards and the many varieties of travel and work permits needed by foreigners in Germany. Some were actively working for London, with means to pass samples back to England via neutral states.

Attempts by Himmler to spread SS activities across the Atlantic virtually came to nothing because Herbert Hoover's FBI had become fully alert to the dangers of Axis and Japanese espionage. All staff at the embassies and consulates concerned were watched, while links from Berlin with the German-American Bund were not pursued. Heydrich had various ideas for independent SD intelligence-gathering operations in USA, but for various reasons these were not furthered; chief among these was his almost total preoccupation with the East.

As soon as Hitler's plans for Operation 'Barbarossa' became known, Heydrich stepped up his operations to gain information in Soviet-occupied territories, and these included the insertion of agents in the Balkans. Yugoslavia and Bulgaria were the two countries in which the SD tried to recruit suitable spies, but the attempts proved largely abortive. Heydrich had to rely on his Poles and some Czechs, but in the latter case he knew of their leanings towards Moscow and needed to be extra cautious. In fact, the case of Czechoslovakia was a vexing one and needed special handling.

The idea to smash the Czech state and reduce it to a vassal state fit only to serve German war production had been Hitler's. Sheer hatred produced a succession of brutally repressive measures which traumatised the population and by an ironic twist led to Heydrich's own death.

Despite fierce determination and disregard for the rights of others, Hitler, and indeed Goebbels, were susceptible to foreign opinion. The diplomat Baron Konstantin von Neurath was chosen as so-called 'protector', but the real power was given to SS *Brigadeführer* Karl Hermann Frank, a German-Czech with a passionate hatred of Czech culture and people. Behind Frank hovered the even greater power of Heydrich and Himmler.

The Germans had been impressed by the impressive fortifications bypassed in their bloodless occupation of the country. There were massive steel and concrete bunkers, some of which were used for rehearsal training by the airborne troops allotted the task of capturing the Belgian forts at Eban Emael in May 1940. Hitler had coveted the great arms works at Pilsen, and owing to the Czech government's failure to heed Lt-Colonel Moravec's warnings, the enemy had been able to capture 600 tanks and 1,000 planes intact. Far worse, and almost incomprehensible, is the fact that the Germans also took the entire gold stocks of the Czech National Bank.

The British had easily recognised the value of maintaining some kind of

'Fifth column' within Hitler's eastern 'bulwark'. They were impressed by the Czechs and made special efforts to assist Moravec and his staff. When the general was bombed out of his very modest suburban house in south London, the British provided him with better accommodation in town. A year after his banishment from Czechoslovakia, Lt-Colonel Moravec had re-established contact with reliable people in his homeland – and a programme of subversion against the German occupiers began. Despite *Gestapo* proof that the provisional head of the puppet Czech government, General Elias, had been in touch with London, Hitler stayed his hand. The Elias team would continue to be tolerated. 'Accounts will be settled with the Resistance movement and Czech personalities who have compromised themselves at a later stage', Hitler said. Von Neurath, despite constant attempts to undermine his authority by Frank, was maintained in office by Hitler, purely as a front and for tactical reasons.

Meanwhile, the truth hidden in the Nazis' velvet glove had already manifested, though covertly, for Himmler had initiated a criminal and inhuman campaign to wipe out the twenty-two-year-old Czech nation by 'Germanisation'. The kidnapping of children following the disgusting atrocity at Lidice in 1942 as a reprisal for the assassination of Heydrich was merely part of a process which Himmler had begun two years before. Himmler had ordered the birth records of suitable Czech children to be

SIPO and SD interrogate Jews in one of the ghettos

- and here direct a Jew into dangerous forced labour

examined for his 'Aryanisation' programme. Demands by some Nazi leaders for the elimination of the 'Protectorate' Bohemia-Moravia (*Böhmen-Mahren*) were resisted by Hitler on the obvious grounds that it would inconvenience his war effort; it seemed senseless to stir up resistance and rebellion among a population so useful to the *Reich.* Therefore, even though Himmler took the initial steps towards assimilation into Germany of the country and its people, the final steps were to be delayed for at least the duration of the war, even though Hitler agreed in the summer of 1940 for the first stage to begin.

In May 1941 Goebbels was able to record in his diary how pleased the *Führer* was with the Czechs for their efforts in war production. Not one case of sabotage had been reported. What the Czechs produced was good, serviceable, reliable and solid. They had proved themselves reliable and hard workers. 'A valuable acquisition for us', Goebbels remarked.

In the period dating from the full occupation of Czechoslovakia in 1939 to 1941, the *Gestapo,* SD and German civil police, plus some auxiliary units, had carted off thousands of suspects. But they had then eased their actions in view of the *Führer's* policy of *rapprochement* – to keep the Czech workers quiescent. Indeed, very little at all was happening in this Nazi province, apart from the squabbling and in-fighting between the local Nazi leaders themselves.

This situation was of course most unsatisfactory to the Czechs and British in London. To have a country under the Nazi jackboot apparently co-operating most fully in the production of war materials for use against the

Allies, and a population who seemed to have settled down to the reality of life under enemy rule, was anathema. Steps would have to be taken.

The Soviets, like the British, had through their agents refrained from actual sabotage, their activities confined to intelligence gathering Moscow's spies operated fairly freely in the sense that the Germans failed to catch them, and though no actual co-operation took place, the Soviets became aware of the British-Czech agents' presence. But in a small number of cases, some Czech agents managed to serve both London and Moscow, bearing in mind that all activities in any way affecting the USSR were faithfully reported to Moscow by Kim Philby of MI6.

In Britain the 3,000 soldiers of the Czech Brigade had been quartered around Leamington Spa, near Warwick, since October 1940. They had escaped from their homeland in 1939, then been chased across France the next year, only just managing to reach England, to see their enemy triumphant across the Channel and the *Luftwaffe* battering Britain. Not knowing if they would ever see their homeland again, these Czechs, like the assorted other displaced Allies (Poles, Frenchmen, Belgians and Dutch, etc.), began to suffer a loss of morale, through hopelessness of the situation. Buoyed though all had been by Hitler's failure to finally subdue Britain through invasion, the inability of their hosts to hit back except by pinprick air raids led to a disheartening situation. Then great dissatisfaction with their officers spread among the Czech soldiers, who saw them as fascists and anti-Semites, much the same as the Germans. This disaffection amounted to near mutiny, and 480 men refused to obey orders. This revolt not only shook their leaders but set alarm bells ringing in the British security department MI5, where it was suspected the Czech units had been infiltrated by Red agitators. That a number were sympathetic to the USSR was undeniable, but then so were many British, both in and out of uniform. The same situation prevailed in Czechoslovakia, especially strong after Chamberlain's leading role in signing away Czech independence in 1938.

How to maintain their comparatively small forces' morale in Britain had become a problem to the various Allied governments in exile. There seemed no immediate prospect of sending them back into Europe to fight the Germans, or indeed of any action at all; only the airmen managed after re-training to hit back at the enemy. At the insistence of the British, the Czech mutineers were split up and transferred to pioneer units as common labourers. Similar problems affected the Poles, many of whom were stationed in Scotland. But their General Sosabowski settled them rather effectively by 'volunteering' many hundreds into a Polish parachute brigade. However, these troops, like those who trained as infantry and armoured units, would have a long wait before going into action in Normandy and Italy. Special problems existed in the Czech units; many of the men were of the better-educated type, who had volunteered to fight, sacrificing everything, with ideals based on hope of an improved society.

Jews indicate the alleged hiding place of an arms cache in a graveyard

The coming invasion of Russia spurred the exiled President Benes to urgently attempt to reinforce his links with the so-called 'Home Army' in Czechoslovakia. The only way to do this was by sending in liaison teams of agents by parachute. Czech volunteers were trained in parachuting by RAF instructors at Ringway Airport, Manchester. Owing to a navigational error, the first agent despatched jumped over Austria and was caught by the enemy. With increased security because of the imminence of Operation 'Barbarossa', *Brigadeführer* Frank feared an uprising in Czechoslovakia once the invasion of Stalin's USSR began. As a result of SD surveillance, several important agents who had been in radio contact with both London and Moscow were arrested; carefully built networks were destroyed by the German SIPO. In one raid, two Czechs were caught in the act of transmitting. One opened fire with a pistol and enabled his comrade to escape by sliding down the radio antenna wire, thereby losing one of his fingers. His friend was dragged off by the *Gestapo*, to be tortured in the Pecek Palace. 'We have successfully uncovered an intelligence ring,' Frank teletyped Heydrich in Berlin, 'not communist, but serving the USSR.' Several transmitters had been found, but these, Frank hinted, were only the tip of an iceberg, there were more. Several organisations were operating against the *Reich*, and as they were still unfound they posed a danger. Frank had been demanding greater powers, over the head of von Neurath, in order to terrorise the Czechs into submission and to betray the subversives among them. Yet, whatever the truth of Frank's beliefs and wishes, the fact was that the most important radio link, the 'Three Kings' transmitter operated by agent A-54, had been lost on the eve of Operation 'Barbarossa'.

President Benes was of the opinion that the invasion of Russia would signal the beginning of the end of Nazi Germany. When it began he was exultant, for he saw that only by spreading the war could hope be gained for the liberation of his country. His fear that Britain would stand aside and watch the two dictatorships ruin each other was dispelled by Churchill's pledge to aid the USSR.

Within a fortnight after 22 June, the German and Allied armies had taken almost 600,000 Russians prisoner. As usual, nothing seemed to stop the Nazi *Blitzkrieg*, and Hitler declared the Red Army broken, and the Soviet colossus smashed, never to rise again. His generals were inclined to agree with him.

Close on the heels of the driving German *Panzern* and infantry went the SS *Einsatzgruppen* (EG), exterminators who were let loose over every area conquered by the military. They began their ghastly work of murdering everyone undeserving of becoming part of Hitler's New Order. The composition of these units is not without interest.

'EG' personnel were drawn not only from different departments of the *Sipo*, but also from the *Waffen*-SS, and all were volunteers. Though members of *Waffen*-SS combat units would not normally have served in such units, there were those nominally in that arm but not serving at the front.

Special Action Group A may be taken as fairly typical as to the composition of such a unit: *Waffen*-SS 340; motorcyclists 172; administration personnel including women 31; SD 35; criminal police 41; *Gestapo* 89; auxiliary police (foreign) 87; order police 33; interpreters 51; teletype operators 3; radio operators 8. The total personnel was 890, or the size of a strong battalion, but size varied.

The EG units were self-contained, and in some cases followed so close on the heels of the invading armies into Russia that they became involved in fighting with the Red Army forces. The very high number of motorcyclists is an indication of their great mobility; the EGs were well provided with their own transport and ranged far and wide into the occupied territory. An EG could vary in strength from a total as high as one thousand to as little as four hundred men and women. The main unit would be divided

A series of photos of an Einsatzgruppe *receiving orders and interrogating suspects in the East*

into *Sonderkommandos* (SK) of twenty to thirty men, *Vorkommandos*, and *Teil-Kommandos*, which were about the size of an Army platoon. The EGs were responsible only to their rear headquarters, who forwarded reports of action taken direct to Himmler via a special radio link. Later, once the occupied zones were settled, regional commands were set up ruled by SIPO chiefs, with EGs on call. Among the most enthusiastic of the EG killers were those locally recruited in Russia and the Baltic states.

All political commissar officers captured in the German invasion were automatically shot by military police or *Sipo* troops on Hitler's order. The chief victims of the EG units, however, were Jews.

Obviously, Heydrich's once exclusive Intelligence Service now included men who were no more than common criminals and mass murderers. It was all a far cry from the pre-war days when the likes of Alfred Naujocks acted as resourceful 'James Bond' types to infiltrate the enemy camp. The SD had in some areas become part of a gigantic killing machine. At the same time, Heydrich's personal power had grown so that he was widely regarded as a man to be feared, and by some perhaps as a likely successor to the *Führer* himself. Whatever Himmler's cunning, he remained to some as no more than a 'chief clerk', not least among soldiers of the *Waffen*-SS, whose disdain for the '*Reichsführer*-SS' grew by the year. But Heydrich served him well, although believing his chief's predilection for crank theories and hobbies was crazy. In fact, by 1941 Heydrich had indeed come to see himself as a force apart, and had in mind goals he did not share with Himmler in any sense.

Press reports in Britain of Nazi reprisals in Occupied Europe concealed a far more terrible reality of wholesale deportations and mass executions, which had nothing to do with reprisals for acts of sabotage against the occupying *Wehrmacht*. Whole regions were to be crushed and transformed through 'Germanisation', which involved a fantastic wave of twentieth-century barbarism. Allied politicians who learned a few facts of these happenings kept silent. While there was little to be done to stop Hitler's murder campaign against innocents, it must be obvious that the acquisition of such facts gave the Allies a very great propaganda weapon, which if properly used might have had effect in blunting the Nazi terror, given Hitler's susceptance to foreign opinion.

As the German blitz smashed deeper and deeper into Russia, Stalin became more desperate for Western help; the first demands for a 'second front' reached London, despite the fact that the British were heavily committed to defending their Middle Eastern bastion against Rommel. The desert war had not so far drawn off any significant German forces. Britain was waging a life-or-death struggle in the Atlantic against U-boats, and the Japanese threat was looming in the Far East. Stalin suggested a British landing in France, which was out of the question. The Soviet leader had no conception of the scale of such an undertaking.

The Czech Intelligence Service had long had links with Moscow, which were belatedly discovered by MI6, who found such contacts useful, again bearing in mind the traitor Kim Philby in their midst. The Soviets, in their great need, graduated beyond the mere gathering of intelligence in Czechoslovakia; well aware of the war factories working full blast for Hitler they demanded a programme of sabotage. The response of the British government was that the Germans would in the long run benefit from premature action in Czechoslovakia. However, Benes, with his honour at stake, could not stand by in London while his countrymen aided the enemy. He was not yet prepared to see blood spilled through the inevitable Nazi reprisals, so argued for RAF raids on the Czech war plants. This request was almost impossible to fulfil owing to the distances involved and the lack of four-engined aircraft in Bomber Command of the RAF.

Yet within Czechoslovakia the communists were a force to be reckoned with; among the workforce there was a strong feeling they had been betrayed by their exiled government and its British ally – their real friends could well lie in Moscow. As a result, a wave of 'go slows' took place, leading to a one-third drop in production, which naturally alarmed Hitler. Benes was pressured by both Moscow and London to continue such actions. He was in a difficult position, being in actual competition in a sense with the other exiled governments for full recognition and aid from their hosts. It was this pressure to aid the Soviets which prompted Benes to call

Himmler inspects the SS guard at Hradcany castle in Prague

on, the now General, Moravec to launch the attempt to assassinate the new Nazi boss in Czechoslovakia.

On 27 September 1941, news broke from Berlin that '*Herr* Konstantin von Neurath' had asked the *Führer* to relieve him on health grounds. *Obergruppenführer* and General of Police Reinhard Heydrich took over as 'Protector' of Bohemia-Moravia. This was dire news for Benes.

Heydrich, it is alleged, intrigued through his man Karl Frank for the post. He wished now to reach out, to further his ambitions, in a sense to command an empire stretching from the Atlantic coast to the Urals. No matter if Hitler was regarded as at the pinnacle of power in Europe, he, Heydrich, was the real power behind the throne. He was tired of doing the dirty work, of cleaning up the sewers in the vast territories conquered by Germany. His chief Himmler was in the process of being ridiculed and failing in his efforts to 'Germanise' Eastern Europe, and Hitler's new faithful paladin, Martin Bormann, and *Gauleiter* Koch in the East were openly contemptuous of him. Himmler's edicts in the region were now largely disregarded by Koch, simply on the commonsense grounds that a policy of deportation and terror ran foul of his need for labour. Hitler, through Heydrich, now planned to convert Czechoslovakia into an SS state, a valuable power and economic base in the heart of Europe. While, on the face of it, Himmler's and Heydrich's interests would seem to have been similar, the former had underestimated his former pupil's cunning and ambitions. Heydrich was after the larger prizes; as each of his targets had been won, so he dreamt up new ones. He secured Bormann's aid in undermining von Neurath and bombarded Himmler with requests to succeed him.

By late 1941 both *Abwehr* and *Gestapo* were in the habit of inflating their reports of 'sabotage' and arrests to improve their ratings in Berlin, so to speak. Heydrich, in order to promote his own future, constantly told Himmler and Hitler that a dangerous situation had been allowed to develop in the Protectorate, which threatened the Greater German *Reich*. These machinations, which involved Frank, probably included the setting up of 'sabotage' themselves, such as the igniting of 100,000 litres of precious petrol. Frank's chief thug and hit man Karl Boehme was regarded even by the *Gestapo* as a villain. He was behind the blowing up of a German children's home.

Frank flew to see Hitler on 20 September, to promote the cause, armed with a briefcase full of evidence proving the uselessness of the then Protector, von Neurath. Frank believed the *Führer* would have no choice, in the face of a rising wave of unrest and sabotage, but to sack the diplomat. However, his time with Hitler was unexpectedly interrupted by the arrival of Heydrich, who, with masterly timing, began inserting his own version of events. He handed Hitler documents listing *Gestapo* and SD reports proving the Czech puppet government's contacts with London and Moscow. This sent Hitler into a rage. He ranted against the Czechs, and to Frank's dismay appointed Heydrich *'Reichsprotektor'*, charged to smash all resistance in Czechoslovakia.

When Heydrich telephoned his wife Lina to give her news of his great promotion, she seemed unimpressed. She had suffered through his affairs with other women and rarely saw him, but was mollified by the thought of more money and a fine new home in Prague. That night, Heydrich went with his family to dine at the Schellenbergs', requesting his deputy and lawyer to check over the document appointing him *Reichsprotektor* in case it contained any limitation on his powers.

When Heydrich's plane touched down at Prague airport, an assembly of Nazi officials and a guard of honour awaited him. He kept them waiting, telling those with him in the aircraft to observe how a top Nazi leader was received. In a speech later to an assembly of Nazi and Czech officials he told them of his steely determination to crush all opposition, to 'put to the wall' all resisters – but reward those who saw the sense of co-operating. In this respect, he proposed raising the fat ration of arms workers by 400 grams per week. Other measures followed swiftly.

Over 400 people were condemned to death following fresh police raids, many of them ex-officers and members of the intelligentsia. Heydrich pursued the same line as the Soviets – any who might provide a new rallying point for resistance cells had to be eliminated. In all, between 4,000 and 5,000 people were arrested, but processing and interrogating them

Himmler in Prague with: Frank, Wolff and Heydrich

*Heydrich and Frank
salute the flag at
Hradcany castle*

proved too slow for Heydrich. He began seeking ways to shift all such prisoners to concentration camps so they could be shot more quietly – 'while
attempting to escape'. It was in these times that the new 'protector' earned
himself the title of 'Butcher' Heydrich.

By December 1941, Heydrich's reports to Berlin, which were printed on
specially large type for Hitler, boasted how he had crushed all resistance
leadership, including a team parachuted in by the Soviets. Heydrich had
also cracked down on the black market; Germans and Czechs who traded
illegally were shot, their goods confiscated and distributed to the Czech
workers' canteens. Heydrich used cunning to woo these Czechs who were
so essential to the German war effort, calling on them to list any grievances
through a trade union group he received at Hradcany castle. He followed

up promises with deals, having 200,000 pairs of shoes released free through workers' councils and increasing the rations of certain key personnel in the arms plants.

On the political front, Heydrich had Prime Minister Elias arrested, tried, and sentenced to death. The sentence was postponed as he saw the politician best served as a hostage for the good behaviour of his people.

For the comfort of his family, Heydrich took over a château about twelve miles outside Prague, confiscated from a Jewish sugar magnate in 1939. Here his wife Lina began a new life, ordering extensive refurbishments, including a new bathroom and swimming pool. Labour was provided from the nearest concentration camp, usually Jews destined for the gas chambers. Lina began collecting German porcelain, probably receiving gifts from Himmler's Allach factory. Considering the growing hatred generated against him by his victims and others, Heydrich was careless of his own security. He insisted on being driven in an open car into the city each morning by his burly chauffeur Klein – without the benefit of an escort. But Himmler insisted on sending an SS guard company to watch over the Heydrich residence.

In October, Heydrich reiterated to his staff that all Jews must be expelled from the Protectorate as soon as possible. The town Terezín (Theresienstadt), was to be made the collecting point for the exodus. Evacuees would be exported to Minsk and Riga, and the 'cleansed' area settled exclusively by Germans. In all, almost 94,000 Czech Jews were removed under Heydrich's programme, and of these only 3,371 survived.

Heydrich with economics minister Funk in Prague

*A new SIPO college is opened
by Heydrich in Prague*

Meanwhile, in London President Benes was pleased to inform *The Times* that up to one-third of Czech war production for the Germans had been lost to 'undetectable sabotage', enough material to equip a whole division. Then, in view of the new situation which had arisen in his homeland, Benes decided on the 'spontaneous act of desperation' (as he called it), the elimination of a top Nazi chieftain. His first choice was Karl Hermann Frank. Benes, still under pressure from the British and Soviets, felt bound to initiate some action, whatever the expected reprisals. He conferred with his Intelligence chief, General Moravec, and the result was Operation 'Anthropoid' – the target being Reinhard Heydrich. The Czechs in Britain hoped his assassination would provide 'a spark which would activate the mass of the people'. In this Benes and his aides were wrong, as he later realised, and in the fashion of politicians caught in the wrong, he tried to deny complicity in the affair. He had been careful to keep his talks with General Moravec off the record.

Since German intelligence from Britain was almost completely provided by MI5, no hint of any scheme to kill a Nazi leader was received in Berlin. Not that it would have made much difference, for Heydrich was insistent that the Czechs should not fear their 'protector'. He believed that by going to work unescorted he was holding the psychological initiative.

Operation 'Anthropoid' relied on just two volunteers, one Czech, one Slovak, both trained parachutists and small-arms experts. For security reasons the Czech Resistance was kept in the dark. The two Czech soldiers selected were Josef Gabcik and Karel Svoboda. They were briefed by General Moravec in London, learning how much importance had been put on the operation, and of the dangers. They could have opted out, but decided to stay with it, though guessing they stood little chance of survival. However, the Czechs were unable to go ahead without the co-operation of SOE, who insisted on further training, and during this Karel Svoboda suffered severe concussion. Dropped from the plan, his place was taken by Jan Kubis.

The British Secret Service played no part in this operation, which following the Czech approach was managed entirely by SOE. Whether the great dangers inherent in such a plot were apparent and pointed out by the SOE chiefs is uncertain. The Nazi reaction was entirely predictable: severe reprisals would be taken against the Czech people. There would also

The aged Czech premier Hacha is 'interviewed' by 'Reichsprotektor' Heydrich

be disruption to the agents trying to rebuild broken networks, which would defeat the main object seen by some doubters, which was the provision of intelligence to West and East. Certainly, MI6 could not have been in agreement with such an operation.

Then, perhaps all too typically, 'Bomber' Harris, not long in the saddle as chief of RAF Bomber Command, refused to release one of his four-engined bombers to transport the two assassins. In desperation, President Benes appealed to the Poles, who had been given a Halifax; but this aircraft crashed in Sweden after an operation over Poland. Not until 28 December was a plane and crew found, when a Halifax of No. 138 Special Duties Squadron became available. General Moravec collected his two agents and rushed them to Tangmere in Sussex, and following a meal and pep talk he saw them off in the Halifax. Also aboard the aircraft were two more Czech teams, codenamed Silver A and B. Both these had been frustrated in previous attempts using ancient Whitley bombers. The Halifax roared away into the darkness, its fuel tanks topped up almost to overflowing, loaded with crew and nine agents.

Following a long, cold and uncomfortable flight, the Halifax arrived over Czechoslovakia, but snow over the landscape below prevented the crew from properly identifying the drop zones. Nevertheless, the Operation 'Anthropoid' agents jumped at 02.24 hrs on 29 December.

Czech Lt-Col Panacek organised Operation Anthropoid

Meanwhile, the former naval lieutenant who had so offended the martinets of the old *Reichsmarine* now held a whole nation in his grip. Heydrich had confirmed his total power over a revamped team of Czech puppet politicians under a replacement for the hostage General Elias. The new premier was called Krejci, who was appointed to rubber stamp Heydrich's orders and carry them out; when he met with his cabinet they were obliged to render their proceedings in German. Krejci pledged full co-operation with the *Reich*. This included the acceptance of Himmler's SS-owned enterprises, which soon began showing a healthy profit. Further, the giant Skoda works was ordered to divert production exclusively for the *Waffen*-SS, which led Albert Speer to complain that the SS was treating the Protectorate as its own province. Heydrich continued to use stick and carrot methods, declaring May Day a public holiday, distributing free tickets to football games, theatres, cinemas and luxury hotels. Nazi propaganda portrayed him as a friend of the workers, while Goebbels recorded:

> The Czechs are working to our complete satisfaction and doing their utmost under the slogan – 'Everything for our *Führer* Adolf Hitler!'

Obviously, the one-third drop in war production had not lasted long. Heydrich's measures had worked, and he felt the situation was well enough in hand to leave for Paris. German reverses in Russia had resulted in a new wave of Resistance activity in France. The German military seemed helpless to prevent it, so Heydrich installed SS *Gruppenführer* Karl Oberg in Paris with full powers to carry out whatever measures he felt necessary. Heydrich's measures were based on his experience in the Protectorate. The situation in France reflected badly on the *Abwehr*, whose reputation was not enhanced by the successful British raid on the radar station at Bruneval. Indeed, Admiral Canaris's stock had fallen. He had failed to provide Hitler with data on enemy radar developments, although the *Führer* always took the keenest interest in war technology. The previous autumn Canaris had been astonished to receive a 'Hitler order' passed by General Keitel giving him the job of assassinating the French Army Commander-in-Chief, General Weygand. He found the idea outrageous, and after asking Keitel the reason for it, discussed it with his staff. Keitel told him the *Führer* believed that Weygand, recently sent to restore order in French North Africa, would instead go over to the British and help them prepare bases in that area. Canaris told Keitel his service was an intelligence agency and did not deal in killing. In fact, Hitler was now considering ordering the *Wehrmacht* into the Unoccupied Zone of France governed by Vichy, which could well have propelled Weygand over to the British. In the event, the German invasion of Southern France was postponed and Weygand stayed put.

German attempts to commit espionage and sabotage in the USA ended in farce or disaster. Hitler blamed this too on the *Abwehr*'s incompetence.

An operation designed to create fresh problems for the British in Ireland also failed, perhaps through no fault of Canaris. The IRA leader Sean Russell was to be transported by U-boat with some henchmen, but he died of a heart attack *en route* and the submarine returned to port. When ten 'enthusiastic young Nazis' were also sent across the Atlantic to commit sabotage, one died of VD at sea. Seven of the nine survivors who landed on the American mainland were arrested immediately and soon executed, the other two jailed.

Next, Canaris was charged with the execution of the French prisoner General Giraud after his escape from German captivity; the admiral refused and Giraud was spirited away on a British submarine.

On 18 May 1942, Admiral Canaris arrived in Prague, humiliated, and compelled to sign a second 'agreement' with Heydrich.

Heydrich decided to apply 'Protectorate' solutions to the problems in other occupied territories. However, his repeated attempts to put his ideas to Hitler were, he believed, baulked by Himmler and Bormann, who he felt had become jealous and alarmed by his rise in status.

Meanwhile, near-disaster had struck the two Czech agents after they parachuted from the Halifax; the difficulties experienced by the RAF navigator had resulted in their being dropped in the wrong place, not near an

Para-agents Sergeants Valcik and Kubis

airfield as planned, but well off course and twenty miles from Prague. Worse, Gabcik had injured his foot in landing and could only hobble along with the help of Kubis. Also, unknown to either, the false papers prepared in London contained errors that any alert German security policeman could spot.

Gabcik buried their parachutes while his comrade made a quick reconnaissance. Soon they had moved away across the snow towards a nearby village, choosing to hide in an old stone quarry. They ate chocolate and bully beef and tried to plan their next move, and obviously they needed to find a doctor to tend Gabcik's foot. They could not know that their enemy was about to move into a heightened state of alert that would place them in even greater danger.

A series of German police successes now uncovered explosives and equipment, which proved that the Czech Resistance were now moving into actual sabotage and assassination. These fears were confirmed. A bomb attack was made on the German ambassador, Franz von Papen, in Ankara. He and his wife escaped, but the would-be assassin was killed. Investigation pointed to the attempt as having originated in the Soviet embassy; Goebbels blamed the British and Soviet Secret Services. This incident late in February was followed by another in March, when the chief of

Lt Opalka and Sergeant Gabcik

235

Heydrich's *Einsatzgruppe* A, Franz Stahlecker, was ambushed and killed by Soviet partisans. In the same month, the *Gestapo* arrested a man acting suspiciously in Prague railway station. He claimed to be a German musician, but in his case the police found a rifle with telescopic sights. Interrogation revealed he had been sent by Moscow to kill Heydrich.

Alarmed by a wave of such incidents throughout their occupied territories, the Germans stepped up their already tight security. Extra guards were placed around the Heydrich home and at his public appearances. But he refused all attempts to have him travel in a closed, armoured car under escort. He would not believe the Czechs would be stupid enough to try and kill him.

Over the following weeks the two agents from London led a harried and highly dangerous existence. They had been extremely fortunate in finding a sympathetic doctor to treat Gabcik's injury, and were able to pass from one safe house to another. This was remarkable in itself, for the country was in great tension, with constant German security checks and raids. Whole streets were being sealed off as houses were searched, people shot at random and a general state of fear and terror engendered. Most Czechs would no longer trust any but their closest friends, fearing infiltration and betrayal, the majority only wishing to lead some kind of life in peace. This was difficult, as there were spy and sabotage groups moving about Prague and elsewhere, from both London and the Soviet side; some were

The assassination scene –

discovered by the Germans, and gun battles took place, with casualties on both sides. The atmosphere was anything but conducive to the job of intelligence gathering by MI6 agents.

While the disasters befalling some of its teams became known in London, no word was received concerning Operation 'Anthropoid'. For week after week Benes remained in a state of ignorance and anxiety, until finally, a coded message broadcast by the BBC received an acknowledgement from another agent – the pair were in good hands. Benes had other worries, as rumours had begun to circulate of peace feelers put out by German opposition groups; the Czech leader became anxious, for should the Allies take them up he feared for the fate of his country. However, the British rejected them, though the Soviets are believed to have entered into secret dialogue with their 'fascist beast' enemy, though nothing came of it.

Not until the morning of 27 May 1942 did the two agents Gabcik and Kubis set off to kill Heydrich. In their battered old briefcases they carried dismantled Sten guns, concealed by grass. Many Czechs now kept rabbits to beat the food shortage and picked grass to feed them. They both wore caps, Gabcik carrying a raincoat, and travelled by train to a suburb of Prague to collect bicycles, one of which was an old girl's model. They strapped their cases to the handlebars. Cycling to the Holesovice district, they were met by their helper, Valcik, the man who had informed London they were safe. Valcik sauntered off along the highway, a mirror

and damaged Heydrich Mercedes

in his pocket for signalling the approach of Heydrich's car. The spot chosen for the attempt seemed ideal, at a sharp bend in the road where the SD chief's driver Klein would have to slow down. They would present a perfect target. Kubis placed himself behind a lamp post and in the shade of some trees, while Gabcik crossed over to wait on a little grassy rise near a tram stop, his Sten gun now assembled and hidden under his raincoat. Then they waited.

The evening before, Heydrich had inaugurated a concert at the Prague Music Festival at which a quartet of pupils from his old home town of Halle had participated, playing examples of his father Bruno's works. Heydrich chatted with German and Czech guests during the interval, his mind no doubt darting to weightier matters, for he was due to fly back to Berlin to see Hitler the next day. A rumour had started that he would not be returning to Prague. Heydrich fully expected to be given plenipotentiary powers to take command in the West. Heydrich was excited at the possibility of actually taking over a nation such as the French. He fully expected he could succeed where others had failed.

The two agents waiting in the Prague suburb on that bright May morning were brave and dedicated. They had sampled the kind of life meted out to their people by the occupiers at first hand and were determined to strike a blow that would shake their hated enemy – at whatever cost.

Nazi police and Czech firemen attempt to flood out the hidden agents

As Heydrich's car slowed before them the two Czechs would open fire and throw grenades into the car. Yet, almost until that very morning, attempts had been made by patriots in Prague to have the attempt called off. These had failed, as Benes was determined to strike at the highest possible level. At 10.32 a.m. Valcik saw Heydrich's car topping a rise not far away, and began flashing his mirror to the waiting pair at the bend in the highway. Gabcik changed his position and cocked his Sten gun ready for action; Kubis readied his bomb. At that moment a tram rumbled along the road towards them – it was too late to call it off.

As Klein eased his foot off the pedal on reaching the bend in the road, Gabcik pulled out his Sten, aimed it and squeezed the trigger. Not one bullet emerged – the unreliable weapon had jammed. Open-mouthed and helpless, Gabcik gaped into the face of his would-be victim as the Mercedes swept past. Heydrich had seen the Czech with the gun, but instead of ordering his driver to accelerate away, he ordered Klein to halt and then stood up in the car, tugging at his pistol holster. Neither Heydrich nor his driver had noticed Kubis, who calmly stepped into the road to toss his bomb. But in the rush of events he now failed and the grenade struck the side of the car. The explosion showered Klein with splinters and shattered glass, the debris also hitting Heydrich. Both Germans yelled in pain, Heydrich slumping down onto his seat – but only for a moment. The Czechs, in those seconds, saw two spare SS uniform jackets thrown up into the air by the blast, falling back onto the tram wires above.

Not apparently badly wounded, both Germans now leapt from the damaged car, pistols in hand. Kubis ran off, his face cut and bleeding through flying debris, Klein in hot pursuit. Heydrich now lurched towards Gabcik, who managed to loose off one shot from his recalcitrant weapon. He saw Heydrich collapse against some railings. He had broken ribs, but much more seriously, some fragments including hair from the car seat had entered his spleen. Gabcik ran off, watched by a host of incredulous tram passengers, as Klein returned to tend his chief, who is alleged to have called out 'Get the bastard!' The tattered, bleeding figure of the most dangerous man in the Nazi hierarchy slid to the ground before the watching crowd. No one moved to assist him.

Obviously, after so many weeks of waiting, the attempt had been bungled. Gabcik panicked, dropping his Sten and running away into a butcher's shop. The proprietor tried to run outside, colliding with the fugitive. Then, outside in the street he hailed the searching Klein, who hurried up and tried to fire at Gabcik in the shop. But his pistol jammed; he gave it to the butcher, ordering him to chase the suspect. The tradesman trotted off a few yards before deciding his own safety was more important.

At the scene of the incident, little was done to remove the bleeding and now unconscious figure of Heydrich until a Czech policeman riding on the tram managed to commandeer a truck loaded with floor polish. The driver helped load Heydrich into the cab; a blonde woman among the crowd had

Traitor Karel Curga is called to identify the bodies

recognised the victim and word soon spread. They soon realised what would soon follow. The ride over tramlines jolted Heydrich to his senses so that he called out for the driver to stop and help him into the back of the vehicle, where he sprawled among the crates of polish until they reached the Bulovka hospital soon after 11 a.m. Heydrich remained conscious while a Czech doctor examined his wounds and cleaned them up. Not until a German doctor in charge arrived was a more thorough examination made, and following X-rays the wounds were soon seen as serious. Heydrich began insisting on more expert help; he was removed to the operating theatre soon after midday. Meantime, the Czech policeman had called the *Gestapo* to report the shooting of an unknown German officer; but the German who took the call did not find the news very unusual, and saw no need for urgent action. Some time passed before three *Gestapo* agents visited the hospital – at the enquiry counter no one seemed to know of the affair. The *Gestapo* men were obliged to walk through the wards before finally discovering the *Reichsprotektor* sitting up on a table while two nurses attended him.

Shocked into action, the alarm was raised. SS troops and more agents were rushed to the hospital, and men were sent to the scene of the attack, where the two Czech agents had carelessly left all the evidence needed by the German police to prove where the operation originated.

As soon as Hitler heard the news he ordered *Brigadeführer* Frank to await the arrival of an armoured limousine he would send, and to post a reward of one million marks for information leading to the arrest of the attackers; ten thousand Czechs were to be arrested and all those already in custody for political offences shot at once. Even the bestial Frank could see the stupidity of this; such measures would play into the hands of the exiles and resisters, possibly stirring up a revolution. Above all, the disruption would interfere with war production. The chief *Gestapo* investigator, Heinz Pannwitz, thought it was the work of parachutists, not the Resistance. But Hitler continued to insist on revenge, appointing police chief Kurt Daluege as temporary *Protektor*; Daluege had been one of Heydrich's rivals, known as a blockhead and called 'Dummi-dummi'. Himmler was so moved by the outrage he burst into tears. It is an interesting study for the student of human nature, that a man so unmoved by the death of millions could be reduced to weeping by the injury of a colleague. He soon recovered, to begin sending teleprinter messages demanding implementation of the *Führer*'s orders.

Hitler and Himmler with Heydrich's two children

241

Other Nazi leaders also voiced their horror, including Goebbels, who decided to arrest 500 Berlin Jews, with warnings that up to 150 would be shot in response to further outrages. Goebbels believed the attack was part of a larger British-Soviet plot to assassinate Nazi leaders – even Hitler.

In Prague chaos reigned, and senior detectives rushed from Berlin found 'an anthill' as scores of SS, military police and *Sipo* milled about in apparent confusion. Some 21,000 police and troops were sent in to scour the Czech capital for the two fugitives; a curfew was announced for 9 p.m. nightly; 36,000 homes were to be searched, SS troops showing their disregard for self-control and discipline by firing everywhere. One of the senior Berlin detectives needed a military escort to regain his hotel in safety.

In London, President Benes had no idea of the terror he had inadvertently unleashed in his homeland as the Nazis argued about just how many Czechs must be executed in revenge. In Prague, the pathetic ex-Premier Hacha offered ten million crowns for the attackers' capture, calling Benes 'Public Enemy No. 1'. Hacha had been bullied into submission by Hitler before the war, and only recently presented the *Führer* with a lavish gift.

Everyone over the age of fifteen was ordered to register with the police at once or be shot. The shoe shop chain of Bata, well known in Britain, used one of its windows to display the items left by Gabcik and Kubis at the scene of the attack. The massive manhunt was even extended into Germany itself, train and bus passengers being scrutinised. Various rumours circulated in

Heydrich's coffin carried through streets lined with SIPO

Berlin, including one that the attack on Heydrich had in fact been plotted by the Nazi leaders themselves, because the Intelligence Service chief turned politician knew too much.

The former premier General Elias was executed on 19 June, by which time some 157 people had been killed in reprisal, among them whole families heard approving the attack on Heydrich; others were randomly shot during the great German search operation. The 7,000 registered doctors in the Protectorate had to swear they had treated no wounded men of the assassins' description. The manhunt disrupted all other subversive activities, and several agents, including two of the Silver teams, had very narrow escapes. Gabcik and Kubis themselves were finally found a haven in the crypts of the Karel Boromejsky Church, near the centre of Prague.

News of the attempt on Heydrich had been announced over Prague radio during the afternoon of 27 May. Benes sent his thanks to General Moravec and had a message of congratulation sent to the one surviving radio link in Czechoslovakia, remarking, 'It is proof to me the whole nation is solidly together'. In a statement issued on 29 May the Czech government in exile exulted in the operation carried out 'against the monster Heydrich', citing it as an act of revenge by the people of Czechoslovakia. The statement also called on the Czechs to aid the attackers and mete out just punishment on any who betrayed them. A similar broadcast was made from Moscow by the Czech communist leader Klement Gottwald.

Heydrich's body lies in state in Hradcany castle

243

Himmler takes charge of Heydrich's sons as the funeral cortege sets off (note gun carriage)

In the Bulkova hospital, Himmler's doctor, Gebhart, believed Heydrich would pull through. The *Reichsführer* called hourly, enquiring as to the patient's condition. By early June, Heydrich had gone downhill. He developed peritonitis and septicaemia and was in great pain, needing frequent doses of morphine and blood transfusions. His spleen, infected by fragments and hair from the Mercedes car seat, was the source of the problem, but Gebhart refused to allow its removal. The Germans had no penicillin, then under development in Britain, so they used sulphanilamide. Heydrich retained some lucidity, perhaps perplexing Himmler who flew to see him on 2 June; the dying man quoted lines from his father Bruno's fourth opera: 'The world is just a barrel organ which the Lord God turns Himself.'

Their conversations, such as they were, are alleged to have touched on philosophical questions of life and death. Did Heydrich in his last hours run through the 'achievements' of his life, wondering what would follow if he died? Or, did he expect to survive and plan his role in a revitalised Third *Reich*?

Heydrich passed away at 4.30 a.m. on 4 June, Generals Daluege and Frank outside the door of his room. The hospital death register noted: '*Reinhard Tristan Heydrich* (cause of death) *wound infection*'.

A grandiose Nazi-style funeral with all the usual trappings took place in Berlin on 9 June for the 'fallen martyr'. The event was the signal for much maudlin sentiment and eloquence by the leadership, who extolled Heydrich as the most typical Nazi hero.

The Czech people cringed as they awaited the inevitable backlash on top of all that had already been meted out to them. Hacha attended the funeral, in the vain hope his presence might denote some kind of apology and thus soften the blows of reprisal. Lina Heydrich did not attend the funeral, though her children did, their hands held by Himmler; she was expecting her fourth child and remained in the château outside Prague.

Hitler had, it is alleged, once referred to Heydrich as 'stupid', but he and his 'cabinet' now saw him as 'irreplaceable'. Too overcome, the *Führer* spoke only briefly, perhaps playing a part he saw as appropriate. He posthumously awarded the dead man the highest grade of the German Order, releasing more of his pent-up venom against the luckless, pathetic Hacha when the Czech tried to pass condolences and blame it all on the British. Hitler agreed the Czechs were intelligent, industrious workers, but this would not deflect him from taking extreme measures.

As a start, 1,000 Jews were transported by special trains to the death camps, two more groups following for the ghetto at Terezín. Of 3,000 Jews sent, only one survived, by jumping from the train. The mass murders in Poland continued under the title Operation 'Reinhard'; the 'resettlement' process was by then well under way. But, as a special example to both Czechs and their allies abroad which was well publicised and filmed, the SS leaders razed the village of Lidice in Bohemia, the idea having originated with Karl Boehme. The village had already been raided in a search for terrorists. A Czech parachutist captured in October 1941 had foolishly carried written addresses of two families there, one of whom had a son in the RAF in Britain. Although fresh searches revealed nothing incriminating among the villagers of Lidice, the *Gestapo* convinced themselves the killing of Heydrich had been organised from that location.

As a result, Boehme's recommendation that Lidice be sacrificed was approved, and at 9.30 p.m. on 9 June the area was cordoned off. The women and children were removed, 199 males were shot, and of the 95 children, only eight were considered worthy of 'Germanisation' under SS families. Sixteen of the children were traced after the war, the rest had vanished. The women were taken to a concentration camp. The houses of Lidice were razed, Labour Corps personnel bulldozing the debris into the earth. *Brigadeführer* Frank arrived too late to witness the killings; Himmler of course had no stomach for the dirty work himself, and is alleged to have swooned on the one occasion an execution was staged in his presence. Frank commented that the earth of Lidice would yield good corn.

The Nazi-Czech propaganda blasts continued as the manhunt still failed to smoke out the culprits. Only Heinz Pannwitz made sense when he dared to suggest mass terror was not working, whereas inducements might. Yet, a new dictate arrived from Himmler on Hitler's behalf, ordering the execution of 30,000 politically active Czechs. But Karl Frank had followed up the detective's idea, offering an amnesty to anyone who had seen or

A monument was built to Heydrich but torn down once the war ended

helped the killers. This resulted in over 2,000 statements flooding in over three days, including an anonymous letter actually naming the two agents. The betrayer was called Curda, one of a group codenamed Out Distance. Amazingly, Curda is said to have been a heavy drinker and an open admirer of Hitler; somehow, his training staff in England had remained in ignorance of this, yet one more example of SOE inefficiency. Curda gave himself up to the *Gestapo* and was soon persuaded to identify more agents from photographs and confess he was a parachutist himself. The story almost surpasses fiction as the hounds of the *Gestapo* followed a trail of clues, raiding house after house in the hunt for Gabcik and Kubis. Eventually they found Mrs Moravec (no relation to the general), known as Marie, who took cyanide when allowed to visit the toilet. Following another suicide among the suspects, the Nazi sleuths removed Mrs Moravec's son to their head-quarters for torture. They tried everything, including the pouring of alcohol down his throat. Then, becoming desperate, the interrogators presented the youth with his mother's head, floating in a fish tank. At this point the Czech boy's senses gave out and he began rambling about a crypt in the Karel Boromejsky Church his mother had told him to use if he was ever in trouble.

It was the final chapter for Gabcik and Kubis, who were surrounded by 700 Germans, the enemy met by bullets and grenades as the trapped agents defended themselves. The SS troops began firing wildly from inside and outside the church and a fire started. After a two-hour battle the besieged men's fire stopped, and when the German soldiers crept into the first crypt they found the bodies of the two men, who had taken poison, while a third lay unconscious. He died in hospital.

However, the dead were not the assassins. When the church preacher was interrogated, he admitted four more men were hiding in the cata-combs. Appeals by Pannwitz over a loudspeaker for the Czechs to give up were rejected, as was a call by Sergeant Curda. This signalled a fresh outburst of gunfire and grenade throwing, and after an attempt by the fire brigade to flood the crypt the Germans threw in tear gas grenades. Pannwitz argued with Frank and the SS troop commander, and finally they sent in a group to storm the Czechs' hideout. The SS soldiers wore gas masks, but were ambushed among the dark recesses and withdrew, dragging two of their number with them. Then, as the SS prepared to hurl explosive charges into the crypt, shots were heard, and when one brave German ventured back inside he saw the two Czechs lying dead. Both had been wounded, but ended it all by shooting each other in the head.

It had taken the Germans six hours to defeat the parachutists, who had armed themselves with eleven pistols.

Himmler and his subordinates had wanted the Czech agents taken alive for interrogation, but also to parade them as tools of the British. In further operations, the two agents of Silver A were tracked down and killed, one of them by Czech police. These agents had hidden in the village of Lezaky.

*The village and population of
Lidice were annihilated by way
of reprisal – the action filmed.
Note Army officers at the scene*

As a reprisal the Germans shot all the adults, leaving two little girls as worthy to be 'Germanised'. The leader of the Jindra group was taken alive and offered to co-operate by restoring the radio link with London. The Germans had found agents' call signs and already had such a scheme in mind, hoping perhaps to parallel the great success in Holland. But this time things went awry, although the Czech spy base in Waldingham was contacted successfully. The correct procedures were not followed and those in England soon realised the enemy were in charge at the other end. There would be no second 'North Pole'.

It was the Czech agent Vanek who talked freely to save his skin, generally running down the British as the betrayers of the Czech people in 1938–9, and the Czech politicians in London who he believed were simply delivering his country into the hands of the communists. Of all the agents despatched, only Vanek survived. Among the many executed were the relatives of agents Kubis and Valcik; Gabcik's people were spared because they were Slovaks, but 4,000 relatives of exiles in Britain were arrested, including Benes's own. Sergeant Curda was rewarded with five million crowns, paid over monthly instalments, and his mother and sister released from jail. Curda then found it expedient to change his name and marry the sister of an SS officer, going on to work for the enemy as an *agent provocateur*. He became a convinced Nazi and was responsible for the arrest, torture and death of new agents and their relatives.

The demise of SD chief Reinhard Heydrich resulted in the death of 5,000 people in reprisal, but was hailed as a victory in Britain, USA and Moscow, during a period of severe Allied reverses. Heydrich was sanctified by the Nazis, and his death mask adorned books and memorials. His château was awarded to Lina in perpetuity by Hitler. *Frau* Heydrich wrangled with the SS over the terms of the gift and the cost of refurbishments carried out by slave labour on her orders.

The Heydrich affair brought much satisfaction at the time to President Benes by focusing world attention on his country, with even greater sympathy expressed when news broke of the terrible atrocity at Lidice. The incredible, blind savagery of the Nazis rebounded on them in the form of world-wide hatred for Germany, and certainly helped to stifle the slight opposition to the massive bombing campaign against the enemy's towns and cities then getting under way. There could be no softening of hearts, though it was the German civilians who would pay the heaviest price. This in no way implies that the strategic air war resulted from Nazi bestiality in Occupied Europe. The policy of trying to bomb Germany out of the war already existed and formed an essential part of British and later American war strategy. But the crimes carried out wholesale by the Nazi regime hardened public opinion around the world, as Japanese atrocities provoked indifference to the smashing and atomic bombing of their cities later.

However, the Nazis tried to shift all responsibility for the horrors unleashed on the Allies, and Benes in particular. The enemy had learned how Czechs in the homeland had tried to have the attack on Heydrich cancelled; Frank made capital of this, accusing Benes of risking his nation from his comfortable bolt hole in London. This propaganda forced a denial from the British Foreign Office, which continued to insist the assassination had been the work of the Resistance in Prague. After the war, no one on the Czech side in Britain would admit the attack had originated with them. In 1942, among the eulogies written (some published), on the

German side, was this from Wilhelm Hoettle, himself a member of the Nazi SD:

> Truth and goodness had no intrinsic meaning for him, they were instruments to be used for the gaining of more power . . . politics were the stepping stones to more power. A man without a moral code.

Schellenberg wrote of Heydrich:

> A born intriguer, with an incredibly acute perception of the moral, human, and professional weaknesses of others . . .

Heydrich had, he added:

> Unusual intellect, matched by the ever watchful instincts of a predatory animal . . . inordinately ambitious . . . in a pack of wolves he must always prove himself the strongest.

16

THE END OF CANARIS

B y May 1942, Heydrich had largely given up his devotion to intelligence work. His working hours were directed towards the pursuit of more power and the destruction of the Jews in Europe. His removal did in a large sense leave a vacuum in Czechoslovakia; Hitler and his henchmen were correct in seeing Heydrich as irreplaceable, as not one of the candidates for the post of '*Protektor*' had anything like the same combination of personal powers – one can hardly term them 'qualities', put to the wrong use. The extermination programme for the Jews was safe in the hands of Adolf Eichmann and the lesser executives capable of running a murder machine. It was Eichmann who, according to one of his deputies, said before the end of the war that he would leap laughing into his own grave, happy in the knowledge that he had five million people on his conscience. It would give him a feeling of extraordinary satisfaction.

At first, the total RSHA structure was taken over by Himmler, before being handed to Kaltenbrunner, while Walter Schellenberg was promoted to head the Intelligence Service, which he did until the end of the war. He was then arrested by the British as a member of the 'criminal SS'. Schellenberg said that in the early days only the 'best kind' of people were to be found in the SS, and it gave members a certain social cachet and prestige. Schellenberg regarded himself as one of these 'best' Germans, who found, agreeably or otherwise, that the spy service they had joined had become tainted as part of an organisation mixed up in wholesale criminality and murder.

The *Reich's* Main Security Office had, by the end of the war, become a huge and complex bureaucracy. Schellenberg said: 'For a beginner it was practically impossible to find one's way in the labyrinth of bureaux, offices, sections, services and sub-sections.' The once small, 'Peoples' Information Service' had swollen like a balloon into a monstrous maze of often competing segments which spelled inefficiency and error.

The young lawyer who saw his path to success via the SS had gained it by the triumphs it achieved. He had personally played the major part in capturing two important British spies; he had tracked down the Vietinghoff brothers, which led to the smashing of the so-called 'Red Orchestra' spy ring in Germany; he had contacted Alan Dulles, the American spy chief in Switzerland; and arrested Admiral Canaris in July 1944, his old friend

Kurt Daluege speaks on the first anniversary of Heydrich's death

of the horse-riding days. His final 'triumph' had been the prodding of Himmler to ask the Swedish Count Bernadotte to try and open peace negotiations with the Allies.

These were the 'successes' pleaded to by Schellenberg in court after the war. Before that he had been returned to the British after arrest in Sweden. Following months of interrogation by his captors in London, Schellenberg was taken to jail in Landsberg, where Hitler himself had sojourned for a while in 1924. During the Nuremberg process, he was called as a witness in various trials of war criminals before his own case came up. On 14 April 1949, he was awarded a modest six years in jail, released with cancer two years later, dying in Italy on 2 April 1952. He was buried in an unmarked grave in the public cemetery in Turin.

It was perhaps no coincidence that plots to topple the Hitler regime only gained real momentum once serious reverses came to Germany in 1943. As indicated earlier, whatever games Heydrich and his SD had played, there had always been opponents of Hitler, both in and outside the

Ernst Kaltenbrunner took over as SD chief

Wehrmacht. The best known have been written up well in more recent years. Lesser names also managed to survive and even escape *Gestapo* detection, such as the supposed '*Oberleutnant* Heinrich Schnitt', named with two other *Luftwaffe* aircrew as working for MI6 for years. They eventually defected across the North Sea in their new Junkers 88 night-fighter. Schnitt was the son of a former secretary to Gustav Stresemann of the old *Weimar* government, and is alleged to have worked with others to feed information to the British via Switzerland from the early days of the war. Schnitt is even said to have touched down in his Dornier bomber at an RAF base one night to deliver a package of data.

If the tale reported long after the war is true, then this *Luftwaffe* pilot must have been the longest-serving German to outwit the *Gestapo* and SD. Certainly, his arrival by daylight later, escorted by Spitfires, has long been reported in aviation journals. But such men had no part in the plot to kill Hitler; they were apart from those who, while feeling Germany under the Nazis was doomed, seemed incapable of action. Others among the military and aristocracy bravely involved themselves in clandestine activity, their security insufficient to stave off the *Gestapo* and other police agencies on their trail. Nevertheless, the attempt to kill Hitler very nearly succeeded. The number of German officers involved in that plot was small, whereas a much larger number were organised into the so-called 'Red Orchestra', the large spy ring run from Moscow and allegedly utilising one hundred radio transmitters. Whatever the *Abwehr*'s failures overseas, it chalked up some notable successes on German and occupied territory. Perhaps there was a chance there for Admiral Canaris to take over and better organise this spy group. It would have been difficult, as he was under surveillance himself, and since the 'Red Orchestra' were Moscow-owned, no doubt the admiral would have nothing to do with them. They included some of the most prominent families in Germany, aristocrats who had long served the state in one way or another, some highly placed in the administration. It seems ironic that such a class should have been recruited by the Soviets, even covertly, but then Moscow would use anyone useful to them.

Leader of this 'Red Orchestra' was Harald Schulze-Boysen, grandson of Grand Admiral von Tirpitz of the old Imperial Navy. Schulze-Boysen was a familiar, rather Bohemian figure in pre-war Berlin. He was one of the showy, slightly comic intellectuals who had found it expedient to recite left-wing poetry, dolled up in black sweater and allowing his blonde hair to grow down his neck. The same kind were to be found in London, armchair revolutionaries who espoused the cause of the radical left but joined no political party. His kind gathered for parties, mouthing foolish platitudes extolling social and political upheaval, in truth apparently having no connection with anything but idleness. They spouted verse to each other, pseudo-Reds hailing the revolution in Russia as a glorious episode in the people's struggle for emancipation. Surprisingly, Schulze-Boysen's mother had connections and put her son into the *Luftwaffe* at the outbreak of war, not to fight of course, but to sit behind a desk in Goering's so-called 'Research Bureau'. Perhaps Schulze-Boysen was in fact a 'Pimpernel' figure, playing the fop, while in truth working against the regime? It seems odd that a man known for his effete lifestyle and left-wing views should be employed in such a leading Nazi's '*Gestapo*' offices, ostensibly spying on any opposition. Obviously, if this was part of Schulze-Boysen's job, then he was well placed to warn those indulging in anti-Nazi activity of any danger.

In the event, according to published evidence, Schulze-Boysen used his privileged position over two years to gather in like minds and build up a great espionage service reporting to Moscow. Since he had never actually joined the Communist Party he seemed safe in Goering's headquarters, since he could never have been admitted into such a job if he had. Schulze-Boysen's spies worked in various *Wehrmacht* departments and were also to be found in the civilian ministries. Among these was Arvid Harnack, nephew of a famous theologian and a brilliant young economist in Walter Funk's Economics Ministry. Harnack had travelled abroad before the war, and while in USA met a girl in Wisconsin University, marrying her and

Most infamous Nazi executioner – Adolf Eichmann

taking his bride back to Germany. Other agents recruited by Schulze-Boysen were Franz Scheliha of von Ribbentrop's Foreign Office and Horst Heilmann in Goebbels's Propaganda Ministry, which also housed an English lad with a German mother. His name unknown, the latter did not spy, but read Goebbels's news bulletins in English for enemy listeners, finally ending up in a concentration camp before the war's end. Another Schulze-Boysen spy was Countess Erika von Brockdorff, who worked in the Labour Ministry.

These were just a few of the more prominent names in the Schulze-Boysen circle, which might have continued to operate until the war's end, but for the capture of two Soviet agents parachuted into the *Reich* in 1942. Neither *Gestapo* nor SD had detected the great spy ring in the heart of the Nazi administration. It was the *Abwehr* which perhaps stumbled onto it and, obliged to alert the other agencies, Walter Schellenberg took up the trail; the case proved so large he was forced to do a great deal of travelling around Germany and outside its borders. Since the two Soviet agents had talked freely, many of the 'Red Orchestra' spies were soon languishing in jail. In all, an amazing seventy-five leaders of the conspiracy were charged with treason, fifty being condemned to death, among them Schulze-Boysen and Arvid Harnack. Mildred Harnack (née Fish) and Countess von Brockdorff were given prison terms, but Hitler intervened and insisted these women be executed, so they were. In Germany in those times the usual method of execution in civilian trials was through the medieval way of beheading. There were no regular gallows available, though many

255

makeshift ones sprang into use in the Eastern territories. In the case of the 'Red Orchestra' spies, a new method was inaugurated: they were strung up from meathooks. This style of execution was also used with the Bomb Plotters.

The awful fate of such victims could not be counted against the new SD chief Schellenberg when his own case came up after the war, as he had only carried out a similar role to the counter-spies of MI5. Yet, pleased though Himmler must have been with Heydrich's successor in that role, the SD had no successes to report against the Western Allies, only against the various Resistance groups. It was not the SD which was blamed for the failure to warn Hitler of the Allied landings in North Africa, for example. When Hitler feared the Allies might invade Spain he used Canaris to sound out General Franco's possible intentions, i.e. would the Caudillo then side with the enemy (as did the Italians later)? Franco, partly in payment for Hitler's help in the Spanish Civil War, had sent his 'Blue Division' to fight on the Russian front as part of the great anti-Bolshevik 'crusade' trumpeted by the Nazis. Losses and suffering in the terrible winter of 1941–2 led to the unit's withdrawal. Attempts by Hitler to inveigle Franco into the general war against the Allies by promising him help in taking Gibraltar failed. Neither Canaris nor von Ribbentrop made much impression on the wily Spaniard. The SD was not involved.

Then, despite having excellent contacts in Italy, the *Abwehr* failed to alert Hitler to the impending dire turn of events in Italy. The fall of the *Führer*'s friend shook him, though the turncoat nature of the Italians was not over-looked. Admiral Canaris did, however, warn General Keitel not to trust the Italian General Badoglio's government, which, following Mussolini's arrest, had assured the Germans of a continued fight against the Allies when they landed in Sicily and then the mainland in September 1943. Keitel failed to pass on the warning because it clashed with information provided by von Ribbentrop's staff in Rome. He would never pass Hitler unwelcome news if he could help it for fear of upsetting him. Canaris had been canny enough to work up a better relationship with the SD, passing *Abwehr* reports to Schellenberg and assessments by both agencies to Keitel. This Canaris did to cover himself and others he knew were playing questionable roles. The man who had remarked to his Colonel Oster in 1940, 'Aren't you people inciting me to commit what is really high treason?' was himself now playing a dangerous game.

Meanwhile, Alfred Naujocks had long been dismissed from the SD. A little black market dealing had come to Heydrich's notice early in 1942, during the tail end of the German Army's great trial on the Eastern Front. Naujocks had great cause to regret his indiscretion and felt understandably bitter against the man for whom he felt he had worked so well. Thrown out by Heydrich, Naujocks was posted to a *Waffen-*SS unit in the 7th Prinz Eugen mountain division, then engaged in 'anti-bandit' warfare in the wild country of Yugoslavia. He was no infantryman, and used his cunning to get

Karl Frank, hung for war crimes

himself ensconced in a supply echelon, eventually becoming a sergeant. By the late summer of 1944 he was drafted as a replacement into what remained of the 12th SS Hitler Youth division in the West, but deserted to the Americans in October. Before that, in late 1943, he had received a letter from an old SD crony giving various news and gossip, including a hint that both SD and *Gestapo* were on the track of 'real culprits' in the *Abwehr* – including 'Old Whitehead'.

Colonel Oster had lost his job; the military lawyer Hans von Dohnanyi had been arrested; Canaris's Division I chief of the *Abwehr*, Colonel Piekenbrock, was gone, legitimately posted to lead a regiment in order to make general. The chief of Division III, Colonel von Bentivegni, was leaving the service, and his successor, Colonel Heinrich, was involved in a serious car crash. One by one, the admiral's oldest and most trusted aides were leaving, and he knew the SD and *Gestapo* were closing in on him.

It is true that Canaris began to work against Hitler's interests in small ways after 1940, when he was asked to assess the Swiss military and economic potential. Hitler toyed with the idea of taking over that small nation for various reasons he thought to his advantage. For example, the Simplon and St Gotthard tunnels allowed better access to Italy; the country's cash and small but expert industries were also useful. Canaris advised such a move futile, largely because of his Swiss connections and sympathies; in his report he told Hitler that the Swiss mountains would enable its army to maintain prolonged resistance, and the country had enough supplies stocked to last at least two years.

Then, when the Germans captured Swiss documents in France, Canaris advised them of the event.

Following Heydrich's success in the Venlo affair in 1939, he had refused Canaris access to the interrogation reports gained from the two captured British agents. The reason was that both SD and *Gestapo* came to believe the trumped-up German military conspiracy ploy invented by Heydrich had in fact a basis of truth – and was connected to the *Abwehr*. However, it took the Nazi security services another five years to really find something to pin on 'Old Whitehead'. Before he was put to death, his *Abwehr* was finally swallowed by the SS and became a mere 'department', its work confined to military intelligence. Long before that, in 1942, the SD had uncovered *Abwehr* probings into home intelligence matters, but despite this clear breach of their agreement, Heydrich took no action; he preferred to watch and wait. His assassination prevented him from reaping a final triumph over his old adversary.

It has been suggested that Himmler and Heydrich were not entirely frank with each other. Whenever the two met, which until May 1942 was fairly often, Heydrich confined himself to passing his chief current reports and facts. He never confided suspicions or ongoing investigations. It is interesting to speculate what his reactions might have been if he had lived to learn of Himmler's early peace feelers. Whatever the opposition practised surreptitiously by the *Abwehr* and others, *Reichsführer* SS Himmler is believed to have first considered replacing Hitler himself following the first great German reverses in Russia in 1941–2, while outwardly the staunchest of *Führer* supporters. Secretly, Himmler was prey to other ideas, using the lawyer Langbehn to pursue very tentative feelers abroad. He sat back, perhaps waiting for the opposition to do the dirty work of killing Hitler, at which point he would intervene and take over as '*Führer*' – to preserve law and order in Germany.

On the same day Canaris met the new Nazi security chief, Kaltenbrunner, two young German students were executed for their part in a plot hatched at Munich University. Brother and sister, the youngsters were killed for indulging in subversive activities in the birthplace of National Socialism. Though details are lacking, their 'plotting' must have been rather more serious than belonging to the jazz movement that sprang

Ernst Kaltenbrunner in the dock at Nuremberg

up in the *Reich* and which was never really cracked down upon by the Nazi authorities. The executions at Stadelheim Prison followed a trial and the usual type of loud-mouthed harangue delivered by the chief judge of the People's Court – Roland Freisler. According to *Gestapo* and SD reports, unrest in Munich followed these deaths; Freisler was to die under Allied bombs later.

On 22 February 1943, Canaris met the SS police chief in the Hotel Regina, the admiral viewing Kaltenbrunner as a huge, ungainly creature with the shape of an Alpine lumberjack. His cheeks were criss-crossed by duelling scars, his manner and way of speaking slow and clumsy. Canaris was incautious enough to express upset over the executions in Munich, Kaltenbrunner making it clear he had no feelings at all in the matter. Realising he had no 'Heydrich' to deal with, Canaris confined himself to hackneyed phrases on the useful collaboration he looked forward to; Kaltenbrunner's response was to launch into complaints against a certain Count he alleged was in contact with the conservative opposition in

Austria, and the Hungarian Intelligence Service who were (Kaltenbrunner said) well-known Anglophiles.

Despite his aversion and caution, and almost bizarrely, in view of their great suspicions and surveillance of him, Canaris often invited Kaltenbrunner, *Gestapo* Müller and Schellenberg to his new *Abwehr* offices. All three guests were well aware of the increasingly precarious position of their host. The Nazis' campaign to subvert and put an end to Canaris and his *Abwehr* had been furthered the previous December, when two of its men were arrested at Prague Customs office for smuggling currency. Whether this was 'in the line of duty' is not known, but the *Gestapo* and SD began twisting the incident into a political affair. Yet, though his men were still trying to gather more evidence, Himmler did not press the case. The 'Cicero' affair by which the *Abwehr* and SD succeeded in wresting secrets from the British ambassador's safe in Ankara did nothing to save Canaris and his service, which provided more meat for the Nazi chopper when the admiral's man in Turkey, Dr Erich Velmehren, defected with his wife to the British – taking secret material with him but pretending he had fled on religious grounds. Hitler's fury grew as more personnel went missing, some of them *Abwehr* men; the *Führer* blamed 'the filthy mess' on Canaris. Hitler's mistress, Eva Braun, had a sister who married SS General Fegelein, and it was he who put it to the *Führer* that it was now time for the *Abwehr* to be absorbed into the SS. Hitler ordered Himmler to prepare, and in February 1944 the *Abwehr* ceased to exist as a separate intelligence service.

Canaris himself lasted a little longer. He was switched to become chief of economic warfare at Eiche, near Potsdam, his family sent to Bavaria. During the afternoon of 20 July, Colonel Claus von Stauffenberg telephoned Canaris at his home at Schlachtensee to announce the death of Hitler. 'Dead?' Canaris shouted, 'For God's sake! Who did it? The Russians?'

Canaris had grown weary and increasingly pessimistic about the plot to remove Hitler, not so much anxious for himself but over the lack of thoroughness and foresight among the conspirators. They seemed to have placed all their efforts into planting a bomb constructed with captured British explosive, with little thought for what must follow. By 5 p.m. Canaris heard from another caller that Hitler had survived, and on reaching his office his deputy showed him a telegram already prepared congratulating 'our beloved *Führer*' on his escape. Naturally, the call to the admiral from the courageous but mistaken Stauffenberg had been tapped by the *Gestapo*, yet more evidence of the lack of security inherent among the plotters. When Canaris reached the office of SS *Standartenführer* Huppenkothen after his arrest, he was shown a transcript of the phone conversation. An old comrade the admiral happened to have bumped into the day before was also arrested. Canaris had been taken away by Schellenberg, direct to the damaged *Gestapo* and SD building in Prinz-Albrecht-Strasse, to be lodged in one of the cells below ground, the door left ajar because of

frequent air raid alarms. There were armed SS guards in the corridor. The prisoners in many cases were shackled, and handcuffed at night. When some prisoners were taken away for interrogation all other doors were closed, and when actual air raids took place they were hurried off to the 'Himmler bunker', as they were too important to be lost. In the shelter they were lined up against a wall, an SS guard standing between each. In these confined circumstances the prisoners soon learned each other's identity, and among them were those who had held rank and high posts in the regime – generals with red stripes on their breeches. They included the former financial wizard Hjalmar Horace Greeley Schacht; Herbert Goering (the *Reichsmarschall*'s cousin); a high court judge; Artur Nebe, former chief of the Criminal Police. Also imprisoned was Pastor Niemoller, the well known ex-U-boat captain of the earlier war who had turned anti-Nazi preacher. His sermons had irritated the regime for long, and the Bomb Plot seemed the ideal opportunity at last to arrest him. Canaris was indeed in somewhat exalted company, recognising the once powerful in chains nearby. Even the former military governor in Belgium, General von Falkenhausen, was present.

The prisoners were kept alive on one-third normal rations, and made to scrub floors. One SS guard jeered at Canaris as he did this demeaning chore, 'You never thought you'd end up swabbing the decks, Admiral!'

SS Colonel Huppenkothen seemed a rather humane type, more like a civil servant in uniform. This gentlemanly manner was only modified when he realised results were not forthcoming from his interrogations. Another interrogator who made appearances was *Gestapo* Müller's representative, Colonel Pantzinger; others taking their turn at the job included three *Gestapo Kriminal Kommissars.* One called Starvitski preferred punching prisoners in the face if their replies dissatisfied him. Each night the prisoners lay on their backs on wooden bunks, tightly handcuffed and forbidden to turn away from the brilliant lights above their heads. The cells were deliberately overheated.

Despite the discomforts, Canaris found his morale improving, because he had discovered the failings of the SD and *Gestapo* interrogators. Their minds and methods were crude, there was no way they could match him mentally. Both prisoners and interrogators knew the war was nearly over. The former tried to prolong proceedings, as indeed did some of their captors, who knew they were in safe jobs and hoped to spin them out.

Himmler had located one of his smaller concentration camps at Flossenburg, close to the old Bavarian frontier with Bohemia. The wood huts had been built to hold up to 16,000 prisoners, but now housed 60,000, most taken out to work daily in the quarries and forests nearby. There was a concrete bunker in the camp built to hold special prisoners, men like Canaris and the former Austrian chancellor Kurt von Schussnigg, the Czech minister of agriculture, a few Greek generals – and fourteen RAF officers. The bunker was split into cells, and No. 21 held the one-time chief of Danish Intelligence, Colonel Lunding, who found a peephole in his cell through which he watched the sufferings outside. Lunding saw between seven and nine hundred executions, many carried out by the use of six ropes attached to rings driven into the projecting concrete roof of a small building. On another spot nearby were knelt those due to be shot, NKVD style, in the back of the neck.

Rudolf Hoess, commandant of Auschwitz, executed by the Poles. Martin Sandberger was chief of SIPO in Estonia and later in northern Italy

While two of the SS guards behaved abominably to their prisoners, another proved quite amiable to Lunding, who learned the identity of the new arrival in Cell 22. It was Canaris, 'one of the blackest and vilest traitors', as the friendly guard remarked. Lunding was intrigued, knowing how Canaris had done his best to protect the Danes from the worst of Hitler's excesses. Perhaps, seeing the end of Nazi Germany, the same guard obligingly passed on prisoners' notes. Lunding learnt the admiral was given better meals than the rest. In March 1945 the SS interrogator-in-chief arrived in the camp, walking with Canaris outside as he questioned him, and learning nothing.

During the night of 8/9 April, an SS *Standgericht* (Summary Court) was held in Flossenburg, attended by Colonel Huppenkothen, who chaired the final 'trial' of several prisoners, including Canaris, who had by then been beaten severely, his nose broken. At six the next morning Canaris and several others were ushered outside, ordered to strip naked, and marched outside to an illuminated yard where they were hanged, one by one. The SS staff then returned to their office, perhaps to complete their reports, other prisoners having to remove the bodies for incineration.

Himmler's hopes of using VIPs for bargaining purposes with the Allies did not include Canaris – he knew too much.

After the war, Huppenkothen was tried three times by the West Germans for these killings, receiving seven years' imprisonment in 1955.

Some of the the surviving VIP prisoners were removed from Flossenburg by the SD as the war ended, but rescued by American troops.

Eduard Strauch and Herbert Kappler, SIPO chiefs in White Russia and Rome

263

*   *   *

Reinhard Heydrich created and built up the Intelligence Service, the *Sicherheitsdienst* of National Socialist Germany. He was its master and driving force from 1931 until May 1942. Heydrich, as explained, was killed not because he was head of the SD, but for purely political reasons, perhaps in the same way Beria might have been removed by one of the Allies had Stalin's USSR invaded Western Europe.

While 'secret' police agencies are maintained by most, if not all, nations possessing any sizeable administrative machines, some grow larger and more sinister than others. The SD was never comparable to Britain's MI6, nor indeed the American counter-espionage agency contained within the FBI. Its only real counterpart was the Soviet NKVD, now well known as the KGB, which somewhat amusingly also originated as and was later termed a 'people's' police service, i.e. to protect the people from hostile infiltration. However, it stepped beyond that parameter to 'oversee' and suppress the population as a whole. Tyrannical regimes, by their very nature insecure at home, rely on such police to maintain their own positions.

As shown, the story of German Intelligence under Hitler was very much that of Reinhard Heydrich and Wilhelm Canaris, both very interesting and in some ways remarkable figures in history. It was always Heydrich vs Canaris, the SD vs the *Abwehr*, and neither the men nor their agencies respected their remit. Both spilled over into areas beyond, both to no great effect. The political intelligence gathered by Canaris at home was to no avail without action, while the military information garnered by Heydrich was all quietly filed away.

As for the *Gestapo*, it meddled in everything – even, one suspects, espionage abroad. The wasteful absurdity of all three Nazi agencies working on home security, for example, serves to prove the muddy fashion in which Hitler arranged his regime. In one case the *Gestapo* inserted a plain female cook into the Italian Embassy in Berlin to spy for them, eventually blackmailing one of the staff into their clutches, a clear case of the *Gestapo* infringing SD territory.

It was unfortunate for Heydrich and his brighter staff that the SD became so enmeshed in criminal and inhuman activities.

BIBLIOGRAPHY

Hitler, A Study in Tyranny, Alan Bullock (Odhams 1954)
The Rise & Fall of the Third Reich, Wm Shirer (Secker & Warburg 1960)
The Game of the Foxes, Ladislas Farago (Hodder & Stoughton 1971)
Canaris, Karl Heinz Abshagen (Hutchinson 1956)
The Second World War Vol I, Winston Churchill (Cassell 1948)
Master of Spies, Frantisek Moravec (Bodley Head 1975)
The Nazi Secret Service, Andre Brissaud (Bodley Head 1972)
Gestapo, Edward Crankshaw (Putnam 1956)
The Order of the SS, Frederic Reider (Aztex Corp 1975)
Marshal Without Glory, Butler-Young (Hodder & Stoughton 1951)
The Goebbels Diaries, Louis Lochner (Hamish Hamilton 1948)
I Was Cicero, Elysa Bazna (Andre Deutsch 1962)
Uniforms of the SS/SD, Andrew Mollo (Historical Research Unit 1971)
One Girl's War (MI5), Joan Miller (Brandon Books 1986)
V2, Walter Dornberger (Hurst & Blackett)
The Führer, Konrad Heiden (Victor Gollanz 1944)
History of the SS, G. S. Graber (Robert Hale 1978)
Goebbels, Helmut Heiber (Hawthorn 1972)
Children of the SS, Henry-Hillel (Hutchinson 1976)
Lucifer Ante Portas, Rudolf Diels (Interverlag Zurich 1949)
The Venlo Incident, S. Payne Best (Hutchinson 1950)
To the Bitter End, Hans Bernd Gisevius (Jon. Cape 1948)
Hitler and I, Otto Strasser (Jon. Cape 1940)
I Know These Dictators, G. Ward Price (Harrap 1937)
Chief of Intelligence, Ian Colvin (Victor Gollanz 1951)
The Last Days of Hitler, H. R. Trevor-Roper (Macmillan 1950)
The Final Solution, Gerard Reitlinger (London 1953)
The Scourge of the Swastika, Lord Russell (London 1954)
Die Geheime Front, Walter Hagen (Linz-Wien 1950)
Die Deutsche Polizei, Werner Best (Berlin 1940)
The Case of Rudolf Hess, J. R. Rees (Ed) (Heinemann 1947)
Heydrich, Charles Wighton (Odhams 1962)
Obergruppenführer Reinhard Heydrich, Callum MacDonald (Macmillan 1989)
Nuremberg Trial Documents, (HMSO 1947)

INDEX